Paris

This book offers a new perspective on French architecture, describing the impact of political history on the architectural development of Paris. Through various stages in history from the Roman to the Medieval, Renaissance and Early Modern and Modern, *Paris: The Shaping of the French Capital* shows how the immense political power of monarchs, the aristocracy and church determined the pace and volume of building in Paris and the extent of town planning. Whereas many other great cities owe their historic importance to trade, and to local government (the City of London being a supreme example), these attributes were largely absent in Paris (throughout most of its history it didn't even have a mayor). Arguably, because of this, gradually over the centuries the French capital emerged as one of the world's most beautiful cities, and now is a metropolis with a population in excess of 2 million.

Paris

The Shaping of the French Capital
A Political Perspective

Paul N. Balchin

Routledge
Taylor & Francis Group

First published in 2021 by Matador

This edition first published in 2023 by Routledge
4 Park Square, Milton Park, Abingdon, Oxon, OX14 4RN
and by Routledge
605 Third Avenue, New York, NY 10158

Routledge is an imprint of the Taylor & Francis Group, an informa business

Publisher's Note
On page 348 there are some errors:
On lines 8, 9 and 10 200 Euros should read 200 million Euros.

ISBN 13: 978-1-032-43254-0 (hbk)
ISBN 13: 978-1-003-36646-1 (ebk)
ISBN 13: 978-1-032-43258-8 (pbk)
Book DOI 10.4324/9781032432540

PARIS

THE SHAPING OF
THE FRENCH CAPITAL

A POLITICAL PERSPECTIVE

PAUL N BALCHIN

Matador
9 Priory Business Park,
Wistow Road, Kibworth Beauchamp,
Leicestershire, LE8 0RX
Tel: 0116 279 2299
Email: books@troubador.co.uk
Web: www.troubador.co.uk/matador
Twitter: @matadorbooks

ISBN 978 1800462 700

British Library Cataloguing in Publication Data.
A catalogue record for this book is available from the British Library.

Printed and bound by CPI Group (UK) Ltd, Croydon, CR0 4YY
Typeset in 11pt Aldine401 BT by Troubador Publishing Ltd, Leicester, UK

Matador is an imprint of Troubador Publishing Ltd

MIX
Paper from
responsible sources
FSC
www.fsc.org   FSC® C013604

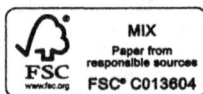

To Alicia

CONTENTS

LIST OF TABLES

LIST OF MAPS

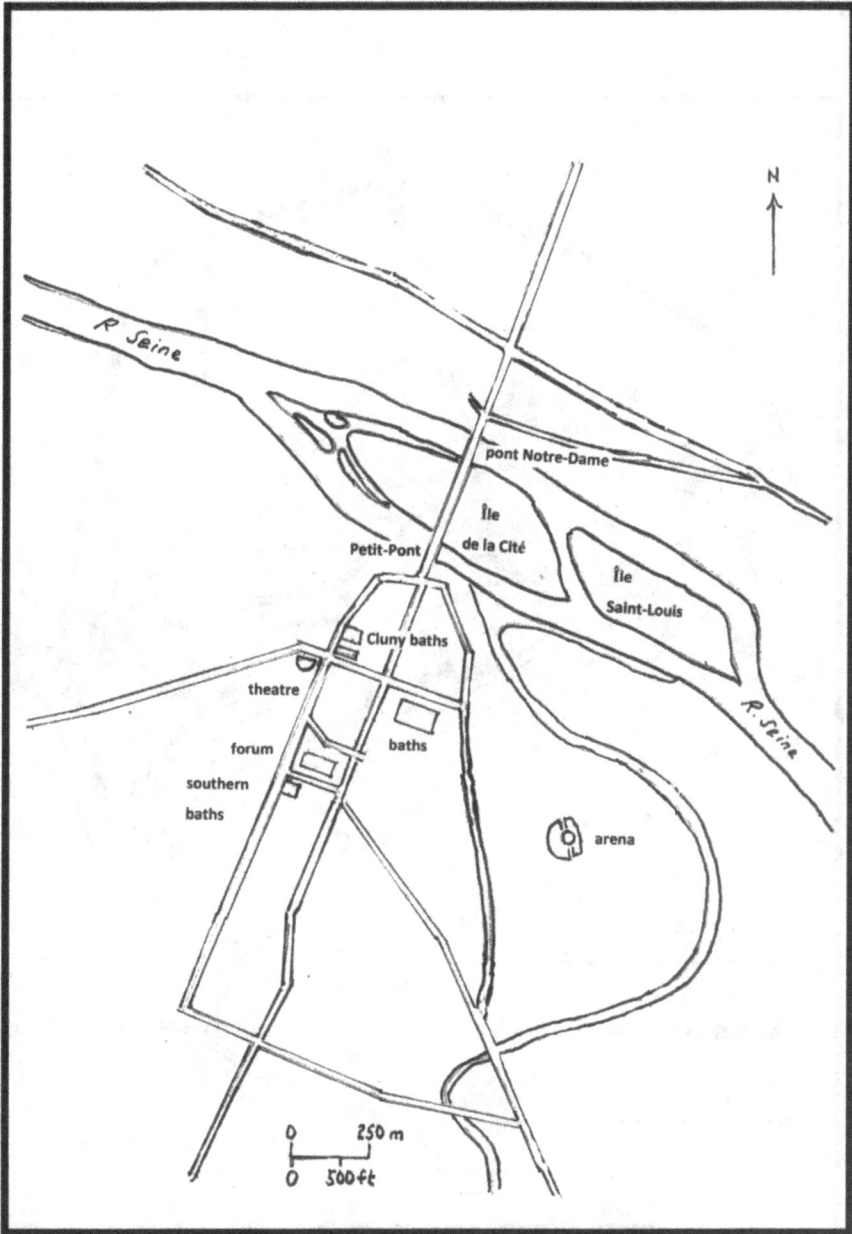

Map 1   *Paris, 1ˢᵗ Century BC to AD 400*

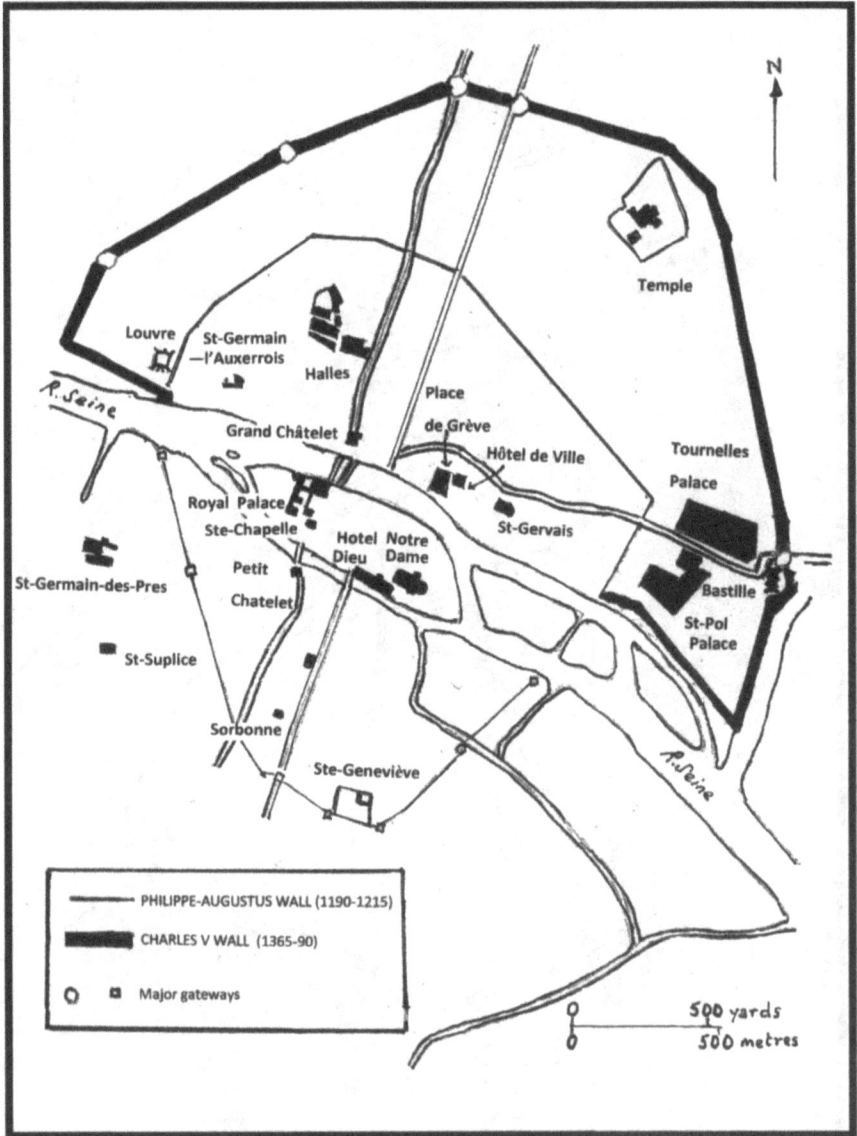

N

Temple

Louvre

St-Germain —l'Auxerrois

Halles

R. Seine

Grand Châtelet

Place de Grève

Hôtel de Ville

Tournelles Palace

Royal Palace

Ste-Chapelle

Hotel Dieu

Notre Dame

St-Gervais

Bastille

St-Germain-des-Pres

Petit Chatelet

St-Pol Palace

St-Suplice

R. Seine

Sorbonne

Ste-Geneviève

PHILIPPE-AUGUSTUS WALL (1190-1215)

CHARLES V WALL (1365-90)

Major gateways

500 yards

500 metres

Map 2   *Medieval Paris*

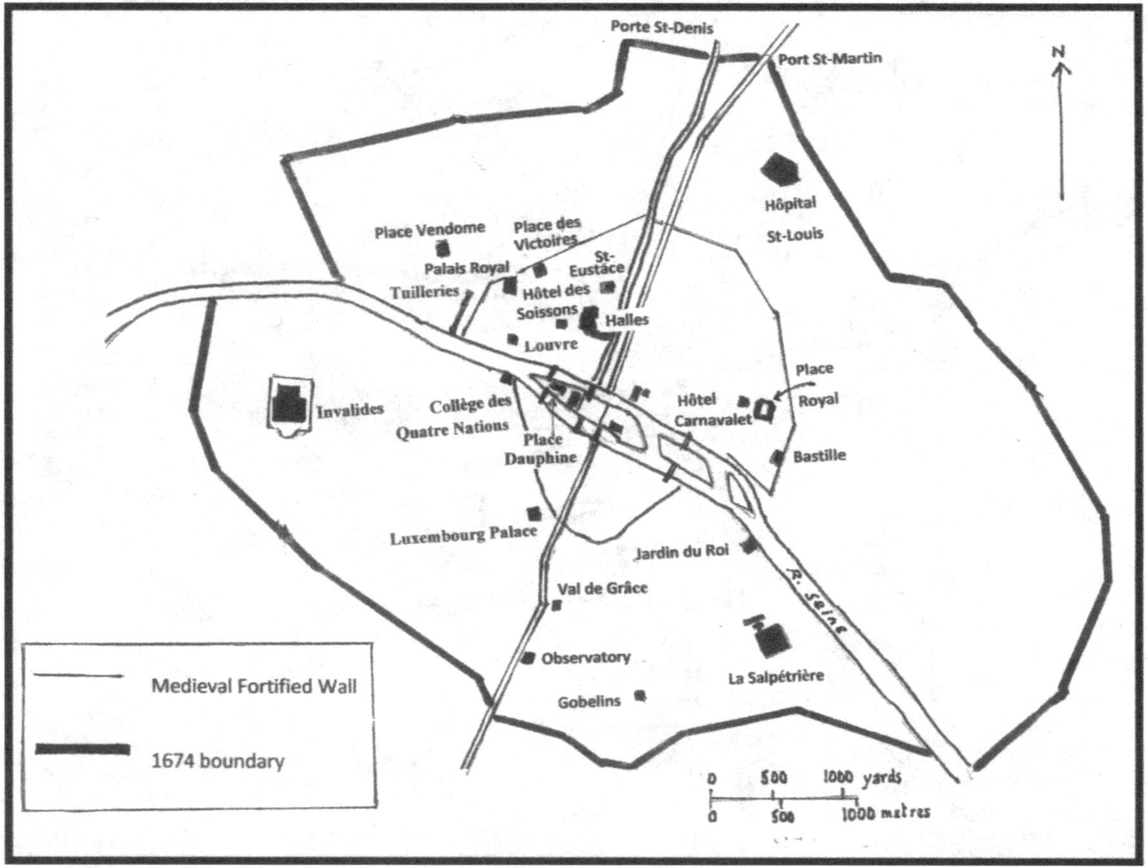

Map 3 *Renaissance Paris*

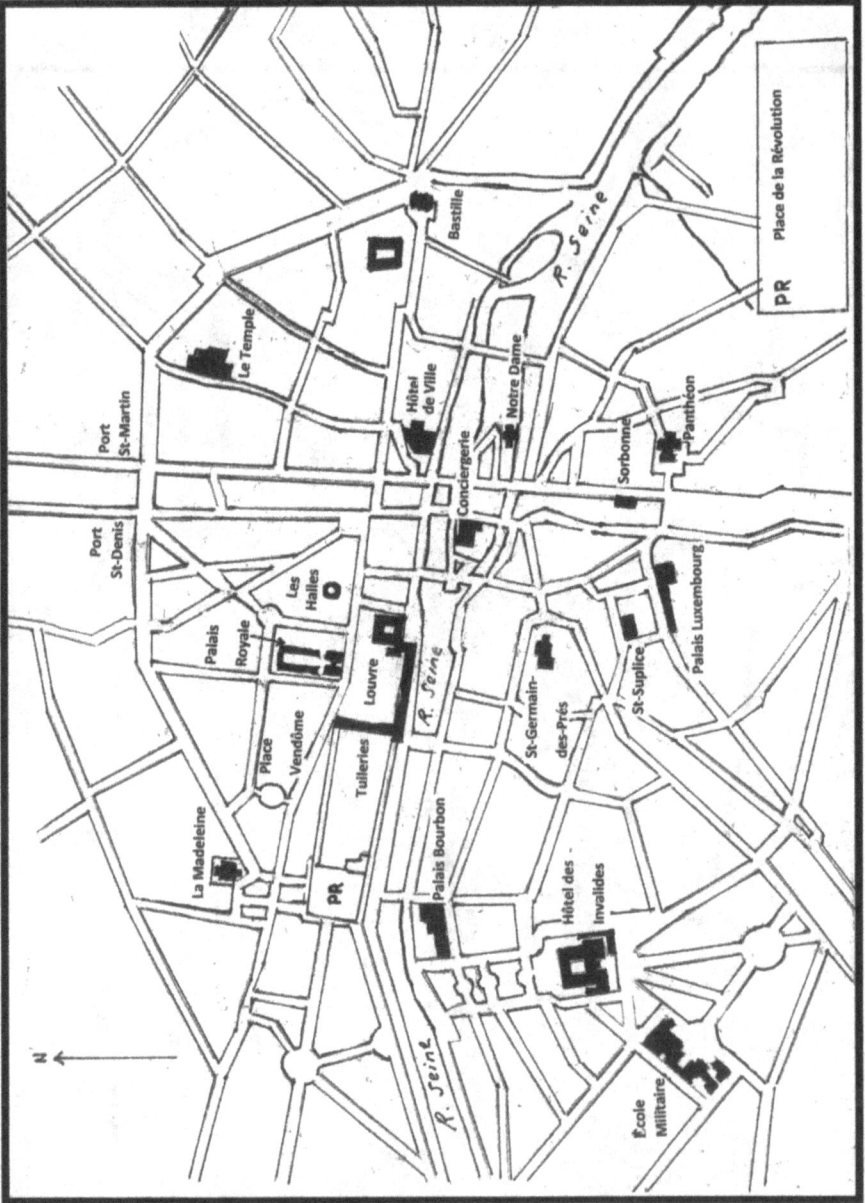

Map 4   *Paris 1715-1815*

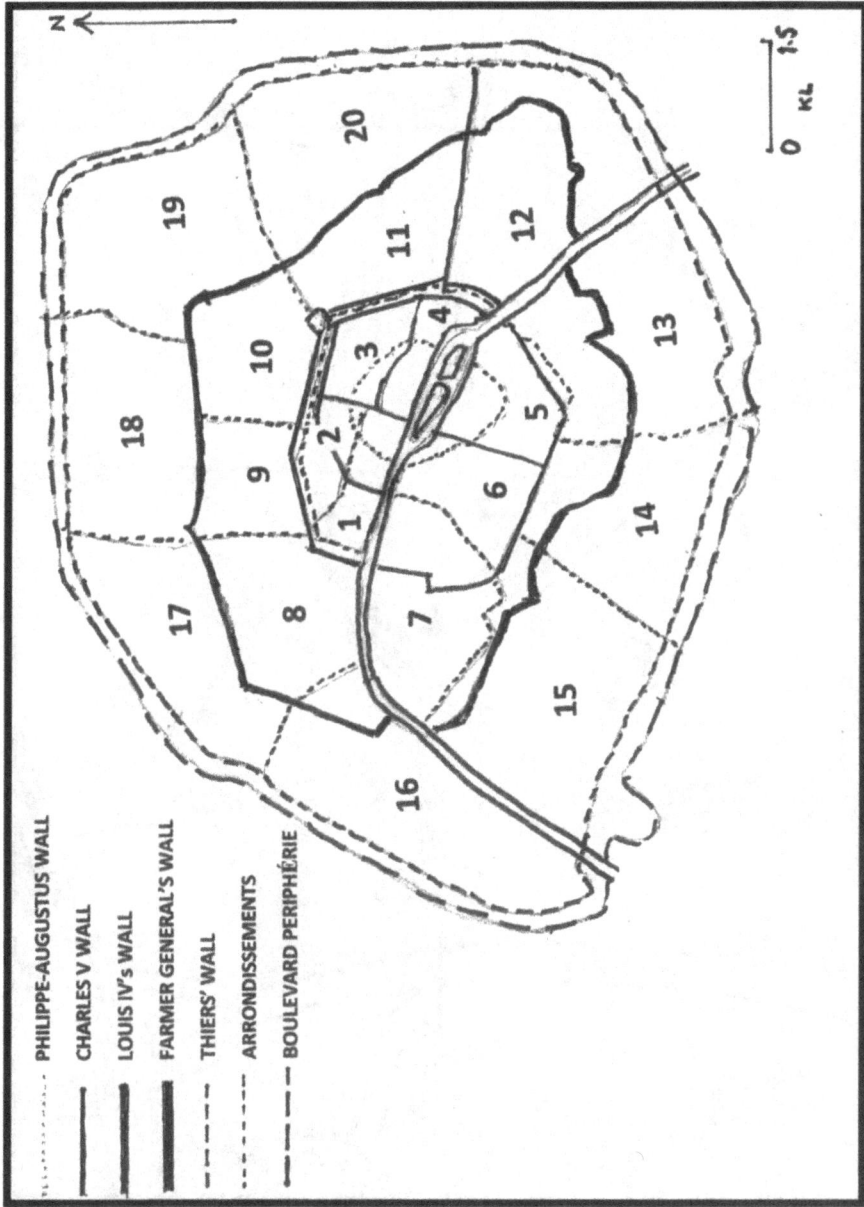

PHILIPPE-AUGUSTUS WALL

CHARLES V WALL

LOUIS IV's WALL

FARMER GENERAL'S WALL

THIERS' WALL

ARRONDISSEMENTS

BOULEVARD PERIPHÉRIE

N

0   KL   1·5

Map 5   *Arrondissements of Paris*

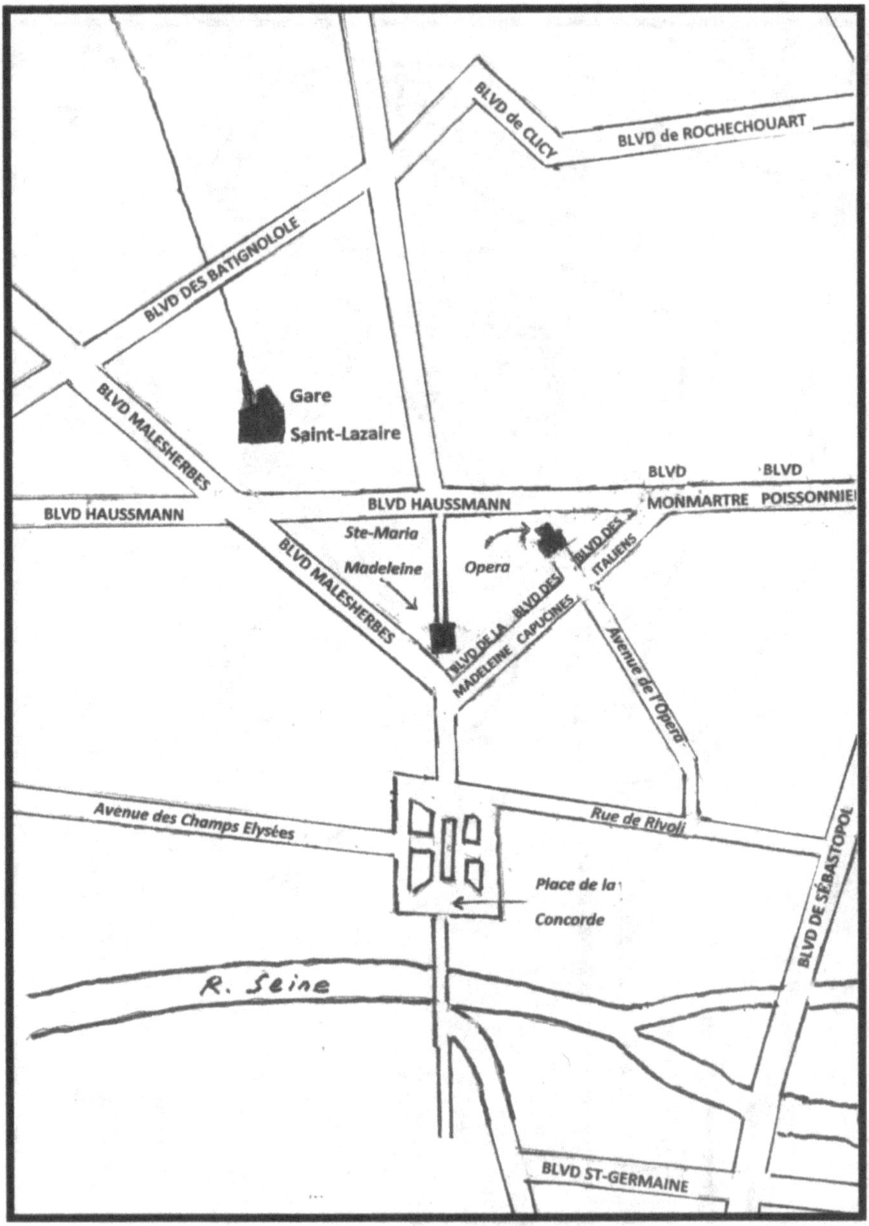

Map 6a *Nineteenth Century Paris: the Right Bank*

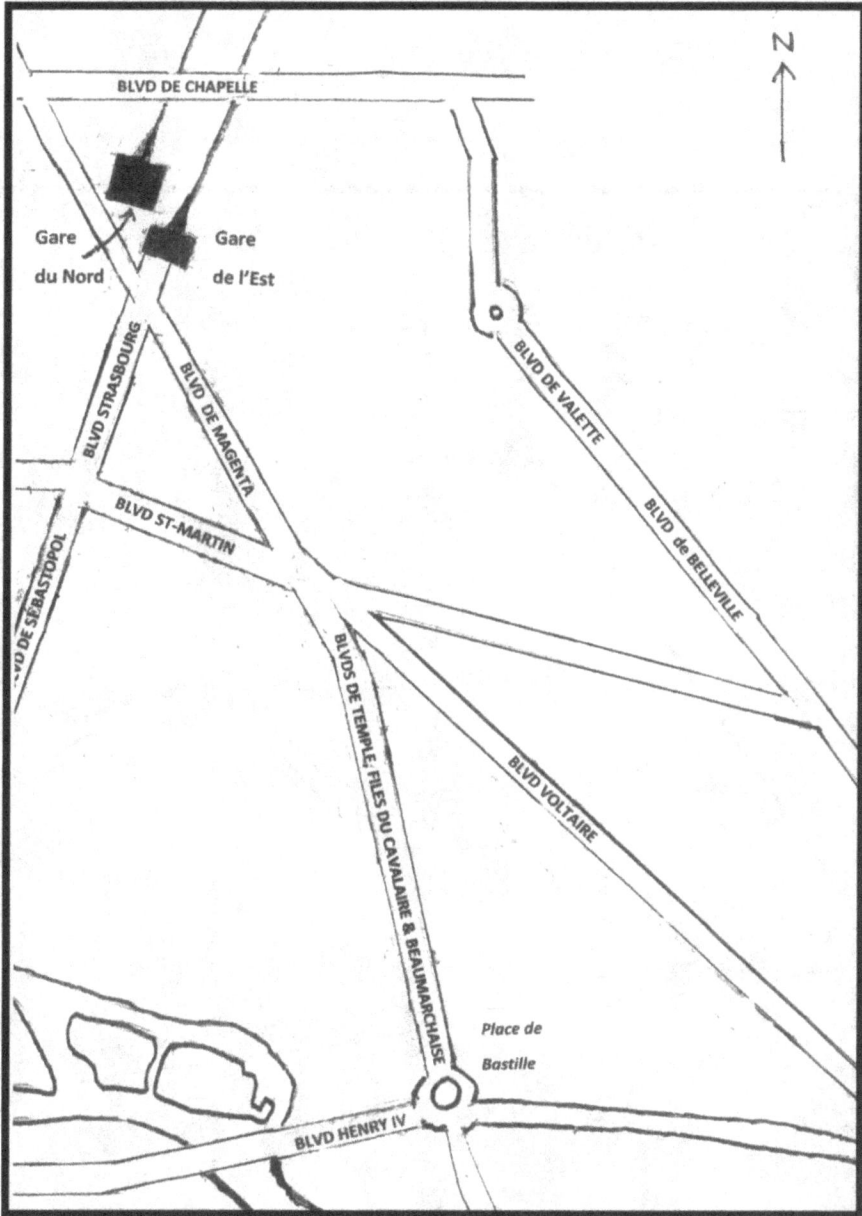

N

BLVD DE CHAPELLE

Gare
du Nord

Gare
de l'Est

BLVD STRASBOURG

BLVD DE MAGENTA

BLVD DE VALETTE

BLVD de BELLEVILLE

BLVD ST-MARTIN

BLVD DE SÉBASTOPOL

BLVDS DE TEMPLE, FILES DU CAVALAIRE & BEAUMARCHAISE

BLVD VOLTAIRE

Place de
Bastille

BLVD HENRY IV

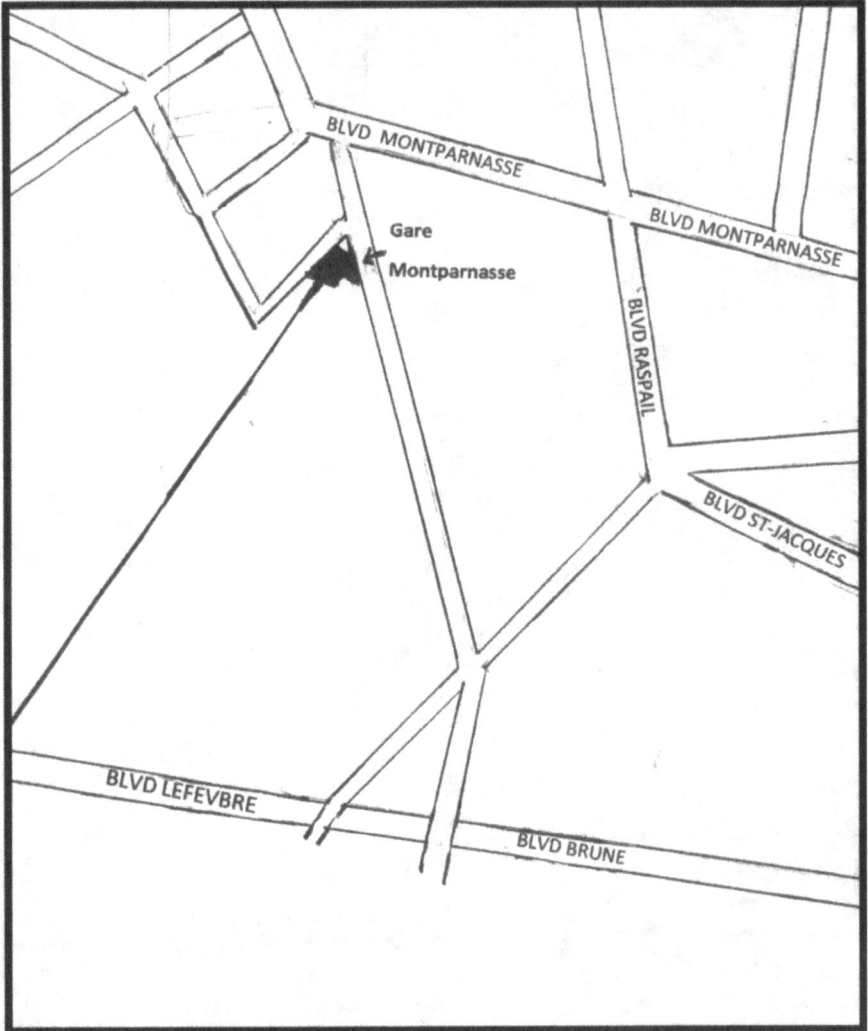

BLVD MONTPARNASSE

BLVD MONTPARNASSE

Gare
Montparnasse

BLVD RASPAIL

BLVD ST-JACQUES

BLVD LEFEVBRE

BLVD BRUNE

Map 7a   *Nineteenth Century Paris: the Left Bank*

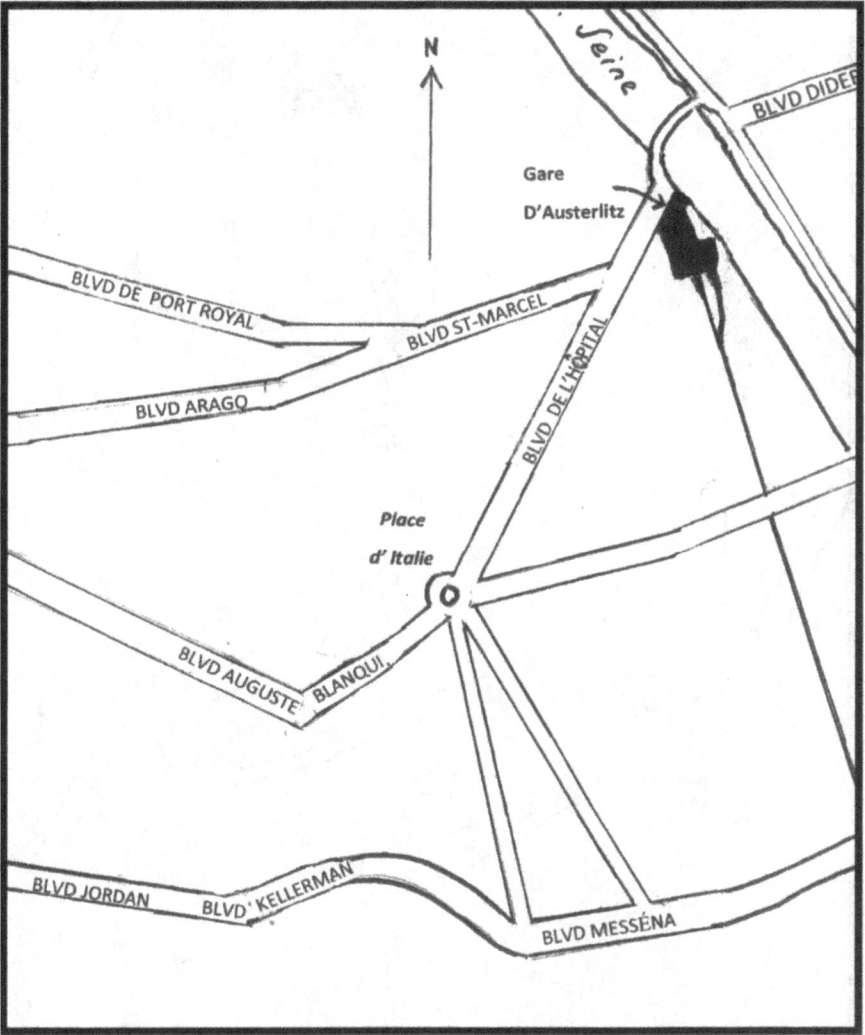

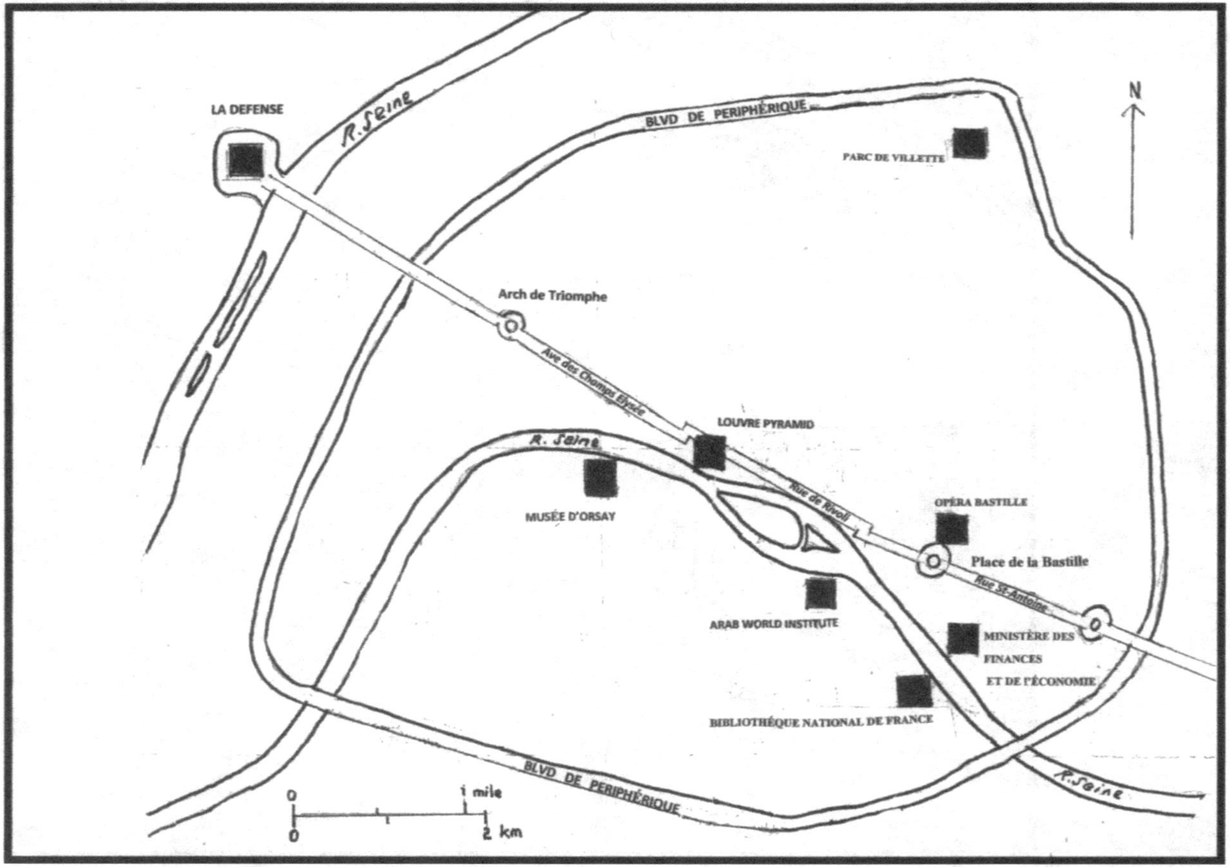

N

LA DEFENSE

Arch de Triomphe

R. Seine

PARC DE VILLETTE

BLVD DE PERIPHÉRIQUE

Ave. des Champs Elysée

Rue de Rivoli

LOUVRE PYRAMID

MUSÉE D'ORSAY

R. Seine

ARAB WORLD INSTITUTE

OPÉRA BASTILLE

Place de la Bastille

Rue St-Antoine

MINISTÈRE DES FINANCES ET DE l'ÉCONOMIE

BIBLIOTHÈQUE NATIONAL DE FRANCE

R. Seine

BLVD DE PERIPHÉRIQUE

0   1 mile
0   2 km

Map 8   The Grand Projects of the late twentieth century

PHOTO CREDITS

All photographs were taken by the author unless stated below.

PREFACE

Paris has been 'shaped' in multi-faceted ways, not least in the latter half of the nineteenth century and throughout much of the twentieth. In fine art, Degas, Manet, Monet, Renoir and Pissaro introduced impressionism to the world in the French capital, with the post-impressionists Seurat and Toulous-Laurec not far behind. In literature, Balzac, Dumas, Zola, Hugo and Flaubert made Paris their home and inspiration; Bizet, Faure, Ravel, Saint Saens, Berlioz, Delibes, Massennet and Debussy enchanted Parisian audiences by their musical compositions. Sight-seeing and places of entertainment have also shaped Paris in the minds of both Parisians and tourists since the late nineteenth century: from the Louvre and the Eiffel Tower, to the café and cabaret culture from the Boulevard St-Germain to Pigallle, while the physical fabric of Paris was fashioned in the neo-baroque style edging towards the art-nouveau style and on to modernism in the early twentieth century. In the political arena Napoleon Bonaparte, Louis Philippe and Napoleon III each attempted to shape Paris as their centre of power, as did Pompidou and Mitterand in the twentieth.

Of course, the history of Paris is not confined to nineteenth and twentieth centuries. Far from it. . Since at least the Middle Ages the French capital has been shaped by an almost continual flowering of the fine arts, literature, musical composition and architectural innovation, while the development of the built environment has been closely determined or influenced by those with political and sometimes ecclesiastical power.

An array of books have been written on the shaping of Paris in each of its different manifestations or more comprehensively across the whole spectrum of the city's growth, but few if any examine concisely the relationship between the political history of the city and its built environment. This book aims – within this context - to fill this gap.

I am particularly indebted to Joe Shillito and his colleagues at Matador in the production of this book, to Maria Bennett for her relentless typing services and to Wendy Baskett for so diligently producing the index. Last, I must thank my wife Alicia for the very great patience she has shown throughout the preparation of this book.

Paul N Balchin

London, 2021

Updated Preface September 2024

In the first quarter of the twenty- first century President Macron, Mayor Anne Hildago and Deputy Mayor Pierre Rabadan each recognised the need to stimulate the economic growth of Paris. Sporting facilities recently become a major land-use requirement prior to Paris hosting the 2024 Olympic Games between 26 July - 11 August, and the Paralympics from 28 August - 8 September. Although the Aquatics pool was completed in 2024, several of the sporting venues were built prior to the games: the Stadt de France (holding track and field events and accommodating around 80,000 spectators) was completed in 1998 to host the football World Cup, La Défense Arena (swimming) was built in 2017, the Olympic village was constructed accommodating 18,000 athletes in time for the opening of the games. Most if not all of these facilities were built within the economically run-down suburb of Seine-Saint-Denis.

However, several of the Olympic and Paralympic events were spread thinly across the rest of Paris: For example, the Marathon from the Hotel de Ville to Les Invalides; the cycling road race starting from the Pont de Jena and finishing at the same point; fencing and taekwondo at the Grand Palais; and the Bercy Arena hosting gymnastics.

The total capital and running costs of the Paris Olympics and Paralympics probably amounted to around 9 billion Euros (£7.8 bn), while the extra sales revenue that visitors contributed was estimated to be about 2,6 billion Euros. Like the London Olympics of 2012, the Parisian organisers extended the public transport network (by building two additional Metro lines) in the years immediately before the games - closing the historical divide between the poorer suburbs and the more prosperous central areas of the capital, with better housing, better public services, better retail and improved tourist facilities.

1

INTRODUCTION

Whether one looks at the cities of the ancient world or at the rapidly developing urban areas of the Third World, "political leaders [have used] architecture for political purposes. It [was] a relationship that occurred in almost every kind of regime and [appealed] to egotists of every description."[1] In Paris this was exemplified most notably by Louis XIV, Louis XV, Napoleon I, and his nephew Napoleon III and more recently by presidents Pompidou and Mitterrand. But cities are not just products of decision-making by a ruling regime, they also determine social attitudes and how we live. As Sir Winston Churchill perceptively said, "We shape our buildings, thereafter they shape us,"[2] a salutary reminder of the celebrated differences and similarities between, for example, a "Parisian" and a "Londoner". It is important to recognise, however, that Paris is unique in being the only commune in France without having had a mayor throughout most of its history. This is in contrast to capitals across Europe that have had mayors continuously in office for centuries, most notably the City of London since 1189 and later Vienna in 1282, Brussels (1380), Amsterdam (1383), Madrid (1393), Lisbon (1801) and Berlin (1809). Only in the years 1789-94, 1848, 1870-71 and since 1977 has the French capital depended on a mayor for its administration and management. Therefore of all capital cities in Western Europe, its planning and development throughout the centuries has been the responsibility of either a monarch or a president exercising their role through an appointed prefect. In this way, the cityscape of Paris has been shaped by decision-making from the highest authority in France and has not always reflected the will of the capital's citizens most obviously at the time of the 1789, 1830 and 1848 Revolutions and the 1870-71 Commune, and more recently in sporadic street demonstrations against centralised decision-making.

In parallel with the political history of Paris, different architectural styles emerged and substantially determined the visual impact of the capital's built environment. Though the Romanesque style was fairly prolific throughout much of France in the eleventh century, little is extant in Paris. It was only with the emergence of Early Gothic between the reigns of Louis VII and Louis VIII (1137-1226) that a new contemporary style had a major impact on the townscape of Paris, only to be superseded by Radiating Gothic in the period from the reign of Louis IX to that of Charles V (1226-1380). Flamboyant Gothic was the next architectural style to emerge, from the time in which Charles VI became king to the death of Louis XII (1380-1515). During the years between the reigns of François I and Louis XIII (1515-1643), the Renaissance style of architecture influenced the design of many notable buildings, but as in Italy, it was superseded by the Baroque, though a very French version of the style. Through most of the eighteenth and into the early nineteenth century, Neo-Classical architecture prevailed, though for much of the nineteenth century Neo-Baroque was dominant. For much of the twentieth century, Art Nouveau, Art Deco, International Modern and Post-Modern styles were widely employed in the continuing development of the Parisian townscape.

SETTING THE SCENE: THE TOPOGRAPHY OF PARIS

Sitting astride the Seine, Paris is only 145km from the English Channel (*La Manche*), and in the past, the French river was wider, shallower, slower-flowing and had a greater tendency to flood than at the present, and was also flanked by marshland – for example in the Marais district of Paris. It flows in a winding direction north-westward to the sea and in Paris is split for 1.9km into two main streams when it passes the Île St-Louis and the Île-de-la-Cité. Within a short distance of central Paris, the Seine is fed by a number of tributary rivers such as the Marne, Essonne, Loing, Yonne and Aube, facilitating "communication from the English Channel in the west towards Alsace, Germany and Switzerland, and through to much of northern, eastern and central France."[3] Though Paris lies on predominantly flat land covered with alluvial deposits, areas of relatively high ground mark the northern and southern topographical borders of the city. On the Right Bank, the land rises to over 60 metres at Chaillot, Montmartre, Belleville and Ménilmontant, and on the Right Bank, it rises to about the same height at Montparnasse. Urban and economic growth has, until the development of modern transport, been concentrated into an east-west belt flanking the Seine and has been restrained by higher ground from expanding northward or southward.

THE ECONOMIC BACKGROUND

Among the many theories of urban growth and the formation of urban land use, two in particular provide an explanation of the development of Paris in Medieval and Early Modern times. The first is the dependency theory that suggests that – under *laissez-faire* – a city such as Paris grows parasitically by exploiting and holding back its surrounding regions. The theory could be even more valid if there was a deliberate attempt by sovereigns to promote the growth of their largest city by conferring upon it the status of capital with extraordinary powers of taxation and expenditure (i.e. taxing the rest of the country and spending the revenue disproportionately at the seat of government). The Swedish economist, Gunnar Myrdal[4] suggested that economic growth follows the principle of "cumulative causation", whereby – once established in a city – economic development promotes further local development – the "spread effect", but this is only at the expense of surrounding areas or other areas elsewhere – the "backwash effect", whereby economic growth in smaller settlements lag behind either absolutely or relatively. Turning from a macro-theory of urban growth to a micro-explanation of urban structure, a Swedish sociologist Gideon Sjoberg[5] posited that a pre-industrial city, such as Early Medieval Paris, normally lacked a central business district, but that the central area nevertheless had pre-eminence over the periphery since – instead of commerce – its focus was governmental and religious, and unlike later industrial cities, it accommodated the homes of the elite whereas the disadvantaged members of the community were relegated to peripheral settlements. In intermediate locations, social areas were further differentiated into distinct quarters according to occupational status or family ties. However, in contrast to most modern cities, there is an absence of functional differentiation in land use, for example the same plots might be used for both housing and work. The resulting pattern of land use was determined partly by cultural values which defined residence in the historic core as the most prestigious and – in the absence of modern transport – by the need for dwellings and places of work to be juxtapositioned[6].

THE EARLY POLITICAL HISTORY OF PARIS

An examination of the political history of Paris from Roman times to the end of the first millennium will show that the growth of the city was for a long time uncertain, and depended very largely on the emergence of a strong ruler and a resilient community, capable together of steering the fledging settlement towards political and economic dominance in its spatial areas of influence. Paris in its very early infancy was inhabited by Celtic tribes during the Bronze and Iron ages, but there is no evidence to suggest that the settlement was any more than rudimentary or that a pre-Roman city emerged either in Paris or anywhere in its immediate vicinity. However, because of its rich rural hinterland and its strategic position in relation to land and river transport, it came under Roman control as an outcome of Rome's attempt to expand its empire and thereby incorporate northern Gaul as much as possible. Defeating local Celtic tribes in 52BC, the Romans – under Julius Caesar – took control of the whole of the middle Seine region, and by the end of the same century a new Roman settlement called *Lutetia* was established on the Île-de-la-Cité and on the Left Bank. Built with locally quarried limestone, *Lutetia* subsequently grew substantially as a planned Roman settlement notable for its grid-iron street pattern and its central north-south thoroughfare on the line of the present-day Rue St-Jacques-Boulevard St-Michel. On the Left Bank, the settlement spread southwards from the Seine "to a little beyond the top of the Montagne Ste-Geneviève [where] a porticoed building . . . combined the functions of a forum with basilica and temple"[7]. Nearby, there was also a theatre, a vast amphitheatre of the Arènes and three public baths (adjacent to the present-day Boulevard Saint-Michel). However, with only around 8,000 inhabitants – compared with 20,000-30,000 in several other Roman cities in Gaul such as Lyon, Reims and Trier – *Lutetia* "was never more than a second rung city throughout the period of Roman rule [and] had little strategic importance"[8], though it became one of the first in France to become Christianised with Dionysius – a Roman or Greek missionary – becoming its bishop in about 250 and canonized as St-Denis after his execution for allegedly posing a threat to the power of Roman emperors. During the second and third centuries, barbarian tribes such as Germanic Alamans from Alsace and Franks from across the Rhine, plundered Gaul, and in 275 caused damage to as many as sixty Gaulish cities including *Lutetia*. Thus, around 300, the inhabitants of *Lutetia* constructed defensive stone fortifications around the Île-de-la-Cité with the aim of protecting themselves against further incursion. However, later in the same century, and throughout the fourth, the city – now called Paris after the local tribe, the *Parish* – was ravaged by war and civil unrest, a situation that was quelled when the Emperor Constantine's nephew, Julian Apostata, arrived in the city to become its governor in 357 where he proclaimed himself emperor after the death of his uncle in 361. Although he established a basilica on the Île-de-la-Cité and witnessed the development of the island as the city's port, Roman rule in Paris and throughout modern Gaul collapsed in the fifth century. Insecurity spread throughout the Roman Empire as Rome was sacked by the Visigoths in 410, and again by the Vandals in 455. Although northern Gaul had been invaded by Atilla the Hun in 451, he failed to take Paris, allegedly because of the piety of St-Geneviève and her followers who prayed for their city's salvation. Geneviève, however, was less successful in both 463-4 and 476 in warding off the pagan Franks who besieged the city and then occupied it in 476.

1   *The Lutetian Arènes, circa 100*

Throughout the Early Middle Ages that followed, Paris experienced a hiatus in her development. After the Romans returned to Rome in defence of their Imperial capital, Paris retained many of the trappings of Roman civilisation as well as being a northern outpost of Christianity. Thus in uniting Gaul, the Frankish king Clovis I – the first of the Merovingian dynasty – made Paris his capital in 508, but after his death in 511 his kingdom was – in German tradition – divided between his four sons into provinces centred on Orléans, Reims, Soissons and Paris, though – because of its special symbolic role – Paris remained capital of all Frankish dominions[9]. In sixth-century Paris, the Merovingian monarch became heavily committed to building ecclesiastical establishments, mainly but not wholly north of the river. The churches of St-Martin-des-Champs, St-Germain-l'Auxerrois, St-Merri, St-Gervais, St-Jacques-de-la-Boucherie, St-Laurent, St-Martin and St-Pierre-de-Montmartre were on the Right Bank; the massive cathedral of St-Étienne was built on the Île-de-la-Cité (near the site of the later cathedral of Notre Dame) together with half a dozen other ecclesiastical establishments; and a dozen churches were built on the Left Bank such as St-Severin, Notre-Dame-des-Champs, St-Julien-le-Pauvre, St-Médard and St-Marcel[10]. However, as the religious importance of Paris increased substantially, the city's political and economic roles diminished, while its urban heritage was being replaced by "one grounded in the countryside."[11] The attraction of Paris as a royal seat also declined and the city was visited less and less by the last of the Merovingian kings in the first half of the eighth century, while the power and responsibilities of the Merovingian dynasty was being delegated to senior royal officials, the '*maires du palais*'. One such 'mayor', Pepin the Short attempted successfully to depose the last of the Merovingian kings and was duly crowned king of the Franks by the pope in St-Denis in 754.

Paris was now a political and economic backwater, and following the death of Pepin in 768, his successor, Charlemagne (after whom the Carolingian line was named), eventually became Holy Roman Emperor in 800 and relocated his capital from Paris to Aix-la-Chapelle (present day Aachen) where, more conveniently, he could advance his imperial aims. But in so doing, he failed to protect Paris from the Viking invaders from Denmark who frequently sailed up the Seine to attack the city and to sack it in 845 – a prelude to a largescale Viking invasion and a ten-month siege in 885-886.

Though the walls constructed against the Franks in the fourth century offered some protection, it was considered essential to renew the city's defences by constructing new fortifications in the 880s under directions from the count of Paris, Odo (r. 882-98). Though Paris in the tenth century was no longer under any threat from further incursion, the city was in very poor shape. Many of its buildings had been destroyed by the Vikings, particularly on the Left Bank and, by the mid-tenth century, Paris "was largely a political irrelevance."[12] However, following the death of the last of the Carolingian kings, Louis V (r. 986-87), the Capetian dynasty assumed power and the decline of Paris was halted and in due course very much reversed.

URBAN MORPHOLOGY

The growth of Paris from the twelfth- to the nineteenth century was intermittently conditioned by the construction of walls that either encircled the built-up area, or enclosed part of the city. Between 1190-

1213, Philippe Auguste funded the construction of a defensive wall around Paris on both the Left and Right Banks in 1190-1213, and beyond the Right Bank section of the wall, a further wall was built by Charles V and his son Charles VI in 1356-83 – a stretch of wall that was extended westward in 1633-36 during the reign of Louis XIII. Then followed, in the years immediately after 1785, the construction of the Wall of the Farmers-General, even further from the centre, but designed not to keep out invaders but literally to act as a customs barrier. Finally, in 1841-44 and even further from the centre of Paris, the French Prime Minister, Adolphe Thiers, ordered the construction of a new outer wall, the eponymously named Thiers Wall, ostensibly to keep enemy armies from taking Paris.

Land on the outer edge of each successive wall tended at first to be sparsely developed or remained open countryside but, as population increased and the need for additional housing and employment became apparent, the built-up area of Paris – often illegally – expanded beyond its current outer wall and formed new *faubourgs* (suburbs), in due course necessitating a further wall. Paris is thus unique among the major cities of the world. Whereas London, Berlin and Los Angeles each expanded into the countryside in a largely unplanned octopus fashion, and other cities such as Turin, Lisbon and New York have been organised on a regular grid, Paris "so often threatened, besieged, or invaded, has from the dawn of time been constrained by its city walls. This has always given it a more or less regular circular form, and it has only been able to extend in a succession of dense and concentric rings."[13]

THE POLITICAL POWER OF ARCHITECTURE AND PLANNING

Throughout much of history, and promulgated by monarchies, republics, the nobility, the merchant class and religious faiths, a significant proportion of property has been developed in order to generate awe, respect and subservience among populations at large. Sometimes property development is the result of an arbitrary decision, but at other times it might be the outcome of market forces or a planning scheme. In examining the history of Paris, or any other major city, it might be useful to consider Deyan Sudjic's observation that "architecture is [and has been] used by political leaders to seduce, impress and intimidate."[14] This view reflects the wisdom of Sir Christopher Wren who posited more than three hundred years ago that *"Architecture has its political Use; public building being an ornament of a Country; it established a Nation, draws People and Commerce; [and] makes the People love their native Country,"*[15] a sentiment that is surely just as applicable to Paris as it is to any other city. But cities are not just products of decision-making whether under feudalism, capitalism or socialism. They also determine social attitudes and how we live.

ABOUT THIS BOOK

After this introduction, Chapter 2 seeks to explain the growth of Paris in the High Middle Ages; Chapter 3 sets out to explore the growth of the French capital in the Late Middle Ages; Chapter 4 considers the development of Paris and its satellite palaces in the Renaissance; Chapter 5 analyses the growth of Paris during the Wars of Religion of the sixteenth century; Chapter 6 discusses how Richelieu and Louis XIII apply the Renaissance to the cityscape of Paris; Chapter 7 focuses on the lengthy reign of Louis XIV and its effects of the built environment of the capital and its royal satellite, Versailles; Chapter 8 examines the growth of Paris during the reign of Louis XV; Chapter 9 describes the impact of the French Revolution and Napoleon's Consulate and First Empire on the structure of Paris; Chapter 10 looks at the effects of the Bourbon restoration on the growth of Paris; Chapter 11 describes how the policies of Napoleon III contributed to Paris emerging as the 'City of Light' in the nineteenth century; Chapter 12 provides a detailed examination of the effects of the Paris Commune (1870-71) on the architecture of the capital, and a consideration of the development of the capital during the 'Belle Époque', 1872-1914; Chapter 13 analyses the effects of the inter-war depression on the shaping of Paris, the impact of the 1895 International Exposition on the Parisian cityscape, and the development of the Modernist School of Architecture on the built environment; Chapter 14 considers the relationship between public policy and the development of the built environment during the seventy or more years after the Second World War, and Chapter 15 concludes by examining the emerging twenty-first century townscape, including the evolving role of mayoral responsibility.

References

1. D. Sudjic. *The Edifice Complex. How the Rich and Powerful Shape the World* (London: Allen Lane, 2005), p.8
2. Sir Winston Churchill, reported in *Time*, September 12, 1960
3. C. Jones. *Paris. Biography of a City* (London: Penguin Books, 2006), p.5
4. G. Myrdal. *Economic Theory and Undeveloped Areas* (London: Duckworth, 1957)
5. G. Sjoberg. *The Preindustrial City: Past and Present* (New York: Free Press, 1960)
6. J. Dickenson, C. Clarkee, S. Mather, M. Prothgeroe, D. Siddle, C. Smith and E. Thomas-Hope. *Geography in the Third World, 2nd Edt.* (London: Routledge, 1996)
7. C. Jones, op cit, p.10
8. Ibid, p.12
9. Ibid, p.28
10. Ibid, pp 29-30
11. Ibid, p.30
12. Ibid, p.35
13. E. Hazan. *The Invention of Paris* (London: Verso, 2011), p.7
14. D. Sudjec, opt. cit., p.2
15. L.M. Soo, *Wren's Tracts on Architecture and Other Writings* (Cambridge: Cambridge University Press, 1998), p.153

2

THE EMERGENCE OF PARIS
IN THE HIGH MIDDLE AGES

INTRODUCTION

Between the years 987 and 1300, the population of Paris grew from around 20,000 inhabitants to about 200,000. As capital of France, its growth was as a result of economic, political and religious factors that made the city the largest and most important urban settlement in the whole of Europe. Both in the ecclesiastical and secular sectors its more notable new buildings displayed, in turn, the Romanesque and Gothic styles of architecture while, in the late twelfth century, population densities increased within the newly built city walls rather than sprawling over the surrounding countryside. To be sure urban growth was not continuous. Throughout the High Middle Ages, France embarked on a series of Crusades to the Levant, and she was frequently at war with her neighbours, particularly England. However, although the development of buildings slowed down during the more severe conflicts, when periods of peace returned construction activity continued its upward path. But with little regard to environmental conditions, further building work often made living conditions worse. High density development – an outcome of space constraints caused by a succession of city walls – was associated with squalor, filth and a lack of sewers, a dichotomy that was to continue until the nineteenth century or beyond.

HUGUES CAPET (R. 987-996)

Following his election as King of France by an assembly of the country's greatest lords, and crowned by the archbishop of Rheims, Hugues Capet made Paris his capital in 987 and founded the Capetian dynasty that remained in power for more than three centuries – or eight if one includes its direct descendants, the Valois and Bourbon. From the late-tenth century until the revolution of 1789-1815 and again from 1815 to 1848, monarchs of Capetian descent (sometimes with the aid of their regents or first ministers) presided over the development of the French capital even when they were living in their Loire and Île-de-France *chateaux*[1]. However, during the High Middle Ages, as many as nine of the twelve Capetian monarchs presided directly over the development of Paris.

ROBERT II PIOUS (R. 996-1031)

It was not Hugues Capet but his successor Robert the Pious who "became the first ruler almost since the Romans to bother seriously about the reconstruction of Paris"[2]. He restored the dilapidated Palais-de-la-Cité that had stood on Roman foundations for a thousand years and rebuilt the abbeys of St-Germain-l'Auxerrois and St-Germain-de-Pres that had been destroyed by the Vikings during their raids on Paris and their subsequent siege of the city in the ninth century.[3]

HENRI I (R. 1031-60)

During the mid-eleventh century, very little building work of note was undertaken in Paris, though in the ecclesiastical sector, the construction of the Romanesque church of St-Martin-des-Champs was an exception. Financed by Henri I, and with its cloister built on the site of an old shrine to St-Martin, the church at the time of its construction was the largest ecclesiastical structure in Paris and was entrusted to Cluny Abbey in 1079. Henri's reign, however, is better noted for the creation of agents of royal power, *prévôts*, who administered *prévôtés* or local units of central government across his kingdom, including Paris. The *prévôt de Paris* was particularly important over the centuries for ensuring that, as far as possible, new development and other local matters were in accordance with the policy aims of the monarch.

LOUIS VI (R. 1108-37)

A substantial amount of construction work took place in the French capital in the twelfth century. To improve defence and trading opportunities, Louis "replaced the wooden Grand Chatelet on the Right Bank with a robust stone tower, and under its protective shadow, there grew up a whole district – the Champeaux – dedicated to commerce and provisions"[4]. Built on some formerly marshy fields to the north of the St-Germain-l'Auxerrois, the Champeaux helped to reduce the level of congestion in the Place de Grève, previously the centre of trade in Paris. Louis also built the Château de St-Germain-en-Laye some 19 km from the centre of Paris in 1122. Intended for his personal use away from the multifarious hazards of the capital, the *château* was expanded and partially rebuilt on several occasions throughout its long history (see below). But Louis was not alone in funding major secular developments. The Knights Templars built their European headquarters north of the Marais in 1119. The building, known as the Temple, was an enormous *donjon* flanked by four towers and provided accommodation at least as secure and accommodating as the king's Palais-de-la-Cité.

In addition to the development of secular land uses and edifices, many ecclesiastical buildings were constructed in Paris in the early twelfth century. Among the most notable are the Abbey of St-Victor (begun 1113), the Abbey of St-Denis (started 1122) constructed under the direction of Louis's adviser, the Abbot Suger, and the eleventh century church of St-Martin-des-Champs converted by Prior Hugo I into a walled priory (1130-42) with a polygonal, Romanesque-Early Gothic choir and circular chapel that anticipated Abbot Suger's magnificent choir in the Basilica of St-Denis completed soon after (see below).

Following the Romanesque, Gothic architecture in France originated around 1140 and in its 'Early' form is displayed at the cathedrals of Sens (c. 1149), Noyon (1145-1228) and Laon (1160-1230). All cathedrals built in this style made use of rib vaults and had higher proportions, thinner members, larger openings and less inert walls.[5] However, the first major example of Early Gothic architecture employed in Paris was secular rather than ecclesiastical. It was neither at St-Martin-des-Champs nor at the Abbey of St-Denis but at the Pont au Change that dates from the early twelfth century.

LOUIS VII (R. 1137-80)

The first of four notable church-building projects undertaken during the reign of Louis VII involved extending the Romanesque church of St-Germain-de-Pres in 1150 by means of an Early Gothic choir with five radiating chapels. Although modified in the seventeenth century (see Chapter 8), the medieval attributes of the building are still very evident.

2   *St-Germain-de-Pres, 1150*

The second project was the construction of the Abbey Church of St-Denis. Built, according to legend, above the last resting place of the third century missionary, the large cruciform church is located some 11 km north of the centre of Paris. It was begun in the early twelfth century and is renowned for pioneering the Early Gothic style of architecture. Standing on the site of the long-since demolished fifth century abbey of St-Denis and replacing a substantial church by Abbot Fulrad built in 750-75, the new basilica was founded by the powerful and influential Abbot Suger (in office 1122-51). Though begun during the reign of Louis VI, it was built mainly in the reign of his successor, Louis VII. Its west front, containing three deep and finely profiled portals, a large rose window and originally two towers (but now one), was inspired by the west front of the great Norman cathedral of St-Étienne at Caen, and was constructed in 1135-40; and its ambulatory, apse and crypt were built from 1140-44. After Abbot Suger's death, the two Early Gothic ends of the new church were still linked by the remaining stonework of the eighth century building.

3   *Basilica of St-Denis, 1135-44*

The third project was the Cathedral of Notre Dame (begun 1163). Though the Abbey of St-Denis was the primogeniture of Early Gothic church architecture, Notre Dame is one of the most iconic buildings in Paris and the finest exemplar of Early and High Gothic design. Situated on the southern half of the Île-de-la-Cité on ground previously occupied by a Gaulish-Roman shrine and a succession of churches destroyed by Norman invaders in the eleventh century, the edifice was founded by Louis VII and built under the direction of the Bishop of Paris, Maurice de Sully. However, neither lived to see its completion. Because of its intricate design, the massive Gothic cathedral was not finished for a further two hundred years. Built in seven stages between 1163-1330, the choir to the east of the transept was constructed between 1163-82 and the three eastern bays of the nave were built from 1180-1200.

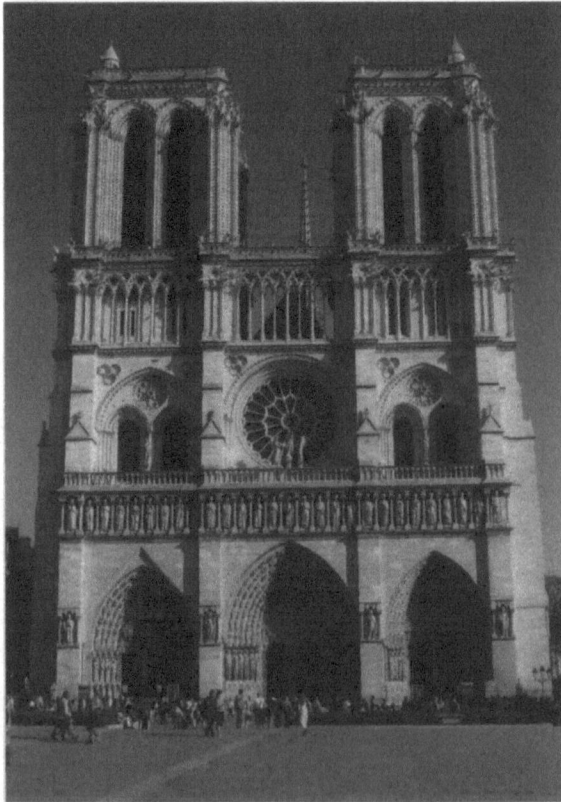

4   *Cathedral of Notre Dame, begun 1165*

5   *Château de Vincennes, started 1178*

The final project is the church of Ste-Geneviève on the Left Bank (*c* 1177). It was built to commemorate the patron saint of Paris, and although it is overshadowed by Notre Dame both in scale and design, it is a notable building since it was reconstructed in the mid-eighteenth century to become the Panthéon, possibly the second finest ecclesiastical building in present-day Paris after the Notre Dame (see Chapter 7).

But church buildings were not the only structures of importance developed during the reign of Louis VII. To defend his capital from potential invaders approaching the city from the Seine downstream, work started in 1178 to construct a substantial citadel, the Château de Vincennes, on the eastern edge of Paris to balance the Louvre on the western edge of the city.

PHILIPPE II AUGUSTE (R. 1180-1223)

However much a city such as Paris is protected against aggression and however well-established it is as a centre of religion and learning, it will not thrive unless it has a sound and diversified economic base. For centuries Paris had been at the centre of the most productive agricultural region of Western Europe, the Île-de-France. It was also located at the crossing of the main north-south and east-west trading routes across France, and situated on a navigable river only 180 km from the port of Rouen where it could easily indulge in maritime trade. However, to exploit these natural advantages, Paris was in need of new market facilities. Therefore on a site north of St-Germain – l'Auxerrois, previously set aside by Louis VI for the establishment of a public market, Philippe Auguste in 1183 ordered the construction of two large stone warehouses "one for grain merchants and the other for a variety of other food sellers."[6] The market was henceforth known as Les Halles, but for over a century it resembled a walled compound securely gated and locked at night rather than a food market.

However, it was very likely that for a while economic growth would be constrained by conflicts on the Continent and overseas. Anglo-French wars ravaged parts of France in 1123-89, 1202-4 and 1213-14, while French forces under Philippe Auguste took a leading role in the Third Crusade to the Holy Land in 1187-92. Philippe Auguste thus found it necessary to levy extraordinary taxes to finance its cost, a practice that set a precedent for the financing of future wars in which France was engaged. Thus, with population and economic growth throughout his reign, and with Philippe Auguste's commitment to the defence of Paris, the cost of administration also rose and imposed even higher taxes on the population of his kingdom throughout his reign. But the burden of taxation might have been even greater had it not been for the French victory over the English at La-Roche-au-Moine in 1214 which led to a flow of revenue from the conquered territory to the Crown. In consequence, the tax yield increased by 160 percent between 1180 and 1203 while there was a concomitant increase in bureaucracy needed to deal with financial matters.[7]

With Paris growing in size – its population reached at least 110,000 by 1200 – and with its economic and political role on the ascent, it was clearly necessary to ensure that its defences were secure. Ten years into his reign, Philippe II Auguste therefore ordered the erection of two surrounding city walls around the capital, the first was on the Right Bank and constructed between 1190 and 1209, and the second was on the Left Bank and built from 1200 to 1215. Over five kilometres in length, three

6   *The remains of part of Philippe II Augustus's city wall, 1190-1209*

metres wide and up to eight metres high, the walls were punctuated by a total of 71 towers 60-80 metres apart.[7] Philippe Auguste also ordered the construction of the Louvre, a robust and square *donjon* some 30 metres high and flanked with turrets. Situated on the Right Bank on the western edge of his city, it looked onto the Seine towards the direction of the Anglo-Norman threat. Built between 1202 and 1223 on rectangular foundations, the outer defences of the Louvre comprised four wings with rounded towers in each corner, while a centrally situated round donjon provided maximum security for the building's defenders. Clearly, the Louvre was not a place for a monarch to reside, but it served its purpose as a major stronghold and treasury. The city walls and the Louvre thus made Paris the most heavily – and most conspicuously – defended military stronghold in western Europe. However, these new structures soon rendered the Grand Chatelet on the Right Bank redundant as a defensive castle, a fate similarly affecting the Petit Chatelet on the Left Bank. The two buildings then served respectively as a court of law and a prison and were demolished in the early nineteenth century.

7   *The original Louvre, 1202-23*

But Paris was not just a centre of commerce and a bastion against invaders. An embryonic University of Paris gradually evolved in the twelfth century and was formerly established by charters conferred upon it by Philippe Auguste and Pope Innocent in 1200 and 1210. A charter of privileges exempted it from civil control, but in practice "the University was [often] haughty in regard to ecclesiastical authority, and always in conflict with Bishop and Pope"[8]. This did not prevent the emergence of the faculties of theology, canon law, medicine and the arts, all of which achieved official status between 1200 and 1240. While theology, canon law and medicine was under the administration of the Chapter of Notre-Dame, the arts faculty was located on the Left Bank on Mont Ste-Geneviève. Each faculty accepted students from four nations according to language or regional origin: France, Normandy, Picardy and England, though the latter soon became known as the *Alemannian* (German) that attracted students not only from England and Germany but also from Scandinavia and eastern Europe. Although the students, and sometimes their tutors, often posed a threat to public order, they "also represented an important sector of urban demand. The Left Bank would have been denuded without them and the service industries they nurtured – from accommodating and catering to manuscript copying and illuminating."[9]

8 *Church of St-Martin-des-Champs, dating from 1060 and altered in 1130-40*

Being only the second university to be established in Europe after the University of Bologna (which dates from 1088), the University de Paris "elevated the name of the French capital, surpassing all others in the fame of its masters and the prestige of its studies in theology and philosophy. It was the magnet for the greatest minds: Thomas Aquinas of Italy . . . Duns Scotus of Scotland . . . Marsilius of Padua and . . . William of Ockham." By virtue of its university, "Paris was the 'Athens of Europe', the Goddess of Wisdom, it was said, after leaving Greece and then Rome, had made it her home."[10]

The construction of churches on the Left Bank in the thirteenth century either preceded or accompanied the development of the University. For example St-Julien-le-Pauvre was started in the twelfth century but finished in the fourteenth, while St-Étienne-du-Mont, north of the church of Ste-Geneviève was begun in 1221 and completed as late as the sixteenth century. On the Right Bank, the church of St-Martin-des-Champs – dating from 1060 and altered in 1130-40 – was completed in the thirteenth century through the addition of a refectory and nave that superimposed the Gothic style on its earlier Romanesque design. By now the High Gothic style had emerged in Paris. This went on to result in the use of rib vaults in more and more churches in the capital, and also in the construction of tall clerestory windows and flying buttresses, motifs inspired by cathedrals such as Chartres (begun in 1195), Reims (1212) and Amiens (1220). Other new adornments included bar tracery and naturalistic sculptured foliage, both introduced at Reims in the early thirteenth century but in due course adopted in Paris. It must be pointed out that since the Church was exempt from taxation, it often found it easier than some of its secular counterparts to target financial resources at new building projects.

Throughout Philippe Auguste's reign, the population density of Paris inside the walls increased dramatically, so much so that the boundary of Les Halles was extended northwards to absorb the St-Lazare fair previously outside of the wall. However, this did not stop congestion within the walls getting worse. The squalor of the streets was appalling (as it was throughout the Middle Ages and beyond), and therefore even in the twelfth century, an attempt was made to enhance the built environment of Paris. Thus, as a reaction to the stench of Parisian mud and effluent passing his palace on the Île-de-la-Cité, Philippe Auguste in 1185 ordered his *prévôt* (the senior royal official) to pave all the main streets in his capital especially the north-south Rues St-Martin and St-Jacques and east-west Rues St-Antoine and St-Honoré leading to each of the city gates, but inevitably progress was slow. Accompanying these measures, open trenches were dug into the centre of each newly paved road to provide a channel for the outflow of sewage into the Seine, often a slow and unhealthy process but probably better than a complete absence of sanitation.

LOUIS IX, THE SAINT (R. 1226-70)

As in the preceding reign of Philippe Auguste, the level of taxation was comparatively high, first to meet the cost of a war with England in 1242-43 and second to finance France's armed contribution to the Seventh and Eighth Crusade in respectively 1248-54 and 1270 – ventures in which Louis took a leading part and was subsequently canonised as St-Louis. With the continual growth in the population and its material needs, there was also a need to finance the escalation of bureaucracy.

9   *Church of St-Germain-l'Auxerrois. 1220-30*

However, a diverse range of notable new and reconstructed buildings were erected during the long reign of Louis IX, but the more important edifices were ecclesiastical. This was not particularly remarkable since the church was very largely exempt from taxation. The first of several important churches, substantially re-built during Louis's reign was the five-aisled edifice of St-Germain-l'Auxerrois, the church possibly becoming the most imposing ecclesiastical building in Paris at that time. Dedicated to the canonised bishop of Auxerre (d. 448), the Romanesque church was reconstructed in the Gothic style shortly after the nearby city wall of Philippe II Augustus was completed. Though the church dates back to the twelfth century when its tower was built, most of the reconstruction work occurred when the church's choir and the southernmost aisle were built between 1220-30.[11]

10   *Sainte Chapelle, 1246-8*

Paris experienced a period of further urban development when, during his long reign, Louis IX built the Hospice des Quinze-Vingts and the theological college of the Sorbonne, and over Roman and Merovingian foundations rebuilt the Palais-de-la-Cité including the magnificent two-storey Gothic church of Sainte Chapelle in 1246-8. Constructed midway across the Palais-de-la-Cité in 1246-48, parallel to the Royal Palace, the enormous Sainte-Chapelle was built by Louis (later canonised as St-Louis) as a shrine for the Crown of Thorns and other passion relics acquired from Venice in 1239. Designed by Pierre de Montreuil who probably drew upon elements of the design of the Gothic cathedral at Amiens (the tallest building in France until the construction of the Eiffel Tower in 1887-89), the chapel is a two-storey rib-vaulted edifice with a western portico, a low ground floor with three aisles for members of the court, and a slender upper floor for the monarchy and the holy relics, terminating in a polygonal choir and an apse. With the side walls and eastern end of the upper floor punctuated by stained tracery windows, its west end is adorned by a magnificent rose window.[12]

Anxious to add an ecclesiastical dimension to his Château de St-Germain, Louis IX in 1230-38 enlarged the twelfth century residence through the addition of the Chapelle St-Louis designed in the current Rayonnant style of French Gothic. But since the château was strategically located on a sharp bend of the Seine to the west of the Louvre, and some 19 km from the centre of Paris, Louis also strengthened the building by the addition of curtain walling and rounded towers.

From 1231-8 further work was undertaken on the construction of St-Denis. Its central nave and transepts with their clerestory windows replaced the older walls; and flying buttresses were put in place to support the upper storeys. But before and after work was undertaken on St-Denis, the construction of Notre Dame continued apace. The western bays of the cathedral's nave were laid between 1200-1225, the west front was pierced by three portals with rich sculptural adornment, and from 1225-1259 the twin towers of the west front were erected. In 1246-47 a new transept was built in the north, and around 1250 the upper reaches of the cathedral (other than its west front) were rebuilt to accommodate huge tracery windows in an attempt to improve the interior lighting of the cathedral, while the buttress system was realigned accordingly. In 1258 the southern façade of the nave was completed together with a new transept; and a magnificent rose window was installed in the south transept by Pierre de Montreuil between 1258-67. Finally, between 1296-1330, choir chapels in the apses were constructed, high windows in the choir were installed, and the choir buttresses were reconfigurated.[13] Diminutive by comparison with Notre Dame, the church of St-Séverin located on the Left Bank was started in the early thirteenth century when its five naves and eight bays were constructed similarly in the Gothic style.

Even in the mid-thirteenth century, the University of Paris did not provide campus accommodation and teaching facilities. Since the accommodation of scholars was at best makeshift, a number of colleges were constructed to remedy these deficiencies. The first to be built after the University's foundation was the Sorbonne, founded by Robert le Sorbon, Louis IX's chaplain. Many others followed and by 1400, the University contained some forty colleges.

Though the population and number of notable buildings of Paris increased substantially during the thirteenth century, the city was without a municipal authority to exercise jurisdiction, influence the development of trade and control the location of new buildings. Though for at least two centuries, the monarch could look to his *prévôt de Paris* to implement royal policy in the capital. In 1264 Louis delegated powers to a newly established municipal authority comprising elected *echevans* (magistrates) and the *prévôt des marchands* (a merchants' provost or mayor) who would also be the head of the *Hanse des marchands de l'eau* (the merchants guild). But at first the authority had nowhere to assemble, except in an improvised Parloi aux Bourgeois and subsequently in the Grand-Chatelet. It was not until later in Medieval Paris that more appropriate accommodation became available (see below).

PHILIPPE IV, LE BEL (THE FAIR)(R. 1285-1314)

With a population of at least 200,000 by the middle of Philippe IV's reign, Paris was by far the largest city in Europe, over twice the size of her nearest rivals Florence, Genoa, Venice and London. Because of its size and importance as the national capital, Philippe established a *Parlement* in the city to perform the roles of a legitimate court with specific judicial and fiscal functions.

But the new institution alone could not be expected to raise sufficient tax revenue to finance wars against the English in 1294-98 and 1300-03, and to meet the ever-rising cost of bureaucracy across the kingdom. Direct and indirect taxes were raised for these purposes, for example the *taille* was imposed on people's property or incomes, while consumption taxes were placed on drink, livestock and salt.[14] At best, taxation was tolerated if it was used particularly to defray the cost of wars against the English, and if it was approved by the Estates-General representing the nobles, the clergy and urban bourgeoisie even though it was only the latter (normally the largest of the three estates) that actually incurred taxation. However, throughout the Middle Ages and beyond, taxation was only introduced at times of dire necessity and it would have been extremely important for a monarch to attempt to impose taxes on a permanent basis.

Compounding the daunting fiscal problems facing Paris, bad weather and poor harvests led to an acute food shortage in the capital in 1305 and for many years after, so that by 1317 seriously inflated prices and reduced nourishment had a dire effect on the living standards of most Parisians.

Because of wars, taxation and poverty, very few secular buildings of note were constructed during Philippe IV's reign, and even work on new ecclesiastical buildings seemed to be suspended. But when secular buildings were erected, there was only scant attention paid to Gothic design. Unlike recently built ecclesiastical buildings, they were relatively insensitive to evolving changes in style and, like Romanesque secular buildings, only accommodated those attributes that were considered appropriate to the needs of the user. This applied particularly to bridge-building. In Gothic style, the Pont au Change was constructed across the northern channel of the Seine to link the Grand Chatelet on the Right Bank to the Palais-de-la-Cité; while the Palais-de-la-Cité was extended by Philippe IV in 1296-13. Looking onto the northern channel, the palace contains three ranges, two of which were framed initially by three towers: Caesar Tower, Silver Tower and Bonbec Tower. The palace accommodates one of the largest halls in Europe, the Grand Salle with its lower storey (built in 1300-10) accommodating the vaulted 'La Salle des Gens d'Armes' (Chamber of the Gentlemen-at-Arms), an extensive room 64 metres long, 27.5 metres wide and 8.5 metres high. In the basement, space was provided for a dungeon and prison.

11   *Palais-de-la-Cité, circa 1300 (renamed Conciergerie in 1358)*

Possibly to defray some of the cost of these developments, Philippe seized the wealth of the Templars. Founded in 1119, the Temple was confiscated in 1312 and handed over to the Hospitallers who were charged a huge sum for its acquisition. The Templars were disbanded, and their leaders burnt, including their Grand Master, Jacques de Molay.

PHILIPPE V (R. 1316-22)

By the time Philippe V ruled over his domain, Paris had become a focus of Christian devotion, and many of the churches that came into being in the High Medieval period were properties of monastic orders such as the Augustinians, Benedictines and Franciscans. It is thus not at all surprising that the majority of these buildings – Gothic in style – were located in the ancient core of Paris where population density would have been at its highest, close to or on the Île-de-la-Cité and within the city walls, though this was less marked on the Left Bank. Of the religious establishments newly built during the reign of Philippe V, the church of St-Leu-St-Gilles, west of the Rue St-Denis is the most notable, though the magnificent church of St-Germain l'Auxerrois was still in the process of reconstruction.

CHARLES IV (R. 1322-28)

With the kingdom of France expanding both northward and southward at the end of the High Middle Ages, the population of Paris – the largest city in western Europe – continued to grow rapidly and reached 250,000 by 1330.[15] By the time the direct line of the Capetians came to an end with the death of Charles IV in 1328, Paris was not only large but of considerable importance as a royal capital, a focus of learning and an ecclesiastical centre. The development of the Right Bank had forged ahead and began to press against the wall of Philippe Auguste, while building work encroached on the fields and water meadows of the unprotected Left Bank ending the spatial isolation of the Abbey of St-Germain-des-Pres. Paris was not only the capital of the largest nation in western Europe, and one of its most dynamic powers, but it also accommodated centres of piety and learning and a wide range of crafts [supported by] the largest and wealthiest concentration of consumers in the west.

REFERENCES

1. A. Hussey, *Paris. The Secret History*, (London: Penguin Books
2. A. Horne (B), *Friend or Foe. An Anglo-Saxon History of France*, (London: Phoenix, 2005), p.107
3. H. Ballon, *The Paris of Henry IV. Architecture and Ubanism*, (London: The MIT Press, 1991), p.15
4. C. Jones, *Paris. Biography of a City*, (London: Penguin Books, 2006), p.149
5. C. Jones, opt. cit., p.156
6. C. Jones, opt. cit., p.160
7. C. Jones, opt. cit., p.160
8. H. J. Ballon, opt. cit., p.253
9. H. Ballon, opt. cit., p.253
10. A. Blunt, *Art and Architecture in France, 1500-1700*, (London: Yale University Press, 5th Edit., 1999), p.112
11. Ibid
12. H. Wischermann, *Paris. An Architectural Guide*, (Verona: Arsenale Editrice, 2005), p.46
13. A. Blunt, opt. cit., p.130
14. D. Watkin, *A History of Western Architecture*, (London: 5th Edit., 2011), p.261
15. C. Jones, opt. cit., p.28

CHRONOLOGY

987-996	Hugh Capet rules France. First of the Capetian line
996-1031	Robert II is King of France
1031-60	Henri I rules France
1060-1108	Philippe I is King of France

11th-12th Century	**St-Germain-de-Pres built**
1108-37	Louis VI, the Fat, King of France
1137-40	Louis VII, King of France
1144	**Basilica of St-Denis constructed**
1147	**The Knights Templar build the Temple**
1163 onwards	**Notre Dame Cathedral built**
1178	**Work begins on the *donjon* at Vincennes**
1180-1223	Philippe II, Augustus, King of France
1181-83	**Les Halles built**
1186	**Philippe II begins to pave the main thoroughfares**
1190-1205	**Philippe constructs a new city wall**
12th Century	**St-Martin-des-Champs**
1200	**University of Paris established by Royal charter**
13th Century	**St-Séverin built**
1190-1300	***Donjon* of the Louvre constructed**
12th-15th Century	**St-Germain-l'Auxerroix**
1223-26	Louis VIII, King of France
1226-70	Louis IX, the Saint, King of France
1231-38	**Further work undertaken on the Basilica of St-Denis**
1246-48	**Sainte-Chapelle built**
1253	**Robert de Sorbon founds the Sorbonne**
1270-85	Philippe III, King of France
1285-1314	Philippe IV, King of France
1301-13	**Conciergerie built (initially the Palais de la Cité)**
1307	Templars burnt
1314-16	Louis X, King of France
1316-22	Philippe V, King of France
1322-28	Charles IV, King of France, last of the Capetian line

3

THE DEVELOPMENT OF PARIS IN THE LATER-MIDDLE AGES

INTRODUCTION

Originating in central Asia, and from the Crimea spreading to the European Mediterranean coast, bubonic plague reached Paris in 1348 and over the following two years brought about 40,000-50,000 fatalities in the French capital, reducing its population by between 30% and 40%. But the Black Death, as it was called, was followed by other major epidemics throughout the 1360s and again in 1375 which in total impeded the population growth of Paris until the early-sixteenth century when its population again reached around 200,000. But the growth of Paris was not only affected by plague; it was severely constrained by the Hundred Years War with England. It was thus within the context of a depleted population and the threat of occupation by an invading power that a succession of Valois kings attempted to a greater or less extent to stamp their mark on the physical development of Paris.

PHILIPPE VI (R. 1328-50)

When Charles IV, the last Capetian king, died without a male heir in 1328, the nearest claimant to the French throne was his nephew Edward III of England, but since the French king-makers debarred him under Salic Law from the succession since he was descended from Charles's sister, Isabelle of France, Charles's nearest male relative to have descended through the male line was Philippe de Valois. Though he was duly crowned Philippe VI, his legitimacy as king of France was disputed by Edward III, heralding the beginning of the Hundred Years War with its inevitable impact on Paris.

During Philippe's reign, there were serious underlying weaknesses in the general wellbeing of the French capital. First, its inhabitants suffered from the privations of a series of famines, particularly in 1315-17; second, many fell victim to the Black Death that alone reduced the population of Paris by at least a third to around 260,000 in the years 1348-52, though the plague was not altogether disastrous since it reduced population density and the degree of congestion in the city and created a shortage of labour that raised wage levels; third, despite these privations, Parisians began to feel the adverse effects of the Hundred Years War that commenced in 1337 and continued until 1453; and last but not least, they feared that they would become victims of internal insurrection.

JEAN II, LE BON (R. 1350-64)

It is remarkable, and some might say insensitive, that during the Black Death, Jean le Bon ordered further work to be undertaken on the Palais de la Cité. In 1350 he commissioned both the addition of the vaulted Cuisines des St-Louis to the Salle des Gens-d'Armes, and the Tour de l'Horloge at the eastern end of the river façade of the palais – increasing its number of towers from three to four. However, Jean's influence on the development of Paris was cut short in 1356 when the French army was defeated by English forces at the Battle of Poitiers in 1356. The French king was captured and imprisoned in London until his death in 1364, leaving Charles the Dauphin to reign in his enforced absence.

Charles would have recognised that by the 1350s Paris had become an important centre of trade. From the Early-Middle Ages, the Pont au Change (as its name suggests) became famous as a location for moneychangers and goldsmiths, and a large open market functioned at the Place de Grève – a gravelly sandbar to the east of the Grand Chatelet. Although the site contained water mills for the processing of grain, the Place de Grève was devoid of permanent buildings and became a vast open-air depository for all kinds of agricultural produce and minerals shipped up and down the Seine. In addition, there had accumulated around it a higgledy-piggledy pattern of narrow streets containing a miscellany of buildings such as slaughterhouses, knackers' yards, butchers, tanners, fishmongers and brothels to name but a few.

Exacerbating congestion, the Place de Grève was the site of the intersection of the main east-west axis of St-Antoine and the north-south thoroughfares of the Rue St-Denis and St-Martin, each of which tunnelled people and goods into the market. But after the Black Death, only a few prestigious buildings would be built in the French capital until the reign of François I two centuries later, while other buildings would change their use. For example in 1357 the *prévôt* of Paris, Étienne Marcel, in need of a new city hall acquired a substantial Gothic edifice in the Place de Grève variously called the Maison aux Piliers, the Marchandise or the Maison du Dauphin, and henceforth it was put to good use as the seat of municipal government for a further two or three hundred years.[1]

However, by 1358 with Jean le Bon still absent from his throne, Paris soon descended into turmoil, notwithstanding attempts by the Dauphin to pacify its inhabitants. Taking advantage of the situation, Étienne Marcel sought to reform the king's role in the governance of France, including the establishment of a 'Commune of Paris' that, in consultation with the monarch, would govern both the capital and the country as a whole. Provoked by the murder of two of the Dauphin's counsellors in February 1358, Charles quickly vacated the capital in order to assemble his troops with the intention of taking the capital by force and eliminating all opposition. However, around Paris, the peasantry ill-advisedly allied themselves with Marcel but their uprising (the 'Jacquerie') was put down at the cost of some 30,000 lives. Marcel consequently sought support from the English and wanted to open the gates of Paris to their army. However, the Parisians regarded this as treason, and he was murdered by one of his cousins in July 1358. Charles consequently re-entered Paris where from 1364 he reigned over his kingdom largely free from internal opposition.

Once again, households now felt sufficiently safe to construct new dwellings. As the Late Middle Ages progressed, side-by-side gabled timber-framed houses were still being constructed, but gradually stone-framing replaced timber and, to reduce the risk of fire, damaged rubble replaced lathe and plaster in the gaps between the spars regardless of whether the building was timber- or stone-framed.[2] By the end of the fourteenth century, half-timbered houses were in vogue or had façades built entirely of masonry such as ashlar. A special form of housing for the monarch or aristocracy emerged in the Late Middle Ages: the *hôtel*. As described by Anthony Sutcliffe, "most *hôtels* stood on large sites with gardens and ancillary buildings. They were generally closed off from the street by a curtain wall or by dour frontages with sparse fenestration. Their main rooms faced an interior courtyard or garden. The principal entry from the street was through a *porte cochère*, defined by massive masonry and heavy wooden doors."[3] Gothic in style, most Parisian *hôtels* were designed by master builders, and featured "pointed and ogee arches, stone window tracery and transoms, and carved decoration in the Flamboyant style,"[4] and were also notable for their tall conical or pyramidal roofs. One of the first outstanding examples of this genre from the Late Middle Ages was the Hôtel St-Pol. Located between the Seine and the east-west axis of the Rue St-Antoine, St-Pol was built for the Dauphin, the future Charles V, on land that he bought from the archbishop of Sens, the Comte d'Étampes and the abbés of St-Maur around 1360. He thought that St-Pol could become a much more agreeable residence than his former home in the Palais de la Cité where he had to confront a popular insurrection and forceful demands from Étienne Marcel, the Provost of the City's merchants. The Hôtel St-Pol was not a *hôtel* in the normal sense; it was "a group of buildings surrounded by gardens and linked by covered galleries that framed a succession of courtyards, a cherry orchard, a vineyard, a *savour* for raising salmon [and] aviaries."[5]

CHARLES V (R. 1364-80)

Taking advantage in a lull in the Hundred Years War with England, and in the absence of internal conflict, Charles V substantially increased the defences of his capital as a safeguard against the possibility of armed attacks on the city in the future. First, he built an additional wall beyond much of that constructed by Philippe Auguste earlier in the century. However, although it was begun in 1365, it was not completed until the 1390s after his death. Confined to the Right Bank, where four out of five Parisians lived and where attack from the north was more likely than from the south, the five kilometre wall increased the total area enclosed by walls from 272 hectares to 439 hectares, but because the Black Death of 1348-9 had reduced the size of the Parisian population by around a third, further congestion was averted at least in the short to medium term.

To further prioritise defence, Charles ordered the construction of the Bastille in 1370-83, a fortress situated at the south-eastern extremity of his city wall in close proximity to the Hôtel St-Pol and on the Right Bank of the Seine. Initially intended to form the St-Antoine gate, a round tower was soon extended to create a substantial fortress, the Bastille. It was rectangular in shape, with a length of 70 metres and a width of 30 metres, and its immensely thick curtain walls – enclosing twin courtyards – were punctuated by eight massive round towers, 25 metres in height, while the whole building

12   *The Bastille, 1370-83*

was surrounded by a wide moat. Facing both inward towards the city and outward towards the countryside, the Bastille was built to quell internal disorder as well as to defend the city from attack from within. It was only in the early seventeenth century that the building, instead of continuing in its role as a fortress, became a prison and it was eventually demolished in 1789 during the French Revolution.[6]

Soon after becoming king, Charles V abandoned the claustrophobic and insecure Palais de la Cité and duly occupied the recently completed Hôtel St-Pol which, apart from providing greater comfort, was close to the protection of the Bastille. Meanwhile, his enormous palace became a royal administrative building, was renamed the Conciergerie after the Concierge or caretaker of the palace, and a decorative clock was added to what became known as the Tour d'Horloge. But in 1370 Charles embarked on a much more ambitious course of action. He ordered that Philippe Auguste's old citadel of the Louvre be replaced by a palace that was both a stronghold and a place of residence. From the time of its construction in the early thirteenth century, it had been deemed an unsuitable building at which to accommodate French monarchs. It was definitely not a royal palace. However, during the reign of Charles V, "windows [were] struck through Philippe Auguste's grimly functional arrow slits and with fancifully decorative pointed roofs superimposed, [the Louvre] became a palace fit for a king,"[7] even though Charles became the last French king to use the edifice as his main residence.

On the extreme eastern edge of Paris, some 6.7 kilometres from the Bastille, Charles completed the construction of the *donjon* at the Château de Vincennes in about 1370, and during the following six years built its ramparts and began work on the chapel in 1379. Though not a new project – work had begun on the property in 1178 under Louis VII – the outlying *château* enhanced the defensive capabilities of the French capital in the fourteenth century as well as providing a royal residence when the need arose.

To the west of Paris, 22 kilometres from the Louvre, Charles V rebuilt the twelfth century Château de St-Germain-en-Laye during the latter years of his reign, as if to balance the strategic importance of Vincennes to the east of the capital. Though the *château* was largely destroyed by the Black Prince in 1346 during the Hundred Years

War, it was reconstructed by Charles within the original thirteenth-century walls and incorporating the surviving thirteenth century chapel built for Louis IX. It was Charles V (r. 1364-80), however, who completed the medieval stronghold. Its most prominent building, its *donjon*, is 52 metres in height and, when completed around 1370, became the tallest fortified structure in Europe. After it was finished, the rectangular site of the *château* – measuring 330 metres by 175 metres – was protected by a curtain wall punctuated by six bastions and three gateways and surrounded by a deep moat. The Medieval *château* was completed by the construction of the Sainte-Chapelle in 1379, reminiscent of its Parisian namesake though smaller and with no lower level.[8]

The construction of new church buildings was virtually absent during the reign of Charles V, though modifications were made to existing ecclesiastical edifices. For example an additional Gothic nave and chapels were added to the north side of St-Denis c.1375[9], and by the early fifteenth century, the final form of French Gothic architecture, the Flamboyant, was spectacularly employed at St-Germain-l' Auxerrois, making use of "ogees in flame-like tracery patterns, and thin faceted mouldings."[10]

CHARLES VI (R. 1380-1422)

During the reign of Charles VI comparatively little building work was undertaken. France was in the middle of a war that unknowingly was to last a hundred years or more, and its financial and other resources were gradually becoming depleted, insufficient to fund more than a handful of prominent Parisian buildings. Three bridges were constructed across the northern channel of the Seine to the Île-de-la-Cité, and a further bridge connected the island to the Left Bank. The first bridge to be built was the aforementioned wooden Pont au Change, constructed in the twelfth century with its name derived from the goldsmiths and moneylenders who subsequently installed shops across the structure. The second bridge completed in fifteenth century Paris was the Pont St-Michel that linked the Île-de-la-Cité with the Left Bank at the Boulevard St-Michel. An earlier version of the bridge, built in 1378, was constructed of stone and had houses built on it, but river borne ice in the treacherous winter of 1407-8 caused it to collapse. The third bridge to be constructed – connecting the Rue St-Martin on the Right Bank to the Île-de-la-Cité was the Pont Notre Dame that in 1412 replaced the Early-Medieval Planches de Milbray (or plank bridge) that had been swept away by floods in 1406. Commissioned by Charles VI, the new bridge was made from solid wood and had 60 houses built across it (30 on each side).

13   *Hôtel de Clisson, 1380-circa 1400*

Though bridge-building dominated construction activity during Charles's reign, some other building work did take place notwithstanding funding constraints. For example the Hôtel de Clisson was constructed c. 1380 and the Hôtel des Tournelles was built in 1388. Of the two, it was the latter that became famous in the history of the Valois line. Early in its life, the building became the property of the bishop of Paris, but he subsequently sold it to the duc de Berry in 1402, who in turn ceded it to his nephew the duc d'Orléans, the younger brother of Charles VI, in exchange for another *hôtel* in the vicinity, the Hôtel de Gixé. However, in 1407, the duc d'Orléans was assassinated and the Hôtel des Tournelles eventually passed to Charles VI who resided there occasionally from 1417 onwards. Like his father, he preferred to live mainly in the Louvre and locate the centre of his administration in the Conciergerie where, between 1380-90, the enormous and magnificent Salles des Gardes in 1380-90 had been constructed together with a dungeon and prison in its basement.

During the early 1400s in the midst of the Hundred Years War, the Burgundians (allies of England) and Armagnacs (supporters of Charles VI) were in armed conflict with each other over the sovereignty of France. This not only divided French loyalties but was fortuitous for the English since under the leadership of Henry V they were able to decimate Charles's army at Azincourt in 1415. During the final years of Charles VI's reign, it is perhaps remarkable that any building work was undertaken in Paris at all. Although few, if any, secular edifices were built, the church of St-Nicholas was started in 1420, and this was followed in 1420-25 by the construction of the nave and remaining aisles of St-Germain-l'Auxerrois.

The English governance of Paris (1422-36) and the reign of Charles VII (1436-61)

Under the Treaty of Troyes of 1420, the English king, Henry V, was betrothed to Caroline – Charles VI's daughter – and was duly declared next-in-line to the French throne. But within two years both Henry and Charles were dead, and instead of the Dauphin, – the would-be Charles VII – ascending the throne, Henry V's son, Henry VI, became the next king of France as well as becoming the new King of England. However, although Paris was under the occupation of *'les goddams'* (as the English forces were known), Henry was in no position to personally rule France because he was still in his infancy, and therefore his uncle, the Duke of Bedford, governed northern and western France as Viceroy for 21 years from the luxury of the Hôtel des Tournelles. During the English occupation, the Duke of Bedford extended the palace by purchasing 3.4 hectares from the nuns of the neighbouring convent of Ste-Catharine. Situated on the north side of the Rue St-Antoine, the Hôtel des Tournelles shared many of the attributes of the Hôtel St-Pol immediately to the south. It was essentially a collection of buildings rather than a single edifice, and it was spread over 117 hectares. It contained 20 chapels, several pleasure grounds, a maze, six kitchen gardens and farmland. The palace was particularly noted for its magnificently decorated council chamber. After the departure of the Duke of Bedford, the property reverted to the French crown.

From 1422, the former Dauphin, now Charles VII the pretender to the French throne, attempted to rule central and southern France from Chinon, but in 1436 his forces – inspired by Jeanne d'Arc – liberated Paris. Within a year of taking the city, Charles decided to use Bourges as a base from which to continue his conflict with the Anglo-Burgundians, but after the Burgundians under Philip the Good switched sides in 1435, Charles's army achieved decisive victories over English forces at the Battle of Formigny in 1450 and Battle of Castillon in 1453, driving them completely out of France except for Calais.

With Paris under English rule (1415-36) and with Charles absent from the French capital throughout most of his reign, the impetus for growth in the city diminished and comparatively little building work of note took place in the secular sector. However, after Charles's defeat of the English, Chinon and Loche, rather than Paris, accommodated the royal court and for a further sixty or more years a succession of French kings neglected Paris and resided in the Loire Valley which, by virtue of its location, provided greater security against foreign invasions, internal incursions or local uprisings, and because of its forested environment, provided excellent conditions for *la chaise*.

Charles, nevertheless, still had responsibility for royal finances. In contrast to earlier Medieval monarchs, he was fortunate in not having to face bitter disputes over the payment of taxes. Altruistically, they "were gradually accepted in principal and for the "common good. The closing years of the reign of Charles V . . . constituted a major phase of political reconstruction, when growing economic activity facilitated a major increase in the revenue of the state."[11] Tax revenue (measured in terms of the currency of Tours) had increased from some 1.7 million to 2.3 million livres tournais between 1439 and 1449[12], but this was of little use to Paris. The revenue was spent mainly on a standing army of 12,000-15,000 men and their artillery and comparatively little on the administration, buildings and infrastructure of the French capital.

REFERENCES

1. D. Gray-Durant, *Paris and Versailles* (London: A & C Black, 2001), p.251
2. A. Sutcliffe, *Paris. An Architectural History* (London: Yale University Press, 1996), p.10
3. A. Sutcliffe, opt. cit., p.9
4. A. Sutcliffe, opt. cit., p.9
5. E. Hazan, *The Invention of Paris* (London: Verso, 2011), p.57
6. D. Gray-Durant, opt. cit., p.258
7. A. Horne (a), *Seven Ages of Paris: Portrait of a City* (London: Pan Books, 2002), p.3
8. D. Gray-Durant, opt. cit., pp. 332-34
9. D. Gray-Durant, opt. cit., pp. 368-69
10. N. Coldstream, *Medieval Architecture* (Oxford: Oxford University Press, 2002), p.40
11. R. Price, *A Concise History of France* (Cambridge: Cambridge University Press, 1993), p.47
12. Ibid

CHRONOLOGY

1328-50	Philippe VI, King of France. First of the Valois line
1338	Beginning of the 'Hundred Years War' (Ends in 1453)
1338-50	The Black Death strikes Paris
1350-64	Jean II, King of France
1355-56	Étienne Marcel seizes control of Paris
1356-63	**A wall around Paris is begun by Étienne Marcel**
1364-80	Charles V, King of France
1364-80	**Charles V continues building a wall around Paris begun by Étienne Marcel**
1370	**The donjon of the Louvre converted into a palace**
	The Chateau de Vincennes was completed
1380-1422	Charles VI, King of France
1380-83	**Charles VI completes a wall around Paris and builds the Bastille**
1380 onwards	**The Hôtel de Clisson is built**
1420-36	Paris directly ruled by England
1422-61	Charles VII, King of France
1453	End of 'Hundred Years War'
1461-83	Louis XI, King of France
1470	**Work begins on the Hôtel de Ville**
1474-1519	**Hôtel de Sens built**
1483-98	Charles VIII, King of France

4

THE FLOWERING OF
RENAISSANCE PARIS

INTRODUCTION

With a population that had shrunk from around 250,000 on the eve of
the Black Death to 100,000 at the beginning of the sixteenth century,
Paris was no longer the largest city in Europe. In 1500, Naples was
substantially larger with a population of 150,000, Milan and Venice had
around the same population as Paris, while London was inhabited by a
population as small as 40,000.[1] Despite a lower population density than
in the first half of the fourteenth century, Paris two hundred years later
was still hemmed in by its Medieval city walls and reliant on only one
substantial bridge across the Seine, the Pont de Notre Dame. In contrast
to most of the thirteenth and fourteenth centuries when French kings
located themselves and their courts in Paris and commissioned a range of
grandiose buildings, Valois monarchs from the mid-fifteenth century to
the early sixteenth- largely eschewed residence in the French capital and
preferred to reside in the Loire Valley or even to lead their armies into
Italy for not inconsiderable periods of time. It was only from around 1515
after François I ascended the French throne that the Renaissance began
to make a major impact on the physical structure of Paris, and only from
the late 1520s that Paris regained its position as the true capital of France.

LOUIS XI (R. 1461-83)

The effects of the Italian Renaissance on France were minimal and sporadic in the late fifteenth century. Architecturally, the first purely Renaissance building constructed in France was the chapel of St-Lazare in the church of La Major at Marseilles in 1479-81. Commissioned by King René of Anjou and the Italian architect, Francesco Laurana, the chapel was not immediately followed by other Renaissance buildings, and it was not until Charles VIII brought back a number of Italian painters and sculptors to France after his disastrous campaign of 1494 that Renaissance influences were again felt in France, but not in the field of architecture. It was only when Louis XII and particularly François I returned from their Italian campaigns in respectively 1513 and 1526 that Italian architecture began to exert an influence on the design of French buildings.

Although Louis XI was attracted to Italy, there was little evidence that he was sufficiently inspired by the Renaissance to import any of its attributes into France. He was also drawn to the Loire Valley and spent a total of "half of his twenty-two-year reign wandering away from Paris [before eventually] dying at his *château* at Plessis-les-Tours".[2] To be in close proximity to the king, the royal court and the political elite also relocated to the Loire, depressing still further the political and economic importance of Paris. Construction activity in the French capital was almost at an all time low. There was, however, an important exception: The Bishop of Sens commissioned a magnificent Gothic residence on the Right Bank in 1475, opposite Notre Dame.

Like his predecessor Charles VII, but unlike most earlier kings of France, Louis enjoyed a steady inflow of tax revenue from a relatively compliant populace, his revenue amounting to 5.1 million livres tournois in 1482 (more than doubling in money terms the 2.3 million livres tournois collected by his predecessor in 1449).[3] But continuing the practice set by Charles, he spent comparatively little of this sum in Paris, preferring instead to commission projects elsewhere in his kingdom and to support his army.

14   *Hôtel de Sens, 1474-1519*

CHARLES VIII (R. 1483-98)

Though residing much of his time at the Château d'Amboise, Charles VIII spent 1494 to 1498 in Italy at the head of an invading French army. Having reached Naples and hoping but failing to secure accompanying forces to embark on a crusade to the Levant, he returned with difficulty to France fighting off Italian forces in the north-west of the peninsula. Meanwhile, France was left in debt and disarray. Apart from the Cluniacs funding the construction of an impressive *hôtel* adjacent to the Roman Baths on the Left Bank in 1485[4], there was very little building work of any sort undertaken in Paris during Charles's reign because of a low level of demand.

LOUIS XII (R. 1498-1515)

Louis, in a no less costly manner than his predecessor, fought a series of wars in Italy, first against Milan in 1499-1504, second against Venice in 1509 and later in lesser campaigns against Italian armies across the peninsula until being driven out of Italy after the Battle of Navarra in 1513. In between the wars, and during the two years after his final return to France, Louis not only resided at the Château de Blois but oversaw the reconstruction of its main entrance block, largely in the Gothic style but with Renaissance undertones.

However, like his immediate predecessors, Louis XII had little interest in Paris, politically, culturally and economically, and because of his military and other commitments, he was both unwilling and unable to provide money for its physical development. Parisian financial resources had been fully stretched by the Italian wars and construction activity almost came to a standstill, but once again the major exception was bridge-building, a municipal priority.

Since the fourteenth century, notwithstanding the construction of the Pont au Change, the problems of communication across the built-up area of Paris were exacerbated by the absence of robust bridges over the Seine with adverse effects on the Parisian economy. Therefore in 1507 work began on a bridge, the rebuilt Pont Notre Dame, that was to survive the test of time until it was replaced in the mid-nineteenth century. It was constructed of stone on which 34 houses of uniform design were built on each side in accordance with a ruling by the municipality. As described by Anthony Sutcliffe, "each house had a single bay, gabled façade of three floors, with an attic in the gable. An inset arcade at ground level was supported by piers set in line with the party walls."[5] With brick façades and dressed stone inserts above the piers of the arcade, the development was much admired by the citizenry of Paris. The length and symmetry of the arcades contrasted sharply with the set-back ground floors that were common in medieval Paris, and anticipated the streetscape of classical Paris in later centuries.[6] Lesser exceptions were the construction of the Hôtel Herouet (c. 1499), the Hôtel de Cluny and Hôtel de la Reine Blanche (both c. 1500), and within the ecclesiastical sector the churches of St-Jacques and St-Merri dating respectively from 1508 and 1515.

Diminished in size since the Black Death of 1348-49, Paris was still environmentally medieval at the beginning of the sixteenth century and continued to remain so until the nineteenth. However, whereas the French capital over this period was gradually adorned by buildings and town planning schemes in a variety of Renaissance, Baroque and Neo-

15 *Hôtel de Cluny, circa 1500*

Classical styles, in the first quarter of the sixteenth century Renaissance architecture, that had rapidly changed the face of so many Italian cities in the fifteenth century, was only just beginning to exert its influence on Paris and its surrounding countryside. Without patrons such as the Medici of Florence, the Sforza of Milan or the Gonzaga of Mantua, Paris had remained an architectural backwater, but the physical structure of the French capital and its outer environs were about to change.

FRANÇOIS I (R. 1515-47)

The Valois dynasty, initially, was not only unwilling to champion the physical improvement of Paris but was disinclined to reside permanently or hold court in its capital. Instead of inhabiting the royal residences of, for example, the Hôtel-St Pol or Hôtel des Tournelles, François I preferred to live in various *châteaux* in the Loire Valley during the first ten years of his reign, in part because of their environmental attractions and proximity to his favourite hunting grounds, but also because they were relatively safe havens from northern invaders, particularly during times of Anglo-French hostility. Thus until the mid- to late 1520s, French foreign and domestic policy would not emanate from Paris but from locations comparatively remote from the former centres of royal power. In France, the decision to declare war or peace on England or the Holy Roman Empire would be made in the Loire Valley rather than in Paris.

It was from the Loire that, in 1515, François I decided to resume his campaign to take over the Milan area after a break of two years, a decision that resulted in a victory for his army and Venetian allies at the Battle of Marignano against a confederacy of forces from the Swiss cantons and Duchy of Milan. It was also from the Loire that François conducted a continuing war against England in response to Henry VIII having joined the Holy League against France in 1511 and claiming the French throne in 1512. Following the cessation of Anglo-French hostilities in 1514, and the Peace of London in 1518 that confirmed the winding up of the Holy League, François in attempting to improve relations with England, established cordial relations with Henry VIII at the Field of the Cloth of Gold in 1520 and negotiated a commercial treaty with England, initiatives that came to naught with the outbreak of a further Anglo-French war in 1522 and, after a new peace treaty in 1525, yet another war in 1528.

16   *Château de Blois, open staircase north wing, 1515-24*

Meanwhile, under the Habsburg emperor Charles V, German and Spanish armies seized Milan from the French in 1521, and in attempting to recover her loss, the French were defeated by Imperial troops at the battle of Pavia in 1525, and François in command of the vanquished army is taken prisoner and imprisoned in Madrid.

Here, François must have reflected on his inability to enjoy the delights of his *châteaux* of Blois and Chambord, some 150km south-west of Paris, but little over a day's journey from the capital. At Blois, he had added a north wing to the existing palace in 1515-24, which sported "a three-storeyed open arcaded loggia on its outer façade . . . [while] on the court façade [its] famous open staircase brings Renaissance detailing and a new monumentality to the traditional stone spiral staircases"[7] of late-medieval France.

He must also have reflected on his inability to enjoy the delights of his Château of Chambord, a hunting lodge in the process of construction east of Blois. Plans for its construction had been drawn up probably by the Italian architect, Domenico da Cortona in 1519 and work on its construction started soon after but was interrupted from 1524 to 1526 by the Italian campaign and François's captivity. Little did François know that,

17   *Château de Chambord, circa 1519 – 50*

on his release, work would continue on the edifice throughout the whole of his lifetime and would only be completed in 1550, three years after his death. With its square keep flanked by round towers and surrounded by a moat, Chambord is essentially a French medieval château, and although its finer attributes are designed in the Flamboyant Gothic style with a forest of turrets, chimneys and dormers, it is also more Italianate than any other contemporary French building. Chambord was nevertheless intended to be a magnificent hunting lodge, and despite its potential attractions, François was determined to create a new power base in Paris following his release from captivity on 14 January 1526. Unequivocally, Paris was once again about to become the royal capital of France.

In a proclamation to the City's council on 15 March 1528, François declared that he intended to reside most of the time in Paris and its environs. Thus, recognising that the medieval *château* of the Louvre was potentially the most fitting and convenient residency in Paris, François ordered the demolition of the old edifice as soon as he returned from his captivity and set his sights on the construction of a completely new palace on the site, but he saw completion delayed time and time again because of financial constraints and his inability to find a suitable architect until the end of his reign in 1547. In respect of finance, François was able to slightly reduce the cost of reconstructing the Louvre by selling off the Hôtel St-Pol as building plots which enabled its site to be redeveloped in a regular manner laid out as a grid[8], and with regard to the design of the Louvre, it is perhaps no bad thing that a start could not be made on the edifice until Pierre Lescot was appointed in 1546 (instead of an inferior architect earlier). But it is indeed poignant that one of the greatest Renaissance monarchs in Europe did not live long enough to see his two most grandiose projects, the development of the Château Chambord and the Louvre palace completed.

Unable to reside in the Louvre in 1528, François lived temporarily and perhaps reluctantly at the fifteenth century Hôtel des Tournelles in the heart of Paris, although he had already established a residency in the Château of Madrid (started 1527) on the outer fringe of his capital. Built at Neuilly on the edge of the Bois de Boulogne, and only 6 km from the centre of Paris, the Château de Madrid (1527) took its name from the Casa de Campo, the destroyed country house of Licenciado Vargas in Madrid where François I had been imprisoned.

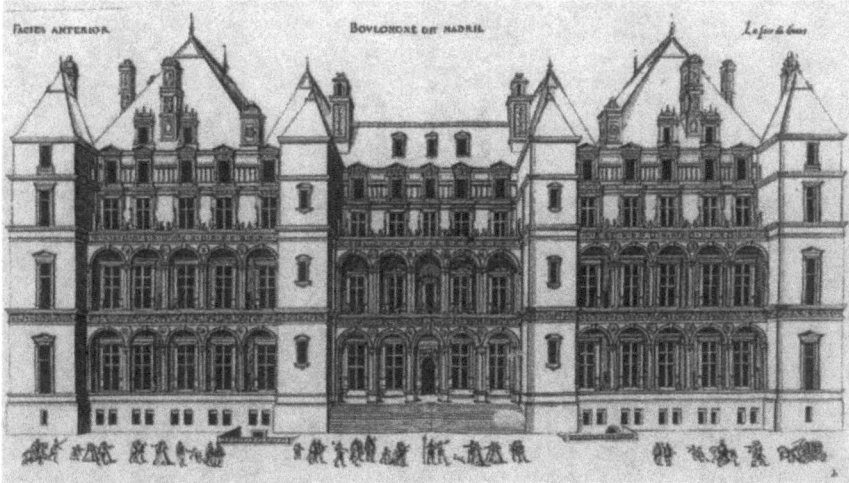

18   *Château de Madrid, started 1527*

The Château de Madrid was part of a group of *châteaux* which soon included the redeveloped Château de St-Germain-en-Laye and the later *châteaux* of Challeau (c. 1545) and La Muette (c. 1570). Though the former *château* was designed by Pierre Gadier, Gatien François (and Girolamo della Robbia who produced the terracotta decoration and might also have modified certain aspects of the design), all four *châteaux* "are of a very singular design, unlike anything else in French architecture. They are of unusual height, decorated with external galleries running between turrets."[9] But whereas Madrid has a high-pitched roof and true *logge*, the others had flat terraces and deep window bays as at Blois. While the design of Madrid is in these respects more Italian than the other three châteaux, its hight pitched roof of Madrid is essentially French. Madrid fell into disuse in the seventeenth and eighteenth centuries and was almost completely demolished in the 1790s. More of a country retreat than the Château de Madrid – though still an important centre of royal power – the Château de Fontainebleau is located only 53 kilometres or a half day's journey by coach from the capital. Built between 1528 and 1540, Fontainebleau presents a sharp stylistic contrast to the Château de Madrid and the other *châteaux* in the Île de France such as Germain-en-Laye, Challeau and La Muette. Whilst these other *châteaux* either look like back to Blois

19   *Corps de Logis, Château de Fontainebleau, 1528-40*

or are reminiscent of Italian models in the complexity of their design and ornamentation, the simplicity of the architecture of Fontainebleau anticipating the emergence of Classicism later in the sixteenth century.

However, in extending and improving the old castle of Fontainebleau, which had been little more than a hunting lodge since the twelfth century, François I and his principal architect, Gilles le Breton, produced "one of the most inconsistently designed châteaux in France,"[10] notwithstanding its very great charm and strikingly graphic vistas. However, despite the design being much of a mismatch, it is unmistakeably French though more Classical than what went before. This is particularly apparent in the case of the Porte Dorée which – despite an illusion of Classicism – is traditionally French. With its three arches, one above the other, the gateway is reminiscent of Luciano Laurana's façade to the Palazzo Ducale at Urbino (1450), but it is not entirely Classical since its arches are flattened rather than rounded, and it is largely asymmetrical. Its two towers are of different widths, the peak of the roof is not centrally positioned and, with an emphasis on verticality, the pediment of each window either cuts into the support of the window above or into the entablature, details more Gothic than Classical.

20   *Porte Dorée, Château de Fontainebleau, 1528-40*

By the 1530s, the only feature of the *château* that was truly Italian was the 60 m long gallery, the Galerie de François I, where, under the direction of Rosso Fiorentino, Mannerism – in the form of strapwork – made its first appearance in France. Under Henri II the gallery was connected to a new ballroom of over 300 m in length. Initially a simple *loggia* in Italian style, it opened onto an oval court but was soon enclosed and transformed into a large reception room that frequently accommodated royal festivals and pageants. Both buildings (the *châteaux* Madrid and Fontainebleau) were constructed on the edge of a forest near the national capital, and both were made up of a long central *corps de logis* with loggias on its two lower storeys and a cubical pavilion at each end. Madrid was influenced by both Italian Renaissance architecture reminiscent of Giuliano Sangallo's Poggio a Caiano near Florence (where its building plan resembled the letter H and its exterior was richly ornamented), and by local styles because of the towers on the corners of each of its four pavilions and its internal layout, are based on the Château of Chambord, and later repeated at La Muette and Challeau.

François saw himself as an absolute monarch whose authority could not be called into question and, as if to demonstrate his power and glory, set his sights on building magnificent *châteaux* for himself and his court in Paris or at least within easy reach of the capital. However, a number of other time-consuming priorities took pride of place. First, to achieve absolute power, he adopted a policy of centralisation. He gradually replaced the *Conseil Étroit* (a tightly-knit body with powers of its own) with the *Conseil des Affaires*, which although larger than the body it replaced, "depended solely on the King and became the chief weapon of his increasingly autocratic direction of the Government."[11] He also phased out the medieval system of finance with one which was administered by central government, while from earlier in his reign he continued to weaken "the power of the nobles by reducing their rights to administer justice and by skilfully enlarging the *domaine royal* at the expense of the other feudal estates,"[12] and by royal decree absorbing the duchies Burgundy in 1529 and Brittany in 1532. Most of the French nobility had little choice but to become courtiers receiving gifts and pensions from their sovereign instead of being dependent on their own sources of revenue. Lesser nobles attended to the day-to-day matters affecting the royal household, while members of the older aristocracy were often appointed as advisers to the King, and through the *Conseil des Affaires* participated in the administration of the kingdom and in the creation of a national identity. Thus, through the Ordinance of Villers-Cotterêts (1539) French replaced Latin, and in the same edict priests were required to establish a registry office in each parish to register local births, deaths and marriages. Second, François was aware that relations between the monarch and the Catholic church had to be preserved, but at some risk. As the outcome of Luther's preaching and writing, the Protestant movement was spreading through much of Europe, including France. Partly because of the influence of his beloved sister Marguerite de Navarre (a conciliator between Catholics and Protestants), François at first adopted a policy of tolerance towards the new movement, hoping that an even-handed approach to Protestantism and Catholicism was the best way of preventing the outbreak of religious strife in his country which might endanger his authority. François also realised that since many German princes had adopted Protestantism, they could prove useful allies in any future struggle with his enemy Charles V.

A policy of religious neutrality was, however, short-lived. On the night of the 17 October 1534, notices appeared on the streets of Paris and in other cities such as Blois, Rouen, Tours and Orléans denouncing Mass, and on the same night a notice was even attached to the door of François's bedchamber at the Château d'Amboise. The so-called 'Affair of the Placards' led to outrage among the Catholic community, and François immediately viewed the spread of Protestantism in his kingdom as a plot against himself. Not only was François very cognisant of his new alliance with the Pope but recognised that the Catholic church was very much "a major political instrument and source of revenue, and as such had to be protected."[13] Protestants were consequently imprisoned and executed and in some areas whole villages were torched. In an attempt to minimise heresy, printing was censored and some notable Protestants such as John Calvin forced into exile. The persecution of Protestants was later codified by the Edict of Fontainebleau (1540), a prelude to the religious wars that bitterly divided France during the latter half of the sixteenth century.

On the world stage, François recognised that France could not compete economically and politically with the Habsburg Empire if his country failed to develop overseas trade, establish colonies and facilitate the territorial spread of the Catholic church. Thus, in 1534 François sent Jacques Carrier to explore the St Lawrence River in Quebec in search of gold and other riches, and in 1541 the king ordered Jean-François de la Roche de Roberval to settle in Canada and to provide for "the Holy Catholic faith". France also developed trade with the Far East. In July 1527, a French trading ship from Rouen was reported by the Portuguese Joa de Baros to have arrived at the Indian port of Diu, and two years later, Jean Parmentier with two ships from Dieppe – the *Sacre* and *Pensée* – reached Sumatra.

Perhaps François's most important priority was the defence of the realm against foreign invasion. He was concerned that France was virtually surrounded by enemies or potential foes. Across her western and eastern frontiers lay the Habsburg Empire, to the north across the Channel was England, and to the south east the Italian states were subject to continual intrusions from both Habsburg and French forces where defeat would weaken the defences of the vanquished. In attempts to protect his nation, particularly from the territorial ambitions of the Habsburg emperor, Charles V, François was engaged in three Italian Wars after his release from Madrid, in 1526-30, 1536-38 and 1542-6. Stemming from his repudiation of the Treaty of Madrid, the War of the League of Cognac (1526-30) involved, on one side, France, the Papacy, the Duchy of Milan, the Venetian Republic and Florence, and on the other side the Habsburg Empire. However, the league failed to produce concerted action. French forces were routed by Charles's army at Landriano, and his 15,000 German mercenaries, the *Landsknechte* marched on Rome and sacked the city in 1527. A humiliating peace (the *Paix des Dames*) was subsequently negotiated by the respective mothers of Francis and Charles (Louise of Savoy and Margaret of Austria) and ratified by the Treaty of Cambrai (1529) which required François having to pay a ransom of 1 million gold crowns for the release of the princes François and Henri (the future Henri I).

21   *Église St-Eustache, 1532-1640*

During the peacetime years that followed, François optimistically attempted to heal relations with Charles V by marrying the Emperor's sister, Eleanor of Austria in 1530 (François's first wife, Claude de France, Duchess of Bretagne, had died in 1524), and commissioning the construction of the Hôtel de Ville in 1532, Paris's substantial new town hall, and the Église St-Eustache, the largest ecclesiastical building in Paris after the cathedral of Notre Dame. With the Hôtel de Ville, François I endowed Paris with a city hall which – because of its palatial dimensions and grandeur – was intended to be worthy of his national capital, then the largest city in Europe. Located in the Marais and overlooking the Place de Grève (now the Place de Hôtel de Ville), a riverside square notorious not only for trading and dealing but also because it was the venue for public executions, the city hall was designed by the Italian Domenico da Cortona, and Frenchman Pierre Chambiges and begun in 1532. Built on the foundations of the Maison aux Piliers, a building acquired by Étienne Marcel in the name of the municipality, construction was halted during the Wars of Religion (1563-1592), and the new city hall was not completed until 1628. It consisted of a two-storey wing sandwiched between two three-storey pavilions that in turn were flanked by two narrow towers of the same height. Shielding its internal courtyard, the front façade was adorned by Corinthian columns and niched statues. On its ground floor, it was pierced by small rectangular windows encased within round-headed recesses (Italian in style), and there were rounded portals positioned at the base of the pavilions and in the middle of the wing. On the first floor, taller rectangular windows extended along the length of the façade, round-headed windows pierced the dormers above the wing and the upper floors of the pavilions, and the frontispiece of the façade was crowned by a raised tympanum enclosing a clock. Notwithstanding its many Renaissance attributes, the Hôtel de Ville – with its three separate pitched roofs and tall chimneys – is unmistakeably French. Within two months of the formation of the Commune in March 1871, the building was evacuated before being set ablaze by its defenders. The present edifice, designed by Theodore Ballu and Pierre Despartes, and built between 1874 and 1884, is a replica of the Renaissance city hall, though it is on a larger scale, more ornate and has lateral wings either side of the main building.

In early sixteenth-century Paris, many churches were embellished and enlarged but very few new ecclesiastical buildings were constructed. The enormous church of St-Eustache, dominating the area of Les Halles, was the major exception. Begun in 1532, and ordered by François I, it was designed by Jacques Lemercier, possibly in collaboration with Domenico da Cortona who also contributed to the design of Chambord. Although overwhelmingly Gothic in style, and with a plan very similar to that of Notre Dame "with double aisles and chapels running round the nave and choir, [and] with transepts that do not project beyond these chapels",[14] the interior of St-Eustache nevertheless contains a proliferation of Renaissance detail. Its tall and narrow arches are mainly round-headed rather than pointed, it has Classical rather than Gothic pilasters, and although there is a very unorthodox use of Classical Orders, for example the height of the Corinthian pilasters are some twenty times their breadth (twice the conventional dimension), the interior of the building is more spacious and its proportions far greater than that found in any other French church of the sixteenth century. Although the Classical features of St-Eustache are confined to its interior, they signify the arrival of Renaissance architecture in the French capital.

However, peace was only short-lived. In preparing for a further conflict with the Habsburg Empire, François sought and obtained help from the Ottoman Emperor, Suleiman the Magnificent, with whom France had been developing an amicable relationship since the 1520s. Together they formed an alliance against Charles V, which involved the Turkish fleet raiding the Italian coast with the later support of François, and after the death of Francesco Sforza, the last duke of Milan, the Italian War of 1536-38 resulted in military operations on a much larger scale than hitherto in which France invaded Savoy and attacked Genoa and Milan while a combined Franco-Ottoman fleet raided Habsburg possessions across the Mediterranean. With Charles V facing the daunting military strength of the Franco-Ottoman alliance, he not only made peace with his two adversaries with the Treaty of Nice, on the 18th June 1538, but also – in his quest to expel the Ottomans from Hungary – secured the treacherous cooperation of François in a venture that was still-born due to Charles's raging conflict in Germany with the Protestant princes of the Schmalkaldic League. In being chivalrously permitted by François to travel across France to suppress an uprising in Flanders against Habsburg suzerainty, Charles was accommodated by the French king at the Château of Chambord, the most magnificent Renaissance residence north of the Alps.

Despite his obvious delight at having built Chambord, François set about improving a medieval *château* at Germain-en-Laye, located close to a bend on the Seine only 20 km downstream from the centre of his capital. Known as the Grand Chatelet from 1122 to the 1360s, it was disparagingly referred to as the Château Vieux from the 1360s to 1539 but since that date – when François commissioned its reconstruction – it has been known as the Château de St-Germain. Its pentagonal plan with turrets in each of its five corners suggests that the *château* – at least in part – may have been designed by the Venetian architect Sebastiano Serlio. With a substantial enclosed courtyard, unique in France at that time, the edifice is reminiscent of some of the *palazzi* and villas of Venice and its *terra firma*. In Italian fashion, the building not only has a flat roof (in contrast to the steep roofs traditionally employed in France) but also has – around the court and encasing rectangular windows – rows of arcades on each of its storeys, and similar arcades on the upper storeys of the externa facades below which the walls are faced with dressed stone pierced by small rectangular windows. The frontispiece of the *château* consists of a pair of triumphal arches, one above the other, in the manner of Francesco Laurana at the Castel Nuova in Naples (1453). Also, as is often the case in the Veneto, most arches on both the court and outside facades are crowned by triangular pediments, while segmental pediments are employed above some of the doors of the turret. As much a diplomatic gesture as an architectural venture, François collaborated with the d'Este dynasty of Italy to build 'Le Grand Ferrare' for Cardinal Ipolito (II) d'Este, son of Lucretia Borgia and the Duke Alfonso I d'Este who had become the newly appointed Papal Legate to France. Designed by Sebastiano Serlio, the Grand Ferrare is now extinct except for its entrance door, but drawings and engravings show the general attributes of the building. It consisted of a *corps-de-logis* comprising of a single flight of rooms, and two lesser winds that stretched forward, one with a gallery and the other with minor rooms. The courtyard so formed "was closed by a wall, broken in the middle by the door that still stands."[15] Though the design of Le Grand Ferrare derives from French *châteaux* of the earlier sixteenth

22   *Church of St-Étienne-du-Mont, extended 1539-45*

century such as Bury and provides a foretaste of the design of many a Parisian town house or *hôtel particulier* built in the seventeenth and eighteenth centuries.

Of the churches that were gradually altered during the sixteenth century, the most notable was the Gothic church of St-Étienne-du-Mont on the Left Bank. Begun in 1492, it was extended by the construction of a new transept in the style of the existing building in 1539, and between 1541 and 1545 decorative stone choir screens were installed, possibly to the design of Philibert de l'Orme. Although in style, the screens – with their spiral staircases and pierced balustrades – were unquestionably influenced by the Renaissance, the principal Classical attributes of the building, notably its portico, were not put in place until the early seventeenth century (see Chapter 6).

The alliance between François and Charles was very short-lived, as was François's rift with Suleiman. However, France and the Ottoman Empire renewed their alliance and were soon at war again against the Holy Roman Empire. The Italian War of 1532-46 was somewhat of a misnomer since extensive fighting took place in France and the Low Countries as well as in Italy itself. The most notable events of the war, however, were the Siege of Nice, when French and Ottoman forces collaborated in the bombardment of the city in August 1543, and Francis's provision of Toulon as a base for the Ottoman fleet and her army to attack the Spanish and Italian coasts from the winter of 1543-44 to the following summer. In 1544 Franco-Ottoman forces confronted those of Charles at the Battle of Cerisole in Piedmont, but under the terms of the subsequent Treaty of Crépy-en-Laonnois, Charles sued for peace because of the financial strain of continuing with this particular war.

In the 1540s, the king was cautious about funding new building work. Though the Italian Wars were over, at least temporarily, France remained in conflict with the Habsburg Empire but not in the Mediterranean. Suleiman was still engaged in the conquest of Hungary in 1543 and with the help of French troops in 1543-44 secured a commanding position in Hungary culminating in the Treaty of Edirne in 1547 with the Habsburgs. The cost of all these wars was enormous. Though the Ottomans lent large amounts of gold to the French crown and although the belligerents generated revenue through the ransoming of enemy ships, continuing conflict stretched available financial resources to the limit, more so in the case of France that, unlike the Habsburg Empire, lacked the gold and silver of the New World to replenish its coffers, and unlike the Ottomans that had access to the enormous wealth of the Levant. Only a year before his death in 1547 were royal coffers sufficiently full to enable work to commence on the reconstruction and expansion of the Louvre. To this end, François commissioned Pierre Lescot to design a *corps de logis* on the south-western section of the *Cour Carrée* (the Square Court of the Palace) though it was left to François's son Henri II to witness the completion of this stage in the Louvre's development in 1552. At the Château de Rambouillet on 31st March 1547, François died at the age of only 52. His legacy is generally considered to be mixed. While he did much to consolidate royal authority and establish a national identity, this was at the expense of religious strife which led France into decades of civil war until the Edict of Nantes in 1598 guaranteed limited freedom of worship. Although he achieved great cultural feats, not least in the development of resplendent buildings, this came at a time when France was embroiled in costly wars and did much to reduce the nation's economic wellbeing.

Henri II (r. 1547 – 59)

Henri II was married to Catherine de Medici, with whom he had ten children including the future François II, Charles IX and Henri III. Born in Florence, Catherine developed a strong knowledge of the Italian Renaissance, not only its visual arts but also its literature including the works of Machiavelli. However, during the early years of her marriage to Henri, she exercised very little political influence as queen. While she was raising a large family, Henri fell increasingly under the influence of one of his several mistresses, Diane de Poitiers, twenty years his senior. Diane took her place at the centre of power, granting favours and dispensing patronage, and throughout his reign supported Henri when he involved France in a succession of wars, with England (1547-50), the Holy Roman Empire (1552-55) and Spain (1555-58), each of which stretched royal finances. Henri also relied very much on the political support of segments of the nobility, most notably the staunchly Catholic Constable of France, Anne de Montmorency and his associates the Guise brothers, Charles (who became a cardinal) and François (the future duc de Guise). However, Henri only lived to the age of forty. Soon after signing the Treaty of Cateau-Cambrésis with Ferdinand I Holy Roman Emperor and Henry VIII of England on 3-4 April 1559 ending the Italian Wars, at the wedding of his thirteen-year-old daughter Elisabeth to Philip II of Spain, he incurred a serious head injury in a celebratory joust at the Palais des Tournelles, and as a result of his injury died on 10 July.

Right from the outset of his reign, Henri had been involved in the development of real estate. Within weeks of his father's death in 1547, and much to the angst of Catherine, he gave the royal Château

23   *Château de Chenonceau, extended 1555*

de Chenonceau in the Loire Valley to his mistress, Diana, who in 1555 greatly extended the building by constructing a built-up bridge across the river. Also as a further gift to his favourite mistress, he commissioned the Château d'Anet close to the Norman town of Dreux, which at 78 kilometres west of Paris was only a short carriage journey away from the capital. Designed by Philibert d l'Orme and begun in 1547, the layout of the *château*, with its three residential wings and lowered entrance wing, resembles the Château de Bury built thirty years earlier. However, for the first time, the entrance wing is detached from the rest of the *château*, a configuration that was adopted "in France for several generations and was occasionally imitated in Elizabethan and Jacobean England."[16] In the view of many, the *château* is De L'Orme's masterpiece. It is thus all the more regrettable that it was partly destroyed or dismantled during the French Revolution and its aftermath. Today, while its entrance wing, one of its other wings and its chapel remain *in situ*, the most important constituent of the château, its *corps de logis*, stands reconstructed in the courtyard of the École des Beaux-Arts in Paris. Dating from the late 1540s, and for the first time in France, its Orders are erected one above the other in the

24   *Château d'Anet, Corps de Logis*
           1547- 1552

25   *Château d'Anet, entrance wing 1552*

correct Classical sequence – Doric, Ionic and Corinthian – as in the Colosseum in Rome.

Built in 1552, and with a monumentality not seen in any other contemporary French building for at least another hundred years, the entrance wing of the Château d'Anet is dominated by its central figure, a carriage entrance reminiscent of a triumphal arch and framed by double Doric columns. The arch is surmounted by a tympanum containing a bronze relief of a nymph and two Victories sculptured in 1543 by Benvenuto Cellini for the Château de Fontainebleau but later presented to Diane by Henri II. Though the entrance consists undramatically of "a sequence of rectangular blocks surrounded by consoles and flanked by two rounded masses which support little terraces"[17], its otherwise drab appearance is redeemed by elaborate open-work balustrades and, at its crown, a clock that supports a bronze stag and two leaping hounds which move at the striking of the hours, a feature that epitomises the inventiveness of the architect. The extant western wing of the *château* is notable, on the one hand for incorporating a number of features not seen previously in France such as regularly positioned windows, the alternation of bays of different widths and the restraint of decoration in the arrangement of the façade, and on the other hand for continuing to employ traditional French elements such as a high pitched roof, dormers, chimney stacks and the vestiges of corner turrets. The extinct eastern wing was, in detail, probably very similar to the western wing, though it incorporated at its centre the chapel, the first ecclesiastical building in France that was based on the Renaissance concept that since the circle is the perfect figure, it is particularly appropriate to employ it in designing the plan of a church.

A very different form of development also emerged early in the reign of Henri II. Since the time of Louis IX (r. 1226-1270), Les Halles degenerated from a well-regulated food market to one where uncontrolled traders, free of charge, plied their goods haphazardly outside of purpose-built halls. Therefore, in 1551, Les Halles was entirely demolished and replaced with finely designed trading halls, hôtels and sumptuous housing. To ease the flow of goods and people, "the old wall of the Halles [was] also demolished, and future access was through regular streets, [while] the allocation of space was more clearly defined."[18]

But it was Pierre Lescot's *Louvre* that was the development project *par excellence*. In contrast to so many Italian *palazzi* of the period, with their emphasis on undecorated masonry, the repetition of standard arches, and unbroken horizontal lines between storeys, the *corps de logis* of the Louvre is overtly ornamental rather than monumental. Also, unlike some Renaissance Italian facades (such as those of the Palazzo Farnese in Rome or the Palazzo Chiericati in Vicenza) which employ sober Doric and Ionic Orders, the *corps de logis* is adorned by pilasters and half columns of the most decorative Orders: Corinthian and Composite. A further difference is that the fenestration of the *corps de logis* is somewhat inelegant compared with the arrangement of windows in Italian *palazzi*. On the ground floor segment-headed windows are encased within round-headed arches; on the first floor the encased windows are positioned below alternating triangular and segmental pediments and, in the attic, the windows are surmounted by cross torches. In essence, Lescot's style is undoubtedly Classical, but a very distinct form of French Classicism with its own attributes and very different indeed from the work of Antonio da Sangallo, Michelangelo or Palladio south of the Alps.

26   *Cour Carree of the Louvre, started 1546*

Pierre Lescot did not confine his work to gigantic royal commissions such as the Louvre. In 1547, at the request of Henri II, he added three Classical viewing arcades onto the rundown face of the Church of the Innocent Children in the Place Joachim-du-Bellay, at the southern end of the rue St-Denis, close to Les Halles. Adorned with sculpture by Lescot's contemporary Jean Goujon, the arcades survived the destruction of the church in the late-eighteenth century, and a fourth arcade was added by Quatremère de Quincy to convert the structure into a free-standing temple and fountain. In the nineteenth century, the Fontaine des Innocents – as we know it today – was completed by the addition of waterfall steps, a reservoir bowl and a cupola. It is probable that Lescot also designed a substantial city mansion for the president of the parliament, Jacques des Ligneris. Constructed in 1548-50, the building – known as the Hôtel Carnavelet since 1579 – features an exuberant *corps-de-logis*, punctuated with symmetrical mullioned windows only broken on the first floor by allegorical bas – reliefs from the renowned workshop of Jean Goujon depicting the Four Seasons.

27   *Fontaine des Innocents, Place de Joachim-du-Bellay, 1547-49*

28   *Hôtel Carnavalet, started 1548-50*

REFERENCES

1. C. Black, *Early Modern Italy* (London: Routledge, 2001), pp. 219-20
2. A. Horne (A) *Seven Ages of Paris. Portrait of a City* (London: Macmillan, 2002), p.69
3. R. Price, *A Concise History of France* (Cambridge: Cambridge University Press, 1993), p.47
4. C. Jones, *Paris. Biography of a City* (London: Penguin Books, 2006), p.101
5. A. Sutcliffe, *Paris. An Architectural History* (London: Yale University Press, 1996), p.12
6. Ibid, p.12
7. D. Watkin, *A History of Western Architecture* (London: Laurence King Publishing, 5th Edt., 2011), p.251
8. E. Hazan, *The Invention of Paris* (London: Version, 2011), p.59
9. A. Blunt, *Art and Architecture in France, 1500-1700* (London: Yale University Press, 5th Edt, 1999), p.26
10. Ibid, p.28
11. Ibid, p.25
12. Ibid, p.25
13. Price, op. cit., p.50
14. Blunt, op. cit., p.30
15. Blunt, op. cit., p.42-3
16. N. Pevsner, *An Outline of European Architecture* (London: Allen Lane, 1973), pp.299-300
17. Blunt, op. cit., p.55
18. Hazan, op. cit., p.65

CHRONOLOGY

1488-1515	Louis XII, King of France
1492 onwards	**St-Étienne-du-Mont**
1494-1657	**St-Gervais-St-Protaise**
Circa 1500	**Hôtel de Cluny built**
1508-22	**St-Jacques Tower**
1515-47	François I, King of France

1527	**The *donjon* of the Louvre demolished**
1532-40	**St-Eustache built**
1546	**Rebuilding of the Louvre as a palace**
1547-59	Henri II, King of France
1547-49	**Fontaine des Innocents built**
1548-50	**Hôtel Carnavalet built**

5

THE RELIGIOUS DIVIDE: IMPLICATIONS FOR THE DEVELOPMENT OF PARIS

INTRODUCTION

Despite its very great political importance in the history of Early-Modern Europe, Paris had relatively few buildings designed in the Renaissance style when François II ascended the throne in 1559. In terms of contemporary architecture, the French capital not only lagged behind Rome, Venice and Florence but also compared very unfavourably with the much smaller cities of northern and central Italy. Like many other urban areas in north-western Europe, its built environment was almost decrepit and squalid, and was only marginally improved, if at all, by the provision of a large open sewer, the *Grand Egout* (that looped westwards from what is today the Place de Republique to an outlet into the Seine between the Pont d'Alma and Place de Trocadéro) and by a few contemporary buildings that had been erected during the early part of the century.

Set in train by municipal legislation in 1554, a ruling from the Hôtel de Ville in 1566 banned overhanging eaves from blocking daylight penetrating the city's streets, while the Crown in the same decade planned to use the familiar process of *lottisement* to sell off parcels of land in the vicinity of the Palais des Tournelles for new areas of habitation, but since the area was unbearably smelly as a consequence of the proximity of the city's sewer, lots did not sell and the scheme was an abject failure.[1] In contrast, in the heart of the Marais, the convent of Ste-Catherine sold off its extensive *contours* from the 1540s to the 1560s, turning "market gardens into prime real estate for precisely the kind of wealthy individuals attracted to Paris by the relocation of the royal court"[2] from the Loire valley. Similarly, the continuing development of the Louvre created an area of prestige houses in its immediate vicinity, and also on nearby sites at Les Halles.

The economic and environmental condition of Paris by 1560 was increasingly geared to the growing demand of the king and his court for luxurious commodities, though private consumption of expensive items was restricted by sumptuary legislation in 1567, albeit to limited effect. Though Parisians no longer wove cloth, "city drapers imported cloths from Bourges, the Beauvaisis and Normandy and dyed and finished them [while artisans worked] with precious stones, ivory, glass and fancy metals [that] were as much in demand as the products of the new trade of cloth making."[3]

Not only was the population of Paris around 300,000 in 1560 – compared to 100,000 in 1500 – it was also bursting at the seams and expanding outside the city walls into *faubourgs* (the suburbs). Since the end of the previous century, the Faubourg of Saint-Antoine had been expanding eastward beyond the Bastille, and soon became noted for its wood-working and furniture-making industries. To the west, the Rue Saint-Honore became a high-status neighbourhood in its own right, and to the north beyond the medieval Porte St-Denis mixed development formed the new suburb of Villeneuve-des-Gravois. Growth on the Left Bank was less pronounced, and mainly took the form of in-fill development within the existing *faubourgs*, rather than expansion beyond their ramparts.

Although the prevailing economic boom had made the French capital the largest city in Europe, its sudden growth and sheer size not only created difficulties for the Crown and its municipal government in attempting to create a city worthy of the Renaissance (if indeed that was their aim), but raised problems about the potential efficacy of its defences, despite the strengthening of the city's ramparts earlier in the century. In the early 1560s, therefore, "a new trench was dug which included the Left Bank *faubourgs*, while tentative steps were taken to extend the Right Bank so as to cover the Tuileries palace."[4]

Despite the initiatives of the Crown and the municipality to enhance the Parisian environment and its economy, Paris largely remained a city of squalor, and its new buildings were arguably less than impressive. In the view of a Spanish nobleman, Gaspar de Vega – relaying his impressions of Paris to his king, Philip II in 1566 – the Louvre "amounted to very little for such a great city. I noticed no notable edifice at all, and the town presents nothing of interest save its size."[5] Though not an objective analysis of the architecture of mid-sixteenth century Paris, de Vega clearly implied that a great deal more needed to be done to make Paris a worthy capital in visual terms. However, this proved to be virtually impossible during the second half of the sixteenth century. French kings and much of the aristocracy were generally more concerned with defending or increasing their political power during the Wars of Religion than with improving the capital's environment.

THE EMERGENCE OF THE REFORMATION

Whereas the Renaissance in French architecture, albeit in its infancy, emanated from Italy in the first half of the sixteenth century, the conflict between Catholics and Protestants in France – that not only divided the Christian church but also destroyed political and social cohesion – was generated at home. To be sure Martin Luther, in pinning his 95 Thesis on the doors of the Castle Church at Wittenburg in Saxony in 1517, unleashed the forces of religious reform in Germany that embroiled the Catholic princes and their early Protestant counterparts in bloody armed conflicts to defend or expand their respective interests. However, it is far from certain that Luther had a major impact on the development of French Protestantism, though it doubtless sowed some of the seeds of religious discontent. It was from Genève that the French reformation originated. It was from here that the reformist ideas of Jean Calvin began to circulate largely through the medium of itinerant preachers, initially attracting people of humble birth and artisanal families. By the middle of the sixteenth century, a national Protestant church was founded, and it soon extended its appeal across the social classes to the many aristocrats and claimants to the French throne who saw the reformed faith as a weapon against Valois power. Thus from 1562 to 1594, the Wars of Religion were fought out across France with a negative impact on the development of architecture in the Île de France and the French capital itself.

FRANÇOIS II (R. 1559-60)

Within a year of Henri II's son, François II, becoming king in 1559 at the age of fifteen, the sickly boy met his untimely death. During this short interlude, the Guise brothers attempted to fill what they saw as a power-vacuum and moved into the Louvre with François and their niece, Mary Stuart, the future Queen of Scots, whom the new king had married the year before.

However, despite François being of sufficient age to rule in his own right, his mother, Catherine de Medici, did not hesitate to exercise the *ex-officio* authority that her son generously conferred upon her. Consequently, she compelled Diane de Poitiers to return Chenonceau to the crown, spoke out against the Guise persecution of the Huguenots (the French Protestants), adopted a moderate stance against religious dissent, and worked closely with Michel de l'Hôpital who had been appointed as Chancellor of France in June 1560. Neither Catherine nor the Chancellor saw the need to punish the Huguenots if they worshipped in private and did not take up arms, an approach confirmed at an assemble of notables at Fontainebleau in August 1560. However, because of an atmosphere of distrust and his undoubted militancy, Louis I de Bourbon, Prince de Condé, the leading Protestant opponent of the Guise family, raised an army in the autumn of 1560 and began attacking Catholic strongholds in the south. Although captured and sentenced to death, Condé was reprieved by Catherine since it was agreed that in the event of Francis's imminent death, the Huguenot Antoine de Bourbon, King of Navarre, would renounce his legitimate claim to the Regency of François's young successor, Charles IX.

It was around 1560 that the construction of the Château d'Ecouen, 18 kilometres north of Paris, was completed. Started in 1538, the construction of the edifice was consecutively under the direction of Pierre Tacheron and Jean Bullant. The *château* is one of the finest in the Île de France and is arranged round a *cour d'honneur*, whose boundaries are defined by square pavilions in each of its four corners, three-storey ranges on its southern, western and northern sides, and [since the early nineteenth century] by a one-storey entrance wing traversing its eastern boundary. Commissioned by Duc Anne de Montmorency, constable of France, in an attempt to enhance his political influence, the "shell" of much of the building is attributable to Pierre Tacheron and has remained largely in its original form until the present day. In essence, Tacheron's design was very traditional since it was based on the quadrangular plan of a medieval bailey castle but, as a concession to mid-sixteenth century taste, corner towers were superseded by pavilions.

It is therefore not until Jean Bullant became involved in completing the *château* that the full majesty of a French Renaissance building emerged. Inspired by his visit to Rome in 1541-43, where he made detailed drawings of ancient buildings and examined current construction projects such as Michelangelo's Capitol palaces, Bullant set out to embellish Ecouen in the Late-Renaissance manner. In the middle 1550s and leaving much of the west and south wings untouched, he built the north wing in its entirety. To its outer façade, he attached Tuscan and Doric columns surmounted by an entablature and giant triangular pediment; and to the courtyard façade he inserted a double portico flanked by pairs of Doric and Ionic columns, and pierced the steep-pitched roofs with dormers of a more classical design than that employed in the earlier wings. On the east-side of the *château*, it was almost certainly Bullant who built the original entrance wing, but although engravings by Jacques Androuet might suggest that it was modelled on de l'Orme's frontispiece at Anet, with the inclusion of a centrally-positioned arched-opening on the middle floor above the portico, its full dramatic effect may have derived from the Porte Doree at Fontainebleau. Rebuilt in the early nineteenth century after its destruction during the French Revolution, the entrance wing comprises a one-storey unembellished wall with a modest central portal, not even a pale imitation of the original wing if du Cerceau's evidence is reliable.

29   *South wing, Château Ecouen, circa 1560*

The final and most impressive of Bullant's work at Ecouen is the courtyard façade that he superimposed on the south wing of the *château*. Its principal feature is the use of four colossal Corinthian Orders arranged in pairs, built either side of double porticos and surmounted by a massive rectangular entablature. Influenced by the Pantheon's portico at Rome, and triggered by Michelangelo's Capitol palaces, Bullant's use of the Colossal Order at Ecouen was not only the first time that the Order had been employed in France since antiquity, but the manner that it was employed was peculiarly French. Whereas "in the Capitol palaces the emphasis is on the horizontal . . . [at] Ecouen the shape enclosed by the Order is nearly square and the vertical lines dominate unchallenged. It was perhaps because a of this strong vertical tendency [in keeping with steep-pitched French roofing] that the Colossal Order soon became popular in France, whereas [in the sixteenth century] it was little used in Italy, except by Palladio."[6]

The Petit Château Chantilly (c. 1560) is second only to Ecouen as a magnificent example of *château* development in the Paris region during the latter half of the sixteenth century. Built by Jean Bullant for Anne de Montmorency, the Petit Château is a long two-storey building

30   *Petit Château, Chantilly, circa 1560*

flanked by two pavilions at right angles to it. The use of a single Order ties together, or even masks, the two storeys of uniform height, while pilasters on the end pavilions rise to the windows of the upper storey that slice through the entablature. Spectacularly, the entrance façade of the building is dominated by a triumphal arch supported by a pair of Corinthian columns, while single vertical strips vertically demarcate the sides of windows on the ground and first floors before cutting through the entablature. Although, Bullant's style might "be regarded as a French form of Mannerism, analogous in certain respects to Palladio's use of interlocking Orders as, for instance, on the façade of the Palazzo Valmarane in Vicenza . . . in his arrangement of the windows at Chantilly, Bullant is taking up again . . . a Late-Gothic tradition."[7]

In the late sixteenth century, in contrast to grand secular gestures in the Île de France, there was little church building in the French capital. However, there is a minor exception. Whereas the church of St-Medard, on the Rue Moffetard, dates back to the twelfth century or earlier, it gained a Late-Gothic nave in the middle- or second half of the sixteenth century, and a Renaissance choir between 1559-86.[8]

CHARLES IX (R. 1560-74)

On François II's death in December 1560, and with Charles IX only nine years of age, Catherine de Medici was appointed by the Privy Council as regent or more specifically governor of France (*gouvernante de France*). However, although she was able to exercise sweeping powers through presiding over the king's council, controlling state business and patronage, and deciding policy, in many parts of France, she was relatively powerless. The rule of the nobles prevailed across much of the country and in the Paris region – the Île de France – the nobility was fiercely Catholic. After a long military and diplomatic career in the services of François I, Henri II, François II and Charles IX, Anne de Montmorency, Constable of France since 1538 – from his *châteaux* at Ecouen and Chantilly – allied himself with François, Duke of Guise and the Marshal Saint-Andre to form the Triumvirate in April 1561 to defend Catholicism. With similar associations taking place on the Huguenot side of the religious divide, doctrinal differences were widening, despite Catherine having issued the Edict of Saint-Germain in January 1562 in an attempt to build bridges across the religious divide. Soon, the first War of Religion was triggered off by the Massacre at Wassy-sur-Blaise in Champagne. On 1 March 1562, the Duke of Guise and his men attacked a Huguenots congregation worshipping in a barn, an incident that killed seventy-four and wounded 104. Though the massacre was celebrated in the streets of Paris, calls for revenge reverberated throughout much of France. Within a month, a Huguenot army was assembled by Prince Louis de Condé and Admiral Gaspard de Coligny and, in alliance with England, it seized town after town in France. During the conflict, centring on Rouen and Orléans, both the leading Huguenot and Catholic antagonists – Antoine de Bourbon, and the Duke of Guise – were killed. With the demise of Guise, Catherine was soon able to bring about peace between the warring sides, the Edict of Amboise ending the war on 19 March 1563.

It was during the subsequent peace in 1563-4 that Catherine began to incur enormous expenditure on the construction of the grandiose palace of the Tuileries, a magnificent royal residence on a site on the western edge to the Louvre and away from the cramped conditions and squalor of much of Paris. She was partly motivated by the unfortunate circumstances

31   *Tuileries, 1563-4*

of her husband's death in the grounds of the Palais des Tournelles only four years earlier, and she would have been very conscious of the fact that her ancestors in Florence and Rome had frequently indulged in a display of wealth as a symbol of power and influence and she was determined to do the same. She thus duly commissioned Philibert de l'Orme to design a grand palace that would occupy the site and act as a symbol of her own authority, and although his plans to build triple courtyards in the proposed building remained but a dream, a single group of Mannerist blocks dominated by a central domed pavilion were built at ninety degrees to the Seine and, facing westward, overlooking a formal garden subsequently referred to as Le Jardin des Tuileries. The palace remained the principal residence of French monarchs for over three hundred years and even survived the French Revolution, but it was irreparably torched by Communards in 1871. Today there is no trace of the building.

In the same year in which Catherine commissioned the Tuileries, Charles IX was declared of age, but from the beginning of his reign showed little interest in government and relied upon his mother to determine and administer policy. Catherine's first concern in her new capacity was to enforce the Edict of Amboise and engender loyalty to the Crown. To this end she embarked with Charles and his court on a progress around France, a journey that lasted from January 1564 until

May 1565 and, with an independent and conciliatory mind, was willing to listen to the grievances of both Huguenots and Catholics. However, Catherine's impartiality, whether genuine or contrived, suffered a serious blow in 1567. On 27 September of that year, Huguenot forces attempted to ambush the king at Meaux, an act of folly that sparked off the Second War of Religion.

Brought to a hasty end by the Peace of Longjumeau of 22-23 March 1568, conditions were now relatively favourable for Catherine once again to increase the stock of royal buildings, but this time not in Paris. On behalf of Charles IX she duly ordered the expansion of the Palace of Fontainebleau by commissioning the Aile de la Belle Cheminee. Whilst the main body of the palace was Classical in concept and constructed between 1528 and 1540 (see Chapter 4), the Aile – designed by Primaticcio in a distinctly Mannerist style – is a single three-storey wing flanked by pavilions and is noted for its impressive double flight of steps from the rusticated ground-level to the *piano nobile* in the Italian manner. Its centrally-positioned portico in the style of a triumphal arch is replicated on the first-floor, and in turn this is surmounted by a prominent dormer window framed by scrolls and crowned by a large triangular pediment, while the steep pitched roofs of the building are pierced by smaller dormer windows capped by segmental pediments. Due to delays caused by the religious wars, Catherine did not see the Aile completed by the time of her death in 1589 and work only resumed during the closing years of the sixteenth century and early decades of the seventeenth.

The short war of 1567-68 was a turning point in the history of France. Believing that all she could expect from the Huguenots was deceit, Catherine was no longer willing to pursue a policy of neutrality and praised the Spanish reign of terror in the Netherlands where Calvinists were slaughtered in their thousands. Wary of her intentions, the Huguenots retreated to the fortified city of La Rochelle but, under Condé, the Third War of Religion soon broke out, this time with the Catholics commanded by Catherine's third eldest son, the Duke of Anjou (the future King Henri III). At the Battle of Jarnac on the 16th March 1569, Conde was killed and was replaced by Coligny as the commander of the Huguenot forces. Following another year of armed conflict, an enormous royal debt compelled Catherine to sue for peace, signing with her adversaries the Treaty of Saint-Germain on 8th August

1570. Catherine further attempted to enhance the security of her realm by arranging a marriage between her youngest daughter, Marguerite and the son of the deceased Antoine Bourbon, Henri de Navarre. But on 21 August 1572, three days after the royal wedding, an attempt was made to assassinate a prominent Huguenot guest, Admiral Coligny, while he was returning to his lodgings after the celebrations. Though his injuries were not serious, both Catherine and Charles IX were fearful that the many Huguenots who were in Paris for the wedding would exact disproportionate revenge for the attempted murder. Therefore, encouraged by the Guises and in a true Machiavellian spirit, Catherine and her son decided to strike first and wipe out as many Huguenot leaders as possible while they were still in Paris. From St-Bartholomew's Day on 24 August and starting with the murder and mutilation of Coligny and quickly degenerating into bloody mayhem, "Groups of killers sacked Huguenot houses and butchered their inhabitants for four days in the capital."[9] The bloodbath soon spread to many parts of France such as Orléans, Rouen, Lyons, Bordeaux and Toulouse and accounted for probably 10,000 lives in all.[10] To Protestants elsewhere in France and throughout Europe and beyond, Parisians were either assassins, religious fanatics or both. But the Saint Bartholomew's Day massacre was not only a particularly ugly episode in a religious war, it was more a horrific feature of an inter-dynastic struggle over who should rule France: the Valois family or the Bourbon-Huguenot faction.

Veuë de l'Hôtel de Soissons bati par Catherine de Medicis, et conduit par Iean Bullont Architecte du Roy.

32   *Hôtel de Soissons, started 1572*

To modern minds, it is astonishing that, during one of the bloodiest times in French history, Catherine audaciously went ahead with the construction of a grandiose residence for herself in the centre of Paris – the Hôtel de Soissons – in the mistaken belief that this would glorify her reign. Catherine would of course have justified her decision since the Tuileries was far from finished and she probably would have needed appropriate accommodation in the meantime. Designed by Jean Bullant, Catherine's new residence was the first *hôtel particulier* in the French capital. Constructed of stone and begun in 1572, the *hôtel* was an extensive three-storey building located on the western edge of Les Halles, and it consisted of a central block of three-bays adorned by a prominent rounded portal on its ground floor, and it was flanked on either side by a pavilion of a similar size and style. In its totality, the central complex was surmounted by three high pitched roofs pierced by dormer windows. At right angles to the main part of the building, wings protruded outwards on both sides to form a *cour d'honneur*, which is demarcated externally by a one-storey arcaded wall. Extending to the left and right of the *cour d'honneur*, two three-storey blocks form the street frontage of the *hôtel*. Although largely demolished in 1748, its 32-metre high fluted Doric column, used by Catherine as an Observatory, is extant and stands proudly next to eighteenth century Bourse de Commerce.

A year after the Hôtel de Soissons was begun, the St Bartholomew's Day massacre produced dismay and outrage amongst the Huguenot communities and triggered off the Fourth War of Religion in which Catholic forces laid siege of the Huguenot strongholds of Sommieres, Sancerre and La Rochelle. The Huguenots soon sued for peace and reluctantly agreed to the terms of the Edict of Boulogne of July 1573 that curtailed many of the concessions previously granted. They were permitted freedom of worship in only three towns: La Rochelle, Montauban and Nimes, but only in the privacy of their own homes. Two years after the massacre, Charles IX died at the age of twenty-three.

HENRI III (R. 1574-89)

Charles IX was succeeded by his younger brother Henri III, but the new king showed little interest in government and depended upon

Catherine and her administrators until the last few weeks of her life. His marriage to Louise Vaudemont in 1575 failed to bring forth an heir and therefore Catherine looked to her youngest son, François, Duke of Alençon to secure the future of the Valois dynasty. Unfortunately for Catherine, François sided with the Huguenot cause, sparking off the Sixth War of Religion (1576-77) in which the Protestant prince fought against the Crown, forcing his mother to give in to all Huguenot demands in the Edict of Beaulieu on 6 May 1577.

Paris being traversed by a major river required a major bridge or bridges for her socio-economic viability and effective governance not least because her administrative and business core was on the Île de la Cité, an island in the middle of the Seine. Thus, by the late-sixteenth century there were as many as four bridges connecting the Île de la Cité with the rest of Paris: the Petit Pont and Pont Notre-Dame (both of Roman origin), and the Pont au Change (dating from the twelfth century) and Pont St-Michel (built in the late-fourteenth century). In 1578, however, Henri III ordered the building of a further bridge, the Pont Neuf, to link the Left Bank of Paris with its university to the Cité,

33 *Pont Neuf, started 1578-79, completion 1599-1607*

34   *Hôtel Angouleme begun 1584, renamed Hôtel Lamoignon 1624*

and the Right Bank – the location of the Louvre and Tuileries. Triumphal arches were to be constructed at each end of the bridge and, as on the Pont Notre-Dame, houses were to be constructed across its span. But in 1579 and 1580 inherent antagonism between the Huguenots and Crown sparked off the Seventh War of Religion, though the flames of conflict were quickly extinguished by the Treaty of Fleix. However, because of the resumption of the war in 1579, work on the bridge was postponed and not resumed until Henri IV ordered a very different structure in 1599 (see Chapter 6).

Soon after the completion of the Hôtel de Soissons, a further substantial *hôtel particulier* was commissioned in Paris in 1584, the Hôtel de Angouleme in the Rue Pavee. Commissioned by Diana of France, illegitimate daughter of Henri III, it was designed by Jean Baptiste du Cerceau very much in a style derived from Bullant. The residence features a narrow *corps de logis* with pronounced flanking pavilions, the use of colossal Corinthian pilasters, while dormer windows – surmounted by broken triangular pediments – are set into the entablature. In 1624, two wings were added to the courtyard, and the building was subsequently renamed the Hôtel de Lamoignon. Recently, the *hôtel* has been restored and has become the Historical Library of the City of Paris. Although very small in number, Parisian *hôtels* of the late-sixteenth century set the scene for the proliferation of town houses in the French capital over the following two hundred and fifty years, but in the late sixteenth century, contemporary design was the exception rather than the rule. In Paris, like so many other European cities, half-timbered buildings – medieval in style – were the norm rather than the exception (see Chapter 3).

Foreign policy and religious conflict took priority over urban development during the later years of the sixteenth century. Because the Catholic League under the duc de Guise allied with Spain and its intention to wage war on the Huguenots, Henri III was obliged to subjugate the Catholic forces in an attempt to achieve a semblance of peace. But since Guise had a stronger army than his own, he wisely conceded to all the League's demands by the Treaty of Nemours, signed on 7 July 1585. The Roman Catholic church was now on the ascendance. Under Spanish leadership, its armed forces waged a campaign against Protestants across Europe, and even attempted to invade England in 1588 and remove her Protestant queen, Elizabeth. But provoked by the duc de Guise, Henri III somewhat reluctantly waged war (the Eighth War of Religion) against Henri de Navarre in 1586-89 to avert the possibility, that under Salic Law, a Bourbon rather than a Valois would inherit the crown. To exacerbate matters, the people of Paris – overwhelmingly Catholic – were becoming dissatisfied with Henri III because of his failure to defeat the Huguenots, thus on 12 May 1588, and with the encouragement of the duc de Guise, barricades were erected in the streets and a popular uprising forced the king to flee the city. Henri III subsequently assembled his court at Blois on 8th September, and dismissed all his ministers without notice, which, in effect, ended Catherine's days of power. On the 23 December 1588 he took even more draconian action. He invited the duc de Guise with eight members of his family to visit him at the Château of Blois and summarily had the duc murdered by the royal bodyguards. On the following day, the duc's brother, Louis II, Cardinal de Guise, suffered a similar fate by being hacked to death in the *château*'s dungeons. Because the duc de Guise was highly popular in much of France, enraged citizens turned against Henri. With criminal charges being brought against the king by Parliament, Henri III fled to Paris to seek asylum with Henri de Navarre, but on 5 January 1589, Catherine died at the age of sixty-nine. After being buried with little dignity at Blois, she was re-interred with more reverence at the Basilica of Saint-Denis. Within months, Henri III's own life was cut short, putting an end to the Valois dynasty. In September 1589, he was murdered by a deranged monk in the royal camp at Saint-Cloud. Some would say that this was a fortuitous act, others that it was disastrous, particularly the immediate impact of political and military events on the well-being of Paris.

During the first five years of his reign, Henri III's successor, the future Henri IV, championed the Huguenot cause while the duc de Mayenne of the Guise family grabbed the baton of the Catholic League. Henri and his troops swept through Normandy and set their sights on Paris. But the French capital prepared to defend itself to the death rather than have a Huguenot king. Following the battle of Ivry on 14 March 1590, in which Henri's army trounced the forces led by the duc de Mayenne, Henri laid siege to Paris in which as many as 40,000-50,000 of its pre-siege population of 220,000 perished, largely as a result of starvation or disease.[11] Over a period of four months (May-September 1590), the economy of the French capital was "damaged by the most crippling siege of any major city since that of Constantinople by the Turks the previous century."[12]

The siege was eventually broken with the help of Spanish forces under the Duke of Parma, and a military stalemate ensued. Henri eventually realised that there was no prospect of a Huguenot king establishing his capital in a fanatically Catholic Paris. Allegedly uttering the famous phrase *"Paris vaut bien une messe"* (Paris is well worth a mass), he successfully endeared himself to the Parisian population, and after receiving mass at St Denis in July 1593 and being crowned in Chartres Cathedral on 22 March 1594, he arrived in the city protected by a troop of 1,500 cuirvassiers (cavalry equipped with armour and firearms), needlessly since there was no armed opposition.

REFERENCES

1. C. Jones, *Paris. Biography of a City*, (London: Penguin Books, 2006), p.122
2. Ibid
3. C. Jones, opt. cit., p.124
4. C. Jones, opt. cit., p.130
5. C. Jones, opt. cit., p.133
6. A. Blunt, Revised by R. Beresford, *Art and Architecture in France 1500-1700*, Fifth Edition (London: Yale University Press, 1999), pp. 85 and 87
7. A. Blunt, opt. cit., p.89
8. H. Wischermann, *Paris. An architectural guide*, (Venice: Arsenale Editrice, 2005), p.42
9. P. Benedict, 'The Wars of Religion, 1562-1598' in M.P. Holt, Ed. 'Renaissance and Reformation in France', (New York: Oxford University Press, 2002), p.156
10. Ibid
11. A. Horne, *Friend or Foe. An Anglo-Saxon History of France*, (London: Phoenix, 2003), p.107
12. Ibid

CHRONOLOGY

1488-1515	Louis XII, King of France
1492 onwards	**St-Étienne-du-Mont**
1494-1657	**St-Gervais-St-Protaise**
Circa 1500	**Hôtel de Cluny built**
1508-22	**St-Jacques Tower**

1515-47	François I, King of France
1527	**The *donjon* of the Louvre demolished**
1532-40	**St-Eustache built**
1546	**Rebuilding of the Louvre as a palace**
1547-59	Henri II, King of France
1547-49	**Fontaine des Innocents built**
1548-50	**Hôtel Carnavalet built**
1559-60	François II, King of France
1560-74	Charles IX, King of France
1564	**Construction of the Tuileries Palace**
1566	**Petit Gallerie of the Louvre constructed**
1572	St-Bartholomew's Day massacre. Thousands of Protestants were killed
1574-89	Henri III, King of France
1578	**Pont Neuf begun**

6

EARLY-BOURBON PARIS

INTRODUCTION

For over three decades, the French Wars of Religion had put a brake on urban development in Paris, the epicentre of the conflict. From 1562 to 1598, few buildings of any merit were constructed in the capital and the application of the Renaissance style of architecture, so effervescent earlier in the century, virtually came to a standstill.

Continuous inter-dynastic street warfare, battles and sieges "fought across the city landscape had left Paris physically wrecked and financially ruined,"[1] but from the beginning of the next century the built environment of Paris was enhanced by decades of relatively uninterrupted development. It was during the reigns of the early-Bourbons, Henri IV and Louis XIII, that the Renaissance, once again, stamped its indelible mark on the architecture and townscape of the French capital, and in contrast to the latter-part of the sixteenth century was not largely confined to influencing the design of *châteaux* in the Île-de-France and elsewhere in provincial France.

HENRI IV (R. 1594-1610)

Notwithstanding the calamitous wars of religion, several years of political stability followed Henri's coronation in 1594. Although he declared war on Spain in 1595, he issued decrees at Folembray in 1596 to end the war of the Catholic League that had been festering across France, and in 1598 signed the Treaty of Ponts de Ce with his former adversaries to end civil war across his kingdom. In the same year, and of at least equal importance, he pacified the Huguenots by the Edict of Nantes which granted freedom of worship and other liberties. The "peace divided" also included economic advance. Henri's superintended of finances, the duc de Sully, reformed taxation and economic policy, funded the improvements of roads and the construction of canals, promoted agricultural modernisation and, by means of mercantilism, promoted overseas trade. On a personal level, Henri helped to maintain political stability and the survival of the Bourbon dynasty through the annulment of his childless marriage to Margaret de Valois and his subsequent marriage to Marie de Medici, who gave birth to the future Louis XIII in 1601. Again, foreign policy strengthened his hold on the reins of power, for in 1604 France and England signed a commercial treaty with each other mutually benefitting their domestic economies.

But foreign policy was but one of Henri's major concerns. On taking up residence in Paris, Henri found that although the built environment of his capital was in an appallingly poor condition, its population – after falling dramatically during the 1589-90 siege – was soaring rapidly. By 1600 it reached around 300,000 and went on to grow to about half a million by 1680. Throughout most of the seventeenth century, Paris not only maintained its position as the largest city in Europe demographically, it also grew spatially at an even faster rate than its population, doubling its area over the period as a whole. With the pressure of population growth, the condition of many of the central areas of the city remained in a deplorable condition or indeed worsened. The paved thoroughfares of the capital were ridden with deep and muddy holes inhibiting the passage of horses and humans alike, and its un-cobbled streets were impassable when it rained. Bridges across the Seine had been badly maintained or severely damaged, for example the wooden Pont-au-Meunier collapsed in 1596 after years of neglect. The absence of funds made it impossible to remedy even the worse instances of urban degradation. As Alistair Home so vividly describes: "[t]he streets were covered with a thick slime of decayed garbage, ashes, urine and faeces, animal and human."[2] Over the course of a decade and a half there were no fewer than three plague epidemics; 30,000 had died in 1580, and a decade and a half later Henri was forced to retire to Rouen to flee *la peste*. Clearly, Paris in the second-half of the sixteenth century – with its population having shrunk to 200,000 by 1590[3] – provided an unsuitable arena for architecture and urban development, and it is probable that if it was left to private initiative alone, the city would have had to wait until well into the seventeenth century before improvements to the built environment were feasible.

Using State funds, Henri therefore attempted to regenerate the built environment of much of Paris, or at least to ameliorate environmental affliction after more than thirty years of devastation and neglect. He took the lead in initiating a series of development schemes that embraced the use of Classical style of architecture that went on to dominate the development of major secular and ecclesiastical buildings and planning schemes for at least fifty years. Notwithstanding the impact upon design by the Dutch style of architecture in Paris (where Italianate motifs were given an idiosyncratic interpretation), Classicism in its "Frenchified" manner became increasingly applied by architects such as Salomon de Brosse, Jacques Lemercier and François Mansart to the development of major buildings in the French capital. Classicism soon became the most sought-after style by major patrons in Paris such as the king himself and his successor Louis XIII as well as by ministers, courtiers and wealthier merchants. Not only was the Classical style fashionable again after a lapse of one thousand years, but as in the past, it was employed to symbolise the political and economic power of its patrons at a time when absolute monarchy was on the ascendance.

Between 1594 and 1610 Henri therefore not only began to refurbish the Louvre but also extended it to make it the political centre of gravity of his reign. This was undoubtedly an expensive project "initiated within months of the king's entry into Paris when the royal coffers were depleted. Yet the project's political value was far from negligible. Construction was intended to stimulate the local building economy, putting masons and carpenters, quarriers and wood sellers, bargees and labourers back to work after the impoverishment of war. The project

35   *Grande Galerie of the Louvre, 1594-1610*

was hard evidence of Henri IV's intention to live in Paris, promising the city a new era of royal beneficience."[4] Part of the project, Lescot's fragmentary *Cour Carrée* was connected to the Tuileries by means of the 400m *Grande Galerie* along the bank of the Seine. Designed by Louis Métezeau and Jacques Androuet du Cerceau, the gallery provided both a series of workshops for artists and craftsmen along its lower floors and an escape route in the event of a political crisis.[5] From the Louvre, the built-up area of the Right Bank expanded eastward within the medieval walls, particularly in the Marais. It was mainly here that architects were obliged to follow building regulations to maintain a relatively straight building line on the street, while – elsewhere in the city – the construction of timber-framed buildings was banned, and attempts were made to keep building heights uniform.

Meanwhile, Diane de France was presiding over the construction of the Hôtel d'Angoulême (later the Hôtel de Lamoignon) (see chapter 5). Begun in 1584, work on the building was interrupted throughout the final years of the Wars of Religion and only resumed after Henri IV succeeded to the throne in 1589, an interruption also affecting the completion of the Pont Neuf.

36   *Pavillon de la Reine, Place Royale, 1605–12 (later the Place des Vosges)*

Henri undoubtedly understood the relevance of town planning to environmental improvement. The first of his planning projects, the development of the Place Royale (1605-12) with its uniform houses, heralded – to its immediate west – the paving over of the old city gutter (*egout*) to form the Rue Neuve-St-Louis (later renamed the Rue Turenne), and, this in turn, stimulated adjacent development in the *coutures* of St-Gervais and the Temple[5]. The Place Royale itself (or the Place des Vosges as it is now known) was built on the former site of the Château de Tournelle, and with private capital injected into the project, the Place des Vosges was developed by Henri from 1605 to 1612 to attract the aristocracy back from their power base in the provinces. Designed by either Louis Métezeau or Baptiste du Cerceau, and inaugurated on its completion by Louis XIII, the Place des Vosges is a true square, with each of its sides being 140m in length, and became the prototype of all the residential squares developed in a host of European cities throughout the following three centuries. Although, of course, there are many examples of planned squares in European cities dating from earlier centuries, particularly the piazzas of northern Italy and Rome, the Place des Vosges – unlike most of its counterparts – is notable for being a residential square with most of its house fronts built to the same design. Each side of the Place des Vosges accommodates nine brick houses with stone-dressed brick façades and, at ground floor level, a uniform vaulted stone arcade surrounds the square. The first and second storeys of the façade are pierced by tall rectangular windows and, resting on the cornices, pedimented dormers protrude from the steeply pitched blue-slate roofs. Near the ridge of the roof (which sharply rises and descends over each pair of houses) discreet small-paned windows illuminate the loft. The central house on both the southern and northern sides of the Place des Vosges is somewhat taller and grander than the other houses in the square and accommodates a tall rounded portal to facilitate access to and from adjacent streets. These prominent buildings were respectively intended for the King and the Queen, but over the years no royal personage has lived in the aristocratic square. However, the square served its purpose. Although, at first, such royal servants as the duc de Sully and Cardinal Richelieu were residents of the square, "[t]he top names of the old sword aristocracy and the new robe nobility of the state administrative service were soon queueing up to purchase,"[6] and for nearly two centuries, the square remained a socially-elite residential area. While the square was originally paved, a central garden was laid out in 1680 and in the nineteenth century, this became a wooded park with a fountain – arguably to the detriment of the visual symmetry of the whole. However, although the social composition of residents of the Place des Vosges became more egalitarian after the 1789 Revolution, the fabric of the square has remained very largely unchanged since built, and in the early twenty-first century the Place des Vosges – after some restoration – is again a high-status residential area.

The Place Dauphine is a further excellent example of seventeenth century civil architecture, though this time the housing was intended to attract merchants and lawyers rather than the aristocracy. Named after Louis XIII's heir, and designed by an architect who is today unknown, the development of the site began in 1607 after its desirability was enhanced by the completion of the Pont Neuf in the same year (see below). The triangular plaza accommodated identical three-storey houses on each of two of its sides and, as was fashionable, their brick façades were framed with ashlar. Although currently some of the

37   *Place Dauphine, started 1607*

houses date from the reign of Louis XIII, most have been altered. Henri planned to develop yet a further square, possibly his most ambitious. It would be known as the Place de France and would be located to the north-east of the city, near the present-day Rue de Bretagne, Rue de Poitou and Rue de Saintonge in the Third arrondissement. Intended as a site for government offices and as an ambassadorial neighbourhood, the scheme had only just got underway when Henri IV was assassinated in 1610 and it was duly abandoned.[7]

But Henri's planning endeavours were not solely concerned with the development of squares. He also promoted the construction of a major new bridge over the Seine, the Pont Neuf. As the first of the new-style bridges, the bridge (still extant), is 278 metres in length and 28 metres in width, and is divided into two separate spans, one of seven arches joining the Right Bank to the Île de la Cité, and the other of five arches connecting the island to the Left Bank. In this respect, the bridge – like its Medieval antecedents – was composed of a series of short arches following Roman precedents. Unavoidably, the bridge was built over an extended period. The initial decision to construct the bridge was taken by King Henri III, who laid its first stone in 1578, and building

38   *Equestrian statue of Henry IV, Pont de Neuf*

work was led by Androuet Du Cerceau and Guillaume Marchand. But construction work was soon subject to a lengthy delay largely because of the Wars of Religion, and work was not resumed until the early years of the reign of Henri IV and the bridge was eventually completed in 1607. The most remarkable feature of the Pont Neuf was that it was the first stone bridge over the Seine that did not support houses in addition to providing a thoroughfare and was the first bridge to be fitted with pavements protecting pedestrians from horses, wagons and mud. For a long time, the Pont Neuf was the widest bridge in Paris. Semi-circular bays were constructed over its pillars without disrupting the flow of pedestrians and transport (the bays were initially used for shops), and

39   *Hôpital St-Louis founded 1607*

at a point where it crosses the Île de la Cité, the bridge is widened on its western side to accommodate a bronze equestrian statue of Henry IV, commissioned by Marie de Medici in 1614, Henri's widow and Regent of France, sculptured by Giambologna and Pietro Tacca, and erected on its pedestal in 1618. From the time of the Pont Neuf's construction, new development was prohibited on the nearby banks of the Seine to allow for an undisturbed view of the Louvre.

Henri's concern for the well-being of his subjects was not reflected solely in his quest for an improved built environment but also in his desire to improve their health. Thus he commissioned in 1607 the Hôpital St-Louis and after it was completed in 1611, it led the way in hospital development in the early seventeenth century. The building was constructed outside of the city walls to accommodate those stricken by the plague. Until the early years of the seventeenth century, the only large hospital in Paris was the medieval Hôtel-Dieu near Notre Dame, but when disease was particularly virulent, it was only able to accommodate a very small proportion of its victims. Designed probably by Claude Chastillon, the new hospital consisted of a walled complex enveloping four wings and eight pavilions surrounding a square courtyard of 120 metres per side, with space for a vegetable garden. On the ground floor of each wing, there was a vaulted storage room and above a high sanatorium. On the western side of the building, outside of its surrounding wall, there was a chapel with a barrel-vaulted hall, groin-shaped transept and semi-circular apses. The hospital's portal, with its high-pitched roof, comprised a massive stone arch with a balcony above embossed with the initials of the royal couple (Henri IV and Marie de' Medici). As was stylistically fashionable, the façades of the building were constructed of brick and its features highlighted in ashlar.

During the reign of Henri IV, the development of Paris occurred on a hitherto unforeseen scale but since the French capital was well endowed with churches, new construction work was confined very largely to secular buildings. The protracted Wars of Religion of the second half of the sixteenth century must still have been in people's consciousness and might well have deterred, at least in the short term, any desire to add to the stock of ecclesiastical buildings or enlarge existing churches. One notable exception to this dearth of church-building was the flamboyant Gothic church of St-Étienne-du-Mont where an imposing Classical portal was added to its west end in 1605.

Despite an extensive amount of development in the French capital, "Henri IV's architects did not perceive Paris as an organic whole . . . Yet as the royal building programme developed, it implicitly demonstrated a growing recognition of Paris as a unified entity, both in the design and programme of the buildings."[8] Whereas Henri's successors were at best ambivalent towards Paris, Henri "regarded Paris not only as the locus of the court but as the primary vehicle for implementing the policies of the crown."[9] In contrast to the future development of grandiose edifices commissioned largely for the glorification of monarchs and the aristocracy, Henri's buildings satisfied the needs of a much wider section of society and established Paris very firmly as the capital of a unified French nation.

Committed to the development of his capital, it might be expected that Henri would resist undertaking major projects elsewhere in his kingdom, but this was a wrong assumption. Henri added quite substantially to the Palais de Fontainebleau by commissioning the Cour Henri IV and the Stable Court with its imposing entrance (attributable to Remy Collin, 1606-09) recalling Bramante's Belvedere niche in the Vatican Palace.

LOUIS XIII (R. 1610-43)

Following the death of Henri IV in 1610 and the accession of his son Louis XIII to the French throne at the age of eight, the Queen Mother Marie de' Medici ruled for seven years as Regent to the young king during his minority. From the beginning of her regency, she was concerned that the French nobility would attempt to grab the levers of power. She had reason to feel under threat since many nobles and royal officials in the early seventeenth century, unlike their ancestors, eschewed residence in the Loire Valley and lived much of the time in Paris that once again became the centre of power. The development of sumptuous *hôtels* gathered in momentum throughout Louis's reign. One of the first notable buildings of this genre is the Hôtel d'Alméras eponymously commissioned in 1611 by Pierre d'Alméras, *Conseiller secrétaire* to the monarch. Designed by Louis Métezeau, an imposing Mannerist pediment embellishes the street entrance which in turn leads inside to the *cour d'honneur* and the main residential building, an elegant stone and brick edifice.

But although royal officials tended to concentrate in Paris, very few aristocrats wished to reside in the capital continuously. They commissioned the development of *châteaux* across the Île de France that although was closer to Paris than that of the Loire Valley was a day or more's journey from the squalor and political in-fighting of the capital. The first grand *château* to be developed in the Île de France during Louis's reign was at Blérancourt (1612). Built for Bernard Potier, and designed by Salomon de Brosse, Blérancourt comprises a free-standing symmetrical block decorated alone by Doric and Ionic Orders and unencumbered by wings but with flanking pavilions positioned at the corners of its forecourt. More than any other French château of the sixteenth and early-seventeenth century, Blérancourt broadly adheres to the ideas of the Italian Renaissance, being "of the same family as Bramante's House of Raphael or Peruzzi's Farnesina."[10] In contrast, de Brosse's Coulommiers (begun a year later) is far more traditionally-

40   *Palais du Luxembourg (garden side) 1615-31*

French. Commissioned by Catharine de Gonzague, Duchess of Longueville, its plan is a variant "of the well-established form with *corps-de-Iogis*, two wings, and a screen enclosing a court."[11]

During the reign of Louis XIII, and as an outcome of the development of the Tuileries as a royal residence, there was "a gradual but clear-cut drift of the city's centre of gravity to the west,"[12] towards and beyond the medieval walls. However, in 1615, as if to emphasise her newly established position at the centre of power, and to demonstrate her independence, Marie de' Medici commissioned the construction of the Palais du Luxembourg. Built on a site named after an earlier owner, the duc de Piney-Luxembourg, and designed by Salomon de Brosse, the Palais du Luxembourg incorporates Mannerist motifs akin to those employed at the Pitti Palace in Florence, the childhood home of the French Queen Mother who wished to replicate many of its features in her Paris residence. As a further reminder of her childhood, a magnificent garden was laid out at the rear of the palace, mimicking the formal Boboli Gardens at her former Florentine home. However, the plan of the Palais du Luxembourg is distinctly French, not dissimilar to that employed at the Château d'Anet. its *cour d'honneur* (or courtyard) is surrounded by three three-storey wings and – on the entrance side – an arcaded screen wall with *aporte cockere*. In addition to funding the development of the Palais du Luxembourg and its extensive garden, Marie took possession of the adjoining Petit Luxembourg, but because the building took sixteen years to complete, Marie – now Queen Mother – could not take up residence because of her seriously weakened position. From the outset of her regency, her approach to government created hostility within the royal council. In 1617, antagonised by the influence of her two Florentine advisers, Concino Concini and Leonora Galigai, Louis XIII – still only sixteen years old – seized power. Concini was executed, Galigai was burnt for witchcraft and Marie and the King's Secretary of State for Foreign Affairs, Armand Jean du Plessis de Richelieu, were accused of treachery and exiled from the French capital.

Thus, because of the ravages of the Wars of Religion still fresh in people's minds and political instability, only a relatively small number of new churches (around 50) were constructed in Paris during the reign of Louis XIII and only a few stand out as striking examples of their genre, but these were mainly Gothic in style with some Classical additions. Despite the general slump in construction activity, the French monarch

41   *Palais du Luxembourg (entrance side) 1615-31*

began funding the embellishment of the façade of the church of St-Gervais-St-Protais in 1616, a commitment continued by Richelieu in the years ahead. Designed by Salomon de Brosse and Clement II Métezeau, the monumental three-storey Classical façade is superimposed on a flamboyant nave built mainly between 1494 and 1578. With building work completed in 1657, the façade is adorned by double columns displayed in the correct sequence of orders: Doric, Ionic and Corinthian, and is crowned by a large segmental pediment. Within a stone's throw of St-Gervais-St-Protais, further work was done on the bridging of the Seine. With royal help, a private entrepreneur, Christophe Marie, successfully circumvented the opposition of the chapter of Notre Dame Cathedral to the development of two new bridges to the Île de Cite (the Pont Marie in 1618 and the Pont Tournelle in 1620).

42   *Church of St-Gervais-St-Protais, started 1616*

In 1619, Louis and Richelieu were reconciled, and thus with little opposition at home, Louis marched his army into Angers and defeated Marie's supporters, the conflict being quelled by the Treaty of Angouleme. In the following year (1620), a revolt by French nobles was suppressed by Richelieu who succeeded in reconciling the Queen Mother and her son. However, religious dissent soon disturbed the peace. In their attempt to regain religious freedom granted by Henri IV, but subsequently diluted, the Huguenots rebelled against Louis in 1621, and fearful of a further war of religion, Louis attempted to suppress dissent by recalling Richelieu to the Council in 1622 and secured his appointment as Cardinal.

Richelieu was very aware that the French aristocracy, regardless of whether it was Catholic or Huguenot, was a political force to be reckoned with, and this was manifested by its attempt to flaunt its wealth and power through the construction of grand *châteaux*. In 1623 Pierre Brûlart de Sillery for example, commissioned François Mansart to redevelop a sixteenth century *château* at Berny. Mansart, though still in his twenties, was more adept than de Brosse at Blerancourt incorporating Classical motifs to his overall design. The new *château* was essentially a stone-built edifice, E-shaped in plan and rising to three storeys at the centre, though its symmetry was broken by the addition of a pavilion to the right of the main block containing the staircase.

To enhance his power and increase his responsibilities, Louis made Richelieu First Minister of France in 1624, a role he performed adroitly until his death eighteen years later. By means of an Anglo-French treaty in 1624, Richelieu attempted to improve relations with England by negotiating the future marriage of Henrietta-Marie, sister of Louis XIII, and Charles, Prince of Wales of England. When the royal wedding took place in 1625 and Charles had been crowned king (Charles I), favourable relations between France and England ensued.

In 1624, with foreign policy now on the backburner, Louis was able to switch his attention to more domestic matters such as enhancing the fabric of his capital city. First and foremost he attempted to enhance the grandeur of the Louvre. In so doing, he commissioned Jacques Lemercier to extend Lescot's fragmentary *Cour Carree* by replicating Lescot's wing to the north of the original edifice and to link it to the original wing by a tall Pavillon, the Pavillon de l'Horloge (later called

43 *Completion of the Cour Carree of the Louvre began 1624*

Pavilion de Sully), the top of which is crowned by a triangular pediment encasing, in turn, a smaller segmental and triangular pediment. The northern end of Lemercier's wing was then continued at a right-angle along part of the northern side of the *Cour Carree*. With work on the Louvre directed by Richelieu, Lemercier's aesthetic contribution to the Louvre was subsequently criticised – not least by the painter Nicholas Poussin – for being overwrought and heavy-handed. This might undoubtedly be a fair comment vis-à-vis the Pavillon de Sully, but the remainder of his contribution was unavoidably conditioned by Lescot's initial work. Overall, however, it cannot be denied that the *Cour Carree* exemplifies the overripe flowering of the French Renaissance style.

Louis, however, was not alone in commissioning imposing buildings. From 1624 to 1630, a relatively small but none-the-less sumptuous palace was constructed for a notorious gambler, Petit Thomas in the fashionable Marais in 1624-30, but since its owner lost his complete fortune after a night's gambling in 1634, and because of the building's aesthetic appeal, it was acquired in 1634 by Maximilien de Bethune, the duc de Sully and former first minister of Henri IV. Designed by Jean-Baptiste Androuet du Cerceau, the Hôtel de Sully – as the building became known – is composed of three wings and a

44   *Hôtel de Sully, 1624-30*

courtyard opulently adorned with carved pediments, dormer windows and eight bas-reliefs in niches representing the four elements and four seasons: a street façade to the south with dominating pointed pavilions looking on to the Rue St-Antoine; and a mini-garden and low-lying palace – the Petit Sully essentially an orangery – to the north.

Meanwhile, Richelieu was endeavouring to further stamp his mark on the architecture of Paris. He commissioned the Église de Ste-Ursule-de-la-Sorbonne in 1625 and, in contrast to the church of St-Gervais–St-Protais, it is the most Classical of all churches in Paris, though some would say that its design is cold and constrained. Designed by Jacques Lemercier and completed in 1642, the church was built afresh and was not an extension of an existing ecclesiastical building. It is without a doubt Roman in style with "its pure proportions, clear spatial relationships and restrained décor."[12] With a barrel-vaulted Greek cross plan and its extended northern and southern arms, both of 49 metres in length, the church is particularly notable for its contrasting west- and north-facing two-storey façades. The former façade, overlooking the street, has an inviting central portal framed by Corinthian columns, and is adorned with carved niches and volutes and surmounted by a large triangular

45 *Église de Ste-Ursule - de-la-Sorbonne started 1625*

pediment, while the latter façade facing the court of the college boasts a "free-standing classical portico with a triangular pediment enclosing a cartouche with the arms of the Cardinal, which makes a striking and unusual end of the college."[14] Like contemporary churches in Italy, it is dominated by a high elegant cupola, which at 51 metres in height is clearly visible from the ground.

But soon a period of peace turned into one of war. In 1627, England aided and abetted the resumption of the conflict between the Huguenots and the French throne. The English king, Charles I, perhaps reluctantly, authorised the Duke of Buckingham to sail from Portsmouth with a fleet to assist the Huguenots in their defence of their western stronghold, La Rochelle. However, because of inefficient

46   *Church of St-Paul-St-Louis, 1627-41*

leadership, the English expedition failed to achieve its objective and, in 1628, possibly because of little help from abroad, the Huguenots at La Rochelle capitulated to the French crown. Meanwhile, as if to compensate for the loss of England as an ally, France signed a treaty of friendship with Spain (in 1627). However, in 1629, the Peace of Susa ameliorated relations once again between France and England, while the Peace of Alais ended the Huguenot revolt.

During the last fourteen and relatively peaceful years of his reign, Louis XIII witnessed further improvements to the fabric of Paris. Whereas in Rome, where the designs of II Gesu (1568-74) pre-date the introduction of the Baroque, the Jesuit church of St-Paul–St-Louis in Paris anticipates the adoption of the Baroque in the French capital. Although the Jesuits had been driven out of Paris in 1595, their return in 1603 led to a gradual revival in their spiritual role in the French capital and their desire for a new church to provide a focus for their liturgical and preaching needs. Supported by Louis XIII in an attempt to quell the expansion of Protestantism, the Jesuits commissioned Martellange in 1627 to build an edifice loosely based on the design of the society's mother church in Rome and, on its completion in 1641, St-Paul-St-Louis shared some of its attributes with II Gesu, such as a façade pierced by three portals with its giant beckoning central portal surmounted by a large segmental pediment, its upper-tier crowned by a triangular pediment and both churches were endowed with a large single dome although they were both barely visible from the ground. There were of course notable differences relating to the use of columns and pilasters, the number of storeys and the use or absence of volutes, but as a statement of ecclesiastical architecture, the similarities were pronounced. In 1628 Richelieu commissioned the church of Notre-Dame-des-Victoires to celebrate the conquest of La Rochelle. Designed by Pierre Le Muet and run by the bare-footed Augustinians, the church is Classical in design with its façade adorned in turn by six Ionic pilasters on the ground floor, four Corinthian pilasters above, and a large gable across the top.

47   *Sisters of the Visitation of Mary*

Established by Ste-Jeanne de Chantal in 1632, the church of the Sisters of the Visitation of Mary (the Visitandines) was one of François Mansart's earlier commissions. However, in designing a church with an arch-framed portal, square-framed rotunda – 15 metres in diameter and 35 metres high – and ring of oval chapels each with square columns arranged beneath a cupola, Mansart "introduces a note of almost Baroque complexity into a building of fundamentally High Renaissance character,"[15] notwithstanding the fact that he largely rejected the Baroque in his future commissions in favour of Classicism.

Despite intermittent residency (mainly in winter), new aristocratic neighbourhoods were gradually established in close proximity to the Palais Cardinal and in the Faubourg St-Honore in the 1620s-30s. A magnificent promenade, the Cours-la-Reine, was also put in place in the 1620s to link the Tuileries to the royal palace at Chaillot. Seven years after becoming cardinal and five years after being appointed as Louis XII's first minister, Richelieu had accumulated sufficient wealth to fund the construction of a residence that – because of its scale and ambitions of its owner – immediately became known as

48   *Palais Cardinal, built in 1620s-30s. Became Palais Royal 1642*

the Palais Cardinal. Designed by Jacques Lemercier, the building was constructed on a site in close proximity to the Louvre to be as close as possible to the seat of royal power. In the manner of a Parisian hôtel of the period, the residence consists of a *cour de logis* with side wings, a *cour d'honneur* and a columned wall with reliefs made of ships' anchors and prows that screen the complex from the Rue d'Honore.

While there were fairly favourable relations between France and her neighbours in the 1630s, political stability at home was far from assured. Marie de' Medici seemed determined to displace Richelieu as the foremost political figure in France and, following a failed coup in 1630, the First Minister exiled her to Compiegne, from where she escaped to Brussels in 1631 and Amsterdam in 1638, eventually to die in Cologne in 1642.

With Marie exiled, she was no longer a threat to peace in France but to protect at least some of the new development that had been recently taking place from any insurrection in the future, an edict of 1634 enacted the construction of new bastions (the Fosse Jaunes) that were to run westward and then south-westward from the Porte of St-

49   *Library of Mazarin converted into the Bibliothèque Mazarin, 1635*

Denis to the Seine. Extending the fortified area of the Right Bank by a third, and swelling its area to 567 hectares, the new bastions enclosed a rapidly built-up area intersected by the east west Rue St-Honore and Rue des Petit Champs, and the north-south Rue de Richelieu. However, building work at this time was not confined to matters military. The personal library of Jules Mazarin, papal nuncio, was transformed into the Bibliothèque Mazarin in 1635. It was accommodated in the Hôtel Tubeuf, a building designed by Jean Thiriot for Charles Duret de Chevry, Controller General of Finance, and initially called the Hôtel Chevry. Constructed from brick and ashlar, and featuring an attractive forecourt, the scale of the edifice was increased during its restructuring in 1645 by the addition of a two-storey gallery wing designed by Mansart.[16]

With security strengthened at home, Richelieu was able to focus his attention on foreign policy. In his attempt to insulate France as much as possible from the Thirty Years War that ravaged the German states between 1618 and 1648, Richelieu confined the French army to the protection of its eastern border by occupying Lorraine in 1633, and in 1635 and 1638 he signed treaties of alliance with the Swedish regent, Oxtenstierna. Thus by 1640, there was little threat from the east during the last eight years of the Thirty Years War. By now, Mansart's style of architecture had enormously matured, so much so that René de Longueil, first Marquis de Maisons and *Surintendant des Finances* before Nicolas Fouquet, commissioned for his frequent use the Château de Maisons, near St-Germain-en-Laye in 1642. With the château being conveniently close to Paris – it was only 30 kilometres or less than a day's journey away – Longueil was easily able to attend to his governmental duties in the French capital. The *château* is a masterpiece in the classical style as interpreted by its architect, François Mansart. Although smaller than its urban counterparts such as the Palais du Luxembourg or Palais Royal (see above), it is more elegant and refined. Standing on a rectangular site bordered by a dry moat and on a raised terrace, the three-storey *château* has a symmetrical façade with a decorative central pavilion and short lateral wings. It is surmounted by characteristic 'mansard roofs' over each of its sections and its skyline is marked by tall chimney stacks. Since 1818, following its purchase by the Parisian banker Jacques Lafitte, the building has

50   *Château de Maisons 1642 (known as Chateau-de Maisons-Lafitte since 1818)*

been known as the Château de Maisons-Lafitte and since 1905 has been owned by the State.

Whereas the French aristocracy demonstrated its predilection for country *châteaux*, the French bourgeoisie created a demand for the development of more modest residences, located particularly in Paris close to the centre of government. Commissioned by the royal secretary and ruthlessly successful state financier Jean-B. Lambert de Sucy, and designed by Louis Le Vau, the construction of the Hôtel Lambert was commenced in 1640 and completed four years later. Built on a riverside on the eastern tip of the increasingly fashionable Île St-Louis, the residence is a brilliant example of a prestigious *hôtel particulier*, and its development demonstrated that an affluent lifestyle was no longer the monopoly of the monarchy and aristocracy but was extended to the new financial elite. In embracing an amalgam of Mannerist and Classical motifs, the *hôtel* features a three-storey wing, an attached rotunda and a rusticated gatehouse piercing its curved street façade. Within, there is a rounded-off courtyard adorned with half columns, while at the rear of the building, the garden façade is supported by monumental Ionic pillars.

51   *Hôtel Lambert, 1640-44*

Like Marie de' Medici, Richelieu died in 1642 and was succeeded by Mazarin who had been residing in his *bibliothèque* prior to his appointment. Richelieu's Palais Cardinal, however, was not inherited by Mazarin as the new cardinal might have wished, but on the death of Louis XIII in 1643, its ownership was passed to the Queen Mother, Anne D'Autriche, and was henceforth known as the Palais Royal.

REFERENCES

1. A. Hussey, *Paris. The Secret History* (London: Penguin Books, 2007), p.137

2. A. Horne (B), *Friend or Foe. An Anglo-Saxon History of France* (London: Phoenix, 2005), p.107

3. H. Ballon, *The Paris of Henry IV. Architecture and Urbanism* (London: the MIT Press, 1991), p.15

4. C. Jones, *Paris. Biography of a City* (London: Penguin Books, 2006), p.149

5. C. Jones, opt. cit., p.156
6. C. Jones, opt. cit., p.160
7. C. Jones, opt. cit., p.160
8. H. J. Ballon, opt. cit., p.253
9. H. Ballon, opt. cit., p.253
10. A. Blunt, *Art and Architecture in France, 1500-1700* (London: Yale University Press. 5th Edit., 1999), p.112
11. Ibid
12. C. Jones, op-cit. p.164
13. H. Wischermann, *Paris. An Architectural Guide* (Verona: Arsenale Editrice, 2005), p.46
14. A. Blunt, opt. cit., p.130
15. D. Watkin, *A History of Western Architecture*, (London: 5th Edition., 2011), p.261
16. H. Wischermann, opt. cit., p.59

CHRONOLOGY

1589–1610	Henri IV, King of France. First of the Bourbon line
1594–98	**Hôtel de Lamoignon or d'Angoulème built**
1595-1608	**Grande Galerie of the Louvre built**
1605-12	**Place de Vosges built**
1607 onwards	**Place Dauphine**
1607	**Completion of Pont Neuf**
1607-11	**Hôpital St-Louis constructed**
1610-43	Louis XIII, King of France
1615-31	**Palais du Luxembourg built for Marie de'Medici**
1624-30	**Hôtel de Sully constructed**
1624-67	**Val-de-Grace built**
1627-35	**Chapelle Ste-Ursule-de-la-Sorbonne constructed**
1627-41	**St-Paul-St-Louis built**
1629 onwards	**Palais-Royal built**

1632-34	**Temple Ste-Marie constructed**
1633-36	**Louis XIII ordered the extension of Philip Augustus's wall**
1634-1736	**St-Sulpice built**
1635	**Hôtel Tubeuf constructed – the oldest building of the Bibliothèque Nationale**
1640	**Hôtel Lambert built**

7

ABSOLUTE MONARCHY AND THE DEVELOPMENT OF PARIS

INTRODUCTION

Around a hundred years after the Council of Trent of 1545-63 had reinforced the Roman Catholic faith in much of Europe in response to the emergence of Protestantism, monarchs in the larger continental countries – Spain, Austria and particularly France – relied upon the Catholic church to underpin the notion of the 'divine right of kings', the perceived *raison d'être* of political absolutism that was carried to extremes in the second half of the seventeenth century. Absolutism, "[a] system of unlimited government in which the governed possess no representation, right to vote or participate in the administration and in which there are no legal or constitutional restraints on the ruler"[1] reached its apogee in the France of Louis XIV (r. 1643-1715). Quite early in his reign, Louis suspended the tax-voting rights of the Estates and rationalised the role of all intermediate authorities between subject and state. In all probability, this would not have been possible had the king not created a standing army and an efficient bureaucracy. Thus, until the Revolution of 1789, "state and monarch were conceived as one and regarded as above the law."[2] Throughout much of Europe, Roman Catholicism and absolutism were inextricably linked to the Baroque style of architecture, its grandiose exuberance being a deliberate reflection of the magnificence of the court and devotion to the "one true faith".

In France, in particular, the connection between religion, politics and architecture was very real. The absolute monarch played a pivotal and commanding role in enhancing the urban fabric particularly in his capital which was going through a period of substantial growth in the second half of the seventeenth century. With a population of 222,000, the population of Paris at the beginning of the century was larger than that of any other city in Europe. By 1700, it had grown to 510,000 but had lost its pre-eminence to London as the continent's largest urban area. The growth of Paris was attributable overwhelmingly to migration from the provinces, as the city's importance rapidly escalated throughout much of the seventeenth century because of the enormous spending power of the monarch and his court and the associated provision of job-creating opportunities.

THE SPATIAL GROWTH OF PARIS
IN THE LATE-SEVENTEENTH CENTURY

Population growth in Paris was not associated with any significant increase in density (it was already very overcrowded) but with an acceleration of urban sprawl after 1670 following the demolishing of the entire circuit of defensive walls. But, by the middle of the seventeenth century, the built environment of Paris had changed very little since the Middle Ages. Despite some remarkable architectural and planning achievements in the reigns of Henry IV and Louis XIII, the Renaissance had had only a minor impact on the physical fabric of the French capital by the time Louis XIV came to the throne in 1643. The city, and particularly districts such as the Marais, was still extremely congested, smelly and unhealthy. It lacked an adequate supply of fresh drinking water, a drainage and sewage system, a suitable means of disposing of waste, and was devoid of street lighting. It was, in this context, that Louis (the *Roi Soleil*), his principal ministers Mazarin and Colbert, and countless courtiers and administrators ambitiously attempted to transform Paris into the 'Rome of the North' and into a capital city worthy of France and fit for the late-seventeenth century and beyond. In this they largely failed. Despite the construction of a number of architectural gems in the French capital during the reign of Louis XIV, it would have been a great exaggeration to claim that, like Augustus Caesar's rebuilding of Rome nearly two millennia earlier, they 'inherited a city of brick and left it marble.' Because of the continuance of squalor across much of the city, it is not at all remarkable that Louis, his court and his government vacated Paris and relocated to Versailles before their work was done.

ABSOLUTE MONARCHY, PATRONAGE AND THE DEVELOPMENT OF PARIS

The very lengthy 72-year reign of Louis XIV was divided into three parts. First, the period from his accession to the throne in 1643 – at the age of five – to 1661, over which time France was ruled by his regent, the Queen Mother, Anne d'Autriche but, more importantly, governed over much of the period by his *Premier Ministre*, Jules Cardinal Mazarin. The second part of his reign covered the years 1661 to 1682 when, after gaining personal control of the levers of power, albeit aided and abetted by Jean-Baptise Colbert, he ruled despotically from Paris; and the final part of his reign – the longest – extended from 1682 to his death in 1715 when his seat of power was firmly established in the Palais de Versailles, 22 kilometres from the French capital. In each of these periods, political events had a substantial though variable effect on the development of the Parisian built environment.

THE POLICIES OF JULES MAZARIN, CHIEF MINISTER OF FRANCE (1643-61)

Though, as Dauphin (1638-43), Louis resided in the Louvre, on his accession he moved with his mother Anne d'Autriche and younger brother Philippe d'Orléans to the comparative safety of the Palais Royal where, since they were less at risk from the Frondeurs (hostile opponents of monarchical power), they remained until 1652. During these nine years, the Crown neither had the resources nor secure circumstances to promote the glory of royal power through the medium of grandiose and awesome buildings. However, in many places outside of the capital, conditions were comparatively peaceful and royal servants showed little hesitation in developing sumptuous *châteaux*, normally with few means of defence. Possibly the best example of this genre from Louis's early days as king was the Château du Raincy in the present-day commune of Le Raincy (Seine-St-Denis), only 13.2 kilometres from the centre of Paris. Commissioned by Jacques Bordier, *Surintendant des Finances* in 1643, and designed by Louis Le Vau in the Baroque style soon after he began his professional career, the building conventionally comprised "a main block with slightly projecting pavilions at the end of the forecourt,"[3] but unusually accommodated a "great oval vestibule in the centre which made a curved projection in the middle of both the garden and court façades,"[4] to an extent a foretaste of Le Vau's magnificent Château de Vaux-le-Vicomte (see below). Falling into neglect during the Napoleonic Wars, the Château du Raincy was demolished in 1819.

But despite the militancy of the Frondeurs, some public officials and members of the aristocracy wished to have more than a *pied a terre* in the capital and thus commissioned the construction of a plethora of *hôtels particuliers*. Like those that followed throughout the seventeenth and eighteenth centuries, they all comprised a *cours de logis* (or main building), and all normally contained two side wings of the same or lower height than the main building, a *cours d'honneur* (a forecourt) embraced by the main building and wings, a frontispiece to the street consisting of a screening wall with a doored gateway (as much for security as for ornamentation), and a walled garden at the rear of the main building. The *cours de logis* is normally of three or four storeys in height (inclusive of an attic within the roof) and tends to be five or seven bays in width. In general, there was a change in the style of the *hôtel* from Baroque in the earlier part of the seventeenth century to a style anticipating eighteenth-century Neoclassicism in the late seventeenth century, early examples of this transition being the Hôtel St-Aignan (begun 1644) and the Hôtel d'Aumont (started 1645).

The Thirty Years War – that had so unremittingly ravaged much of the Continent – ended in the Peace of Westphalia in 1648, with its terms ratified in the same year by the Treaty of Munster and Treaty of

52   *Hotel St-Aignan, 1644-47*

53   *Hôtel d'Aumont, 1645-56*

Osnabriick. Of the victorious combatants – France, Holland, Sweden and an array of German states – France had most to gain from the terms of the Peace. She absorbed all Habsburg lands and claims in Alsace, while several German states placed themselves under her protection, leading to a further weakening of Habsburg power. However, many of the advantages that could have accrued to France toward the end of the thirty-year conflict were dissipated by the outbreak of civil war in France: the Fronde. Hostilities arose because *Parlement* and the nobility resented losing their "feudal" liberties as a consequence of Mazarin's policies of centralisation.

Like his predecessor Richelieu, Mazarin aimed at subjugating all those who had political power below the Crown and its servants. Following the arrest of certain recalcitrant members of *Parlement* in a show of force, Paris erupted in rioting and rebellion and, to avoid possible danger, Anne fled Paris with the young king and his courtiers on 13th September 1648. Following the Peace of Westphalia, the French army under the prince de Condé – on behalf of the Crown – besieged the French capital in January 1649 and put down the insurrection. However, no sooner had the first Fronde (the *Fronde Parlementairs*) ended, than a second Fronde, headed by princes, began. Commencing in 1650, the conflict was essentially a struggle between Condé, who had joined forces with the Parisians, and France's other great soldier, Marshal Turenne, who supported Anne and the King. Though civil war waged between the armies of Condé and Turenne throughout provincial France, Paris was the epicentre of tumultuous conflict and was reduced to a miserable state of anarchy, culminating in much bloodshed and the torching of the Hôtel de Ville.

Since the first eighteen years of Louis XIV's reign was plagued by civil war and international conflict, it is not surprising that the Crown and its servants invested very little in the development of the built environment in the 1640s and 1650s. They neither had resources nor secure circumstances to promote the glory and trappings of royal power through the medium of grandiose and awesome buildings. Even so, the magnificent church of Val-de-Grace was constructed according to the designs of François Mansart (who was responsible for the lower storey up to the entablature) and Jacques Lemercier (who completed the rest of the building). Like the church of the Sorbonne, the Val-de-Grace is

54 *Val-de-Grace, 1638-1667*

stylistically derived from the great Baroque church of Sant'Andrea della Valle in Rome. The lower storey of the façade has a monumental portico surmounted by a pediment, while its upper storey – also pedimented – is flanked by *volutes*, but the building is particularly distinguished by a magnificent dome, 19 metres in diameter, on a very high drum supported by *consoles*. Though the church was initiated during the reign of Louis's father (Louis XIII) in 1638, construction proceeded slowly during the Frondes and was only completed in 1667.

Soon after in 1670–76, the comparatively small church of Notre-Dame-de-l'Assomption was built in the Rue de St-Honoré. Designed by Charles Errard, the ediface is noted for its prominent dome.

With the coming of age of Louis in 1651, the Frondeurs had lost their pretext for revolt and terminated hostilities when, on the eastern fringe of the city, the battle of St-Antoine (1652) ended in stalemate putting an end to the last great revolutionary struggle in France, until the year of reckoning, 1789. Though Louis had had to grant generous terms to the rebels, in return he expected loyalty and obedience. As if to confirm his new-found power, he was crowned at Reims in 1654, and almost immediately sought to underline his authority by uttering his famous words to a recalcitrant *Parlement: "L'Etat, c'est moi.*" However, he was not omnipotent internationally and failed in the short run to deliver peace. War with Spain was unresolved by the Treaties of Munster and Osnabruck, and continued for a further decade but, following an Anglo-French victory over Spanish forces at the Battle of the Dunes in 1658, Louis ensured that the Pyrenees in 1659 not only fixed the border between France and Spain but ceded the whole of Rousillon and various towns in the Spanish Netherlands to France. As an outcome of the treaty, and with an immense dowry of 500,000 gold *ecus*, in part to seal favourable relations between France and Spain, Louis married his cousin, Maria Theresa, daughter of Philip IV of Spain in 1660, but despite some improvement in his personal finances, the French Crown was still very much in debt and, as a result of a long and costly war with Spain, the French treasury faced bankruptcy.

With the disappearance of the Frondeurs from the political arena, Louis XIV and his family returned from the Palais to the Louvre in 1652 and began to consider redeveloping and expanding their new

55   *Notre Dame de l'Assomption, 1670–76*

residence in keeping with the ever-increasing needs of the monarchy. Public officials similarly surmised that the time was ripe to develop real estate in the French capital, for example Pierre de Beauvais (whose wife was a Lady-in-Waiting to Anne d'Autriche) commissioned the Hôtel de Beauvais (1655) noted for its impressive Baroque courtyard; Pierre Aubert funded the construction of the Hôtel de Fontenay (1656) with its curved gateway; the Count of Lauzun built the Hôtel de Lauzun (1656-57) that dispensed with a forecourt and other notable external features except a balcony; and Jean Baptiste Amelot de Bisseuil funded the construction of the Hôtel Amelot de Bisseuil (1658) that has a magnificent double-sided tympanum above its gateway with the latter's skilfully-carved doors.

It was also after the Frondes that Mazarin ordered the construction of the Hôpital de la Salpêtrière, the first major scheme in the French capital during Louis's reign. Founded in 1656 and constructed on the site of a disused gunpowder factory (built on the edge of Paris in 1634), the Hôpital de la Salpêtrière derives its name from saltpetre (potassium nitrate) used in the manufacture of explosives. The new building was originally intended as a general hospital, but it soon became a home

56 *Hôpital de la Salpêtrière, founded 1656*

for sick and socially disadvantaged women and children, and in 1684 a prison for prostitutes was added to the main structure. Designed by Louis Le Vau and Pier Le Muet, the long austere structure of the hospital eventually contained a cloistered courtyard from which stemmed four halls each 24 metres in the manner of a Greek cross, though only the north wing was completed in the late seventeenth century (the remainder of the building was finished in 1765). The hospital also contains a largely unadorned chapel comprising an octagonal altar room surmounted by a centrally partitioned dome, 20 metres in diameter and illuminated by picture windows in circular arcs. Designed by Libéral Bruant, the chapel was built between 1660 and 1677. La Salpêtrière is now a general teaching hospital.

The austere magnificence of the La Saltpetriere is at least matched by the Hôtel des Invalides, founded by Louis XIV in 1671 under the overall supervision of the Marquis de Louvois, his minister for war. Designed by Libéral Bruant, the hospital was built to provide a convalescence home for 4,000 to 6,000 disabled war veterans. South of the extensive Esplanade des Invalides and the 196 metres northern façade of the hospital with its sixth-floor dormer windows and

57   *Hôtel des Invalides – north entrance –*
         started 1671-74

58   *Hôtel des Invalides - cours d'honneur facing north - 1676*

magnificent central pavilion, Les Invalides comprises a main cloistered courtyard (or *cour d'honneur*) measuring 102 x 64 metres, 14 smaller courtyards and 17 kilometres of corridors. Four refectories flank the length of the main courtyard, while somewhat gloomy dormitories, an infirmary (now the Institution Nationale des Invalides) and a priests' wing are dispersed around the smaller courtyards. Bruant's direct involvement in the construction of Les Invalides was cut short in 1676 when Hardouin-Mansart was appointed to supervise the construction of a chapel (subsequently referred to as the 'soldiers' church') to the south of the *cours d'honneur*. Loyal to the original designs of Bruant, the soldiers' church – starkly classical – is but part of a much larger ecclesiastical complex dominated magnificently by the Dome Church of Les Invalides. Designed by Jules Hardouin-Mansart, and begun in 1677, the edifice has a Greek cross plan 52 metres x 52 metres and a centrally-placed double-drum buttressed externally by a colonnade of paired columns on its lower storey and – above a surrounding balustrade – *volutes* on its upper storey. Above, a gilt-encrusted three-layered ribbed dome of 106 metres in height and almost 30 metres in diameter is crowned by an ornamented gilt lantern. Although in designing the domed church, Hardouin-Mansart was doubtlessly inspired by the churches of his great-uncle François (notably the Val-de-Grace and Ste Marie-de-la-Visitation) and Charles Errard's Notre Dame de l'Assomption, the Dome is – to an extent – more overtly Roman baroque with its dome not dissimilar to that of St.Peter's, but – in its two-storey columned façade – provides a foretaste of eighteenth-century Neoclassicism.

59   *Hôtel des Invalides, - cours d'honneur facing south - 1676*

60   *Dome church of Les Invalides - 1679–90*

TABLE 7.1
PROMINENT *HÔTELS PARTICULIERS* IN PARIS
DEVELOPED IN THE REIGN OF LOUIS XIV

Hôtel St-Aignon, Rue de Temple, *built for the Compte d'Avous and designed by Pierre le Muet*

Hôtel d'Aumont, Rue de Jouy (1645), *built for Marshal Antoine d'Aumont and designed by Louis Le Vau and François Mansart*

Hôtel de Guenegaud, Rue des Archives (1648), *built for Jean François de Guenegaud des Brosse, and designed by François Mansart*

Hôtel de Beauvais, Rue François-Miron (1655), *built for Pierre de Beauvais, and designed by Antoine Lepautre*

Hôtel Salé or Aubert de Fontenay, Rue de Thorigny (1656-59), *built for Pierre Aubert, Seigneur de Fontenay, and designed by Jean Boullier de Bourges*

Hôtel de Tallard or Amelot de Chaillou, Rue des Archives (1658), *built for Jacques Amelot de Bisseuil, and expanded in 1702-04 according to the design of Pierre Bullet.*

Hôtel Sagonne-Mansart, Rue des Tournelles (1674-85), *built for and designed by Jules Hardouin-Mansart*

Hôtel de Libéral, Rue de la Perle (1683), *built for and designed by Libéral Bruant*

Hôtel de Brancas, Rue de Tournon (c. 1700), *built for Jean Baptiste Terrat, the Marquis de Chantosme, and designed by Pierre Bullet*

Hôtel de Soubise (now housing the National Archives), Rue des Francs-Bourgeois (1704), *built for François de Rohan, Prince de Soubise, and designed by Pierre Alexis Delamair*

Hôtel de Rohan-Strasbourg, Rue Vieille-du-Temple (1705), *built for the Prince Bishop of Strasbourg, Armand G. Max de Rohan, and designed by Pierre Alexis Delamair*

Source: Wischerman (1997)

61   *Château de Vaux-le-Vicomte-1657-1661*

One of the last notable buildings to be erected during Mazarin's ministry was the Château de Vaux-le-Vicomte, a Baroque edifice near Melun some 55 kilometres from Paris. Funded by Louis's *Surintendant des Finances*, Nicolas Fouquet and designed by Louis Le Vau, the *château* was built from 1657 to 1661, and is without doubt "one of the greatest houses of the century."[5] By having a projecting central block, porticoed and pedimented, the *château* is not particularly unusual, but atypically it lacks a *cour d'honneur* and also differs from most others of its genre by incorporating a massive Italianate elliptical salon surmounted by a dome and a lantern, and by having a curved garden façade.

However, in each of the four corners of its rectangular plan, substantial pavilions with giant Ionic pilasters are given a French flavour by their high-pitched slate roofs. Surrounded on three sides by a false moat, its main rooms look onto a large formal garden designed by André Le Nôtre, which to an extent renders Fouquet's residence reminiscent of the Château de Maisons built a decade or more earlier.

To his undoubted displeasure, the superintendent of finances was forced to cut short his use of the *château*. Influenced by Jean-Baptiste Colbert, Louis was convinced that Fouquet would only have been able to have afforded such a magnificent building and to turn it into a great centre for fine feasts, the arts and social gatherings by misappropriating public funds. Within a year of building work being finished, Fouquet was arrested and imprisoned for 17 years, while the *château* was sequestrated by the king, only to return to Madame Fouquet in 1671. Whether or not Louis was envious of Fouquet because Vaux-le-Vicomte was more magnificent than any of the king's country residences we will never know, but what is certain is that Fouquet's *château* inspired Louis to build in due course a rural edifice even more magnificent and on a substantially larger scale: the palace of Versailles.

JEAN-BAPTISTE COLBERT'S STEWARDSHIP AND THE DEVELOPMENT OF THE BUILT ENVIRONMENT; 1661-1682

Following the death of Mazarin and the incarceration of Fouquet in 1661, Louis XIV abolished the posts of *Premier Ministre* and *Surintendant des Finances* and appointed Jean-Baptiste Colbert to the new and more regulated post of *Controlleur Général des Finances*. With Colbert as his trusted minister, Louis now ruled supreme, a task that was reinforced by financial reforms introduced over the period 1661 to 1667. Between these years Colbert converted a deficit of the equivalent of £8 million into a surplus of £9 million, and largely as a result of revenue gained from *aides* and *douanes* (customs duties), the *gabelle* (a tax on salt) and the *faille* (a tax on land), royal revenue tripled by the time of his death in 1683. Apart from ensuring that an adequate supply of tax revenue would fill the Crown's coffers, he recognised that buildings needed to be constructed to facilitate industrial and commercial activity if mercantilist aims and objectives were to be realised. If France was to prosper, it was essential that the value of exports exceeded that of imports to ensure that, as payment, there would be a net inflow of gold and silver to increase the national stock of wealth. To this effect, Bourbon rule had boosted the Parisian silk industry since the late-sixteenth century and Colbert, in particular, supported the manufacture of luxury goods in order to reduce the country's dependence on imports.[6] With funds allocated accordingly, a large-scale manufacturing complex was established in the 1660s at Les Gobelins in the Faubourg Saint-Marcel in the south east of the city. Under the direction of the king's foremost painter Charles Le Brun, Les Gobelins produced a range of goods for the royal court such as sculptures, fancy ironwork, cabinetwork and tapestry, but Les Gobelins also produced luxury products for the general home market and for export. Although Les Gobelins dominated manufacturing activity, there were other centres of industrial output. At Chaillot, in the west of the city, carpet production was undertaken in the Savonnerie house of the Hôpital General, while smaller scale manufacturing was organised at Reuilly on the outer edge of the Faubourg Saint-Antoine to the east of the city[7].

The French economy was undoubtedly in a stronger position than hitherto. Colbert's extremely efficient administration not only encouraged the growth of exports from the silk, glass, iron and shipbuilding industries, but also sought to reduce French independence on foreign imported goods and thus produced a favourable trade balance and in consequence an inflow of silver and gold from her trading partners. Colbert also encouraged the development of colonies in the Americas, Africa and Asia, all in the name of mercantilism and the importance it attached to foreign trade surpluses. Newly gained economic strength

62   *Les Gobelins – 1660s*

might well have encouraged Louis to embark on two wars, one short, one prolonged, over the years 1667 to 1679. The first, waged in 1667-68, was the War of Devolution in which Louis successfully advanced French claims on parts of the Spanish Netherlands. Almost without a battle, he acquired 12 fortified towns including the key cities of Lille, Douai and Tournai, territorial gains that were subsequently confirmed by the Treaty of Aix-la-Chapelle (1668). The second, between 1672 and 1679, was the Dutch War "a carefully planned war of unprovoked aggression against [a] prosperous tiny neighbour [Holland].[8] Allied to England and Sweden, but opposed by a coalition of Holland, Spain and the Empire, France seized Franche-Comte, a number of towns in the Spanish Netherlands and, further afield, Haiti – acquisitions confirmed by the Treaty of Nijmegan in 1678. Because of his success, both domestically and internationally, Louis – in the view of many of his subjects and allies – had become the *Roi Soleil* (or Sun God).

63   *College des Quatre Nations, begun 1662*

Notwithstanding Louis's long-term aim, Paris rather than Versailles became the focus of new development in the 1660s-70s. Begun in 1662, and at the bequest of Mazarin, the College des Quatre Nations was established by Colbert to provide an advanced education for 60 adult students from the four provinces allotted to France by the Treaty of the Pyrenees: Alsace, Artois, Piedmont and Roussillon. Located on the Left Bank opposite the Cour Carrée of the Louvre, the college was designed by Louis Le Vau in a style reminiscent of Roman Baroque, and with its "domed church flanked with wings curving forward . . . presents a dramatically effective ensemble not to be paralleled in French architecture of the seventeenth century."[9] Though the building has been called the Institut de France since 1795, until that year it accommodated six seventeenth century institutions: the Académie Français (founded by Richelieu in 1635), the Académie Royale de Peinture et de Sculpture (founded by Mazarin in 1648), the Académie des Inscription et Belles-Lettres (founded by Colbert in 1666), the Académie des Sciences (founded by Colbert in 1666), the Académie de Musique (founded by Colbert in 1669) and the Académie d'Architecture (founded by Colbert in 1671).

64   *Eastern façade of the Louvre started 1666*

Across the Seine, and initially under Mazarin's direction, Louis Le Vau completed the Cour Carrée of the Louvre between 1659 and 1664 and, after a fire, rebuilt and extended the Galerie d'Appollon (the main floor of the Petite Galerie) between 1661 and 1664. At this stage in the development of the Louvre, Le Vau's work – unlike that at the College des Quatre Nations – was still typically seventeenth-century French with "richly carved classical motifs, professional rather than inspiring."[10] But after Colbert commissioned Le Vau, Charles Le Brun and Claude Perrault in 1667 to become collectively responsible for the construction of the 183m long eastern façade of the Louvre, work on the Louvre produced a building of outstanding architectural quality. With its flat roofline, crowning central pediment and 52 monumental coupled-Corinthian columns and pilasters, and notwithstanding certain Baroque qualities reminiscent of Bellini (such as the rhythmical spacing of the coupled columns), the magnificent eastern façade is probably "the most accomplished classical building of its date north of the Alps."[11]

65   *Paris Observatoire constructed 1667-72*

Despite the short War of Devolution between France and Spain (1667-8), public development projects continued unabated not least within the field of science. Although in Western Europe the Scientific Revolution started in the sixteenth century, it was well underway by the early seventeenth, particularly within the field of astronomy. Galileo (1564-1642), born in Pisa, was the first astronomer to use the telescope, and what he saw in the universe convinced him of the truth of Copernicus's view that the earth rotates on its axis around the sun. Very soon in Paris, an observatory was established to advance the understanding of astronomy. Funded by Colbert and designed by Claude Perrault, the first national observatory in France, the Paris Observatoire, was constructed between 1667 and 1672. Located outside of the city walls (where the sky was comparatively smoke-free), the Observatoire is a three-storey square block with an angular porch on its northern façade and two octagonal pavilions to the south where it backs onto a covered terrace. Its external walls built of smooth sandstone are pierced by arched windows, and internally the building has a 23 metre deep, climate-controlled cellar for the apertures of the telescope, and ornately vaulted halls[12]. As an example of seventeenth century architectural rationalism, the building in addition to being an observatory (its prime function) also serves as an assembly hall for the Académie des Sciences (founded in 1666) and accommodates its collection.[12]

During the 1670s, the pace of *hôtel* development in Paris decelerated, possibly because Louis was spending less and less time in Paris. It was becoming clear that he intended in due course to relocate his administration and his court to Versailles. Only one *hôtel* of note was therefore developed in the capital, the Hôtel Sagonne-Mansart (1674). Built for the Comte de Sagonne and designed by Mansart, the *hôtel* is particularly impressive on its garden side where Ionic double columns at ground floor level support a continuous balcony along the full length of the main building.

However, in the 1670s Louis was not quite ready to move to Versailles since the palace was still far from complete. As an interim measure, the king spent an increasing amount of time at his principal rural base, the Château St-Germain-en-Laye, a building that was extensively improved to accommodate his needs in the years 1664-

66   *Château St-Germain-en-Laye 1664-80*

80. But not content with this substantial residence, he commissioned other *châteaux* in the Île-de-France for his occasional use. The first of these, located in the forest of St-Germain-en-Laye, is the Château de Val (1674), a narrow one-storey building with a central salon leading to a small apartment on one side and to four rooms of various shapes on the other. Designed by Hardouin-Mansart, the whole building is "completely opened to the surroundings by a series of arched French windows,"[13] clearly anticipating the development of the architect's Grand Trianon at Versailles (see below). The second building, situated north-east of Versailles, is the Château de Clagny (1676). It was built for Madame de Montespan (the king's mistress) and more than any other of Hardouin-Mansart's early commissions, the *château* anticipated the eventually completed Palais de Versailles. Its plan consists of a series of very long narrow wings either side of a domed grand salon.[14] The last of his country houses, the Château de Marly (1679) at Marly-le-Roi, was commissioned by Louis as a place of entertainment and consisted of a "centralised pavilion with two lateral rows of small pavilions for [his] courtiers."[15] But other notable patrons also commissioned *châteaux* in the region in the 1670s, for example the Duc de Chevreuse, Colbert's

son-in-law, funded the construction of the Château de Dampierre (1675) in the commune of Dampierre (Yvelines), a residence with a fairly conventional layout but with a large central *ressaunt* bordered by two blocks with numerous uniform openings and surmounted by large Mansard roofs.

FINANCIAL STRAINS AND THE
GLORIFICATION OF THE REALM: 1682-1715

During the long final-period of Louis's reign, two inter-related series of events had a dire effect on the State budget and undid much of Colbert's skilful efforts in securing financial stability. First, two years after Colbert's death in 1683, and in his attempt to achieve a religiously unified nation, Louis revoked the Edict of Nantes of 1598 and so prohibited the public practice of any religion except Roman Catholicism. Fearing the near extinction of Protestantism in France, about 200,000 Huguenots fled the country and took their many skills with them to Protestant states such as England, the United Provinces and Brandenburg, with a damaging though not ruinous impact on the French economy.

Not least because of the resentment shown by host countries to the energy and enterprise of Huguenot refugees, the Revocation of the Edict of Nantes provoked anti-French sentiment in Protestant countries. Badly advised by the French Minister of War, the Marquis de Louvois, Louis swaggered threateningly across the international stage and provoked most of his neighbours, Catholic and Protestant alike, to unite against him in the War of the League of Augsburg (1687-97). With no allies, and opposed by the United Provinces, England, the Empire, Spain, Savoy, Brandenburg and Bavaria, Louis deployed his vast army – now the most formidable force in Europe – to annex a plethora of cities in the United Provinces and the Spanish Netherlands, as well as incorporating Strasbourg in his realm, while his navy achieved victory at sea at the Battle of Beachy Head. However, because of the pressure of widespread international opposition and the near-certainty of an unsustainable war, Louis was obliged to sign the Treaty of Ryswick in 1697, returning most of the occupied territories to their former sovereign owners, but retaining Strasbourg to signify the importance of the Rhine as the border between France and the Empire. Within four years, France was involved in yet another war, the War of the Spanish Succession. Now supported by Spain and Bavaria, but still opposed by the United Provinces, England, the Empire, Savoy, Brandenburg and now Portugal, Louis attempted to secure the Spanish throne for the House of Bourbon, through its claimant Philippe duc d'Anjou, in the face of a rival claim from the Habsburgs, in the person of Charles, Archduke of Austria. Losing battles at Blenheim (1704), Ramilles and Turin (1706), Oudenarde and Lille (1708) and Malplaquet (1709), the French – after staging a remarkable recovery in their military fortunes in 1712 – eventually conceded defeat and concluded an honourable peace with Great Britain and the United Provinces at the Treaty of Utrecht (1713), and with the Empire at the Treaty of Rastatt and that of Baden (1714). Under these settlements, the duc d'Anjou was recognised as Philip V, King of Spain and ruler of the Spanish colonies, but Spanish territories in the Netherlands and Italy were partitioned between Austria and Savoy, while Gibraltar and Minorca were retained by Great Britain as invaluable naval bases.

Second, against the advice of Colbert and almost regardless of expense, Louis removed his residence, court and seat of government from their temporary rural retreat at the Château de St-Germain-en-Laye to the larger and more sumptuous Palace of Versailles, where they remained from 1682 until the king's death in 1715. In view of the newly-created magnificence of the Louvre, it was one of the great ironies of political and architectural history that its patron Louis found it necessary to relocate his residency from Paris to Versailles, less than ten years after the work that he had commissioned on the Louvre was complete. In settling in Versailles, Louis was clearly no longer willing to base his regal activities in the French capital (or even at St-Germain), and predicted that Versailles – 20 kilometres from Paris – would offer him security from the potential hostile Parisian mob, a more agreeable physical environment, more control over the political activity of his nobles, and isolation from the scandals of the capital. However, he must have been aware that an extravagant project such as the construction, management and maintenance of the Palais de Versailles would seriously deplete his coffers and that, with fewer financial resources, his persistent wars would be financially debilitating and would, very nearly, bankrupt the State. With inexplicable timing and complete disregard for completing claims on government expenditure, he funded the remodelling of the palace in the midst of the Dutch war, and in the year in which the War of the League of Augsburg commenced (1688), he commissioned more and more work on the palace's gardens.

67   *Marble Court, Palace of Versailles 1660s*

Designed mainly by Louis Le Vau, Jean Hardouin-Mansart and Ange-Jacques Gabriel, and built between 1661 and 1756, the Palais de Versailles not only accommodated the royal family and its favourites but over 20,000 nobles, administrators, soldiers, servants and tradesmen, and became "the most spectacular monument to absolute kinship ever seen in Europe."[16] Built initially between 1623 and 1631 as a hunting lodge for Louis XIII, the brick building was initially extended by Le Vau in the 1660s by adding two projecting wings (also of brick) to the original *corps de logis*, and creating within the enclosed space a *cour d'honneur*, known as the Marble Courtyard because of its marble paving stones. He also decorated each of the three blocks around the courtyard with antique urns and marble busts and adorned the main block with a gilded balcony on its first floor. The Marble Courtyard looks out through elaborate grillwork to courtyards designed for Louis XIV: first the much larger Royal Courtyard that was accessible only to royal carriages, and then in turn to the Ministers' Courtyard and Mansart's original gateway grill.

68   *Palais de Versailles, 1661-1756 with wings projecting on either side of the original cour d'honneur.*

Extending either side of the *corps de logis*, and designed by Le Vau in 1669, lengthy three-storey wings, in total 402 metres long, overlook the formal garden of the palace stretch southward and northward. Initially, with a recessed centre, the garden façade was eventually completed in 1678 by Hardouin-Mansart who incorporated the Galerie des Glaces (the Hall of Mirrors) into a space between the two wings, and dramatically rebuilt the north and south wings giving the whole of the garden façade a length of 580 metres. The immense façade pierced by its 375 windows is adorned throughout its length with giant pilasters on its first floor, interspersed by three pairs of columns in its central pavilion and two pairs in each of its side pavilions. Hardouin-Mansart also designed the palace's two-storey Baroque chapel that was incorporated into the northern wing and finished in 1710. To an extent Baroque, and with its flat roof and balustrade adding elements of Classicism, the Palais de Versailles not only introduced the *Louis Quartorze* style of architecture but influenced the design and development of a host of similar palaces throughout much of Europe during the eighteenth

69   *Grand Trianon, Palais de Versailles, 1687*

century. Versailles demonstrated that it was possible not only to provide an absolute monarch with an enormous and sumptuous residence but also an overwhelmingly large centre of political power.

However, probably the finest feature of Versailles is its formal gardens, initially designed by André Le Nôtre. With work beginning in 1662, woods to the west of the palace were cleared to form a wide axial vista in which formal terraces and pathways descend to a wide canal that appear to lead endlessly into the far distance, and on each side formal avenues radiate out into the surrounding landscape. Throughout, the gardens are richly ornamented with pools and statuary, and with low ornamented shrub beds geometrically laid out. There are also artificial grottoes, open-air temples and theatres. Most interesting of all is the Grand Trianon, a miniature palace of pink marble built for Louis XIV in 1687. Designed by Hardouin-Mansart and Robert de Cotte, the building with its own diminutive formal garden provided a retreat for the king and his mistress Madame de Maintenon from the protocol of court life.

70   *Chapel Royal, Palais de Versailles, 1701-10*

Work on the further development of the palace, including the construction of the Chapel Royal (1701-10), continued uninterrupted throughout most of the War of the Spanish Succession. Although extravagance and insensitive timing is a charge that can be readily levelled at the king, he established a unique though stifling ambiance for the exercise of power, the like of which the world has never known. As Alistair Home so vividly comments: Louis "lived among some 10,000 courtiers, virtually without a guard. For all the numbing grandeur of Versailles, the *ennui* must have been excruciating. Where absolute rulers had secret police, or barbed wire, or a Berlin Wall, the secret weapon of the Roi Soleil and his Bourbon successors was boredom."[17] Equally equivocal, Roger Price argues that the "huge cost of construction was from the point of view of the monarchy money well spent. It increased the dependency of the upper nobility and meant that they could be more closely supervised [but, on the downside] it also ensured that kings [who emulated him, and there were many] were to be more than ever isolated from other forms of reality."[18]

71   *Hôtel Libéral Bruant, 1683*

But in Paris, and largely among the aristocracy, the demand for new *hôtels particuliers* revived in the 1680s since it was no longer feared that the exodus of Louis, his court and his administration from the capital would endanger the social role and financial viability of the capital. Mainly located on the western fringes of the city, a plethora of prestigious residences were therefore developed, the first of which was the Hôtel de Libéral (1683), an edifice decorated by rounded niches with busts set within the curved façade of its *corps de logis* and crowned by a large ornate triangular pediment. This was followed some years later by the Hôtel de Brancas (1700) noted for its Classical (or even Neo-classical) simplicity as demonstrated by a sparing use of flat pilasters and a triangular pediment centrally placed on the façade of the main building. Then followed the Hôtel de Soubise (1704) with its nine bay façade and impressive portico supported by four pairs of Ionic columns on both its ground and first storeys, and a crowning triangular pediment above; the Hôtel de Rohan-Strasbourg (1705) with its centrally placed crowning pediment distinctly Classical or Neo-classical in design; and the Hôtel Amelot de Gournay (1712) with its circular courtyard, oversized pilasters on the façade of its *corps de logis*, and its low wings.

72   *Hôtel Soubise, 1704*

73 *Hôtel de Rohan Strasbourg, 1705*

Town Planning

The improvement of the local environment

While the initiatives of wealthy patrons produced a supply of magnificent buildings during the late seventeenth- and early eighteenth centuries, a range of public policy measures helped to determine the physical wellbeing of Parisians during the same period. Heeding the catastrophe of the Great Fire of London in 1666, the city authorities of Paris prohibited new private buildings from being constructed of wood and plaster and instead insisted on stone and, to ease the flow of traffic as well as to reduce the risk of fire spreading, overhanging houses were demolished. In addition, the city's Lieutenant of Police, La Reynie, introduced extensive programmes of street paving and street widening during his long period of office (1667-97) and put in place much more efficient street cleaning than hitherto. A large ring-sewer on the Right Bank was also introduced, while on the Left Bank the River Bièvre was used as an open sewer. There was also a vastly improved provision of street lighting, and after 1700 a new system of fire fighting was provided, facilitated by the use of Dutch fire pumps. Collectively, these measures went hand-in-hand with the westward development of Paris towards the Faubourg St-Honore and beyond but were less successfully applied eastward particularly in the congested Marais.

GATEWAYS

Since antiquity, urban buildings have been designed to symbolise the magnificence and power of the ruler. With the construction of the massive Porte St-Denis (1671-3) and Porte St-Martin (1674) this tradition was exemplified in late-seventeenth Paris on a grand scale. To commemorate Louis XIV's victories in the War of Dutch Devolution, and designed by Nicolas François Blondel and Michel Anguier, the 23 metres high Porte-St-Denis is a bulky triumphal arch spanning the northern end of the rue du Faubourg St-Denis. Only 300 metres to the east, and at the northern end of the Boulevard St-Martin, the Porte St-Martin was built to celebrate the Sun King's annexation of the Franche Comté. Designed by Pierre Bullet, a student of Blondel, a gateway is a more sober monument than its neighbour and is shorter being only 17 metres in height.

74   *Porte St-Denis, 1671*

75   *Place Victoires, 1681-85*

The architect of the Porte St-Denis, Blondel, had become the first Director of the Académie d'Architecture in 1672 and "drew on the king's patronage and vision to promote a style of unprecedented harmony"[19]. Not only was he responsible for introducing schemes of urban improvement in the older areas of the city but in the case of new development, made straight lines the 'norm'. He was thus influential in Louis XIV's decision to demolish all the city's walls and to replace them with raised and tree-lined 'boulevards', though it was not until late in the eighteenth century that boulevards appeared on the Left Bank (it is interesting to note that Haussmann's *grands boulevards* of the nineteenth century – the Boulevards Temple, Beaumarchais, Filles-du-Calvaire, St-Martin, Bonne Nouvelle, Montmartre, des Italiens, Madeleine, Poisonnieres and Capucines followed almost exactly the line of boulevards established between 1656 and 1704). Since the military engineer Sebastian Le Prestre de Vauban had constructed a dense network of fortresses and earthworks along the eastern frontiers of France intended to protect the country from foreign invasion, it was assumed that Paris could, without risk, become an open-city, thus paving the way to a range of planning projects that previously would have been impracticable. The most famous of all boulevards is the Champs-Élysées. Built after 1667 and landscaped by André Le Nôtre, the boulevard is 3 kilometres long and 71 metres wide and extends north westwards in a straight line from the Jardin des Tuileries, designed by Le Nôtre in 1664.

Some 900 metres downstream from Henry IV's 1607 Pont Neuf, the Seine had been traversed by a new wooden bridge in 1637 funded by the entrepreneur Le Barbier and linking the Quai de Tuileries and the Rue du Bac. The structure – like that of the Pont Neuf – was devoid of tenement buildings. However, its life was short-lived. At Louis XIV's expense and designed by Pere F.Romain, the wooden bridge was replaced in the 1680s by the Pont Royal, a new five-arched stone structure that – like its predecessor – was uncluttered by buildings. By the end of the seventeenth century, the whole stretch of the Seine between the Pont Royal and Pont Neuf, with the Tuileries and Louvre on its Right Bank and the College des Quatre-Nations on its Left, had in effect become "a kind of public amphitheatre where fireworks, river jousts and ceremonial water processions were held".[20] Perhaps more importantly, the bridge facilitated an improvement in transportation across the Seine to the benefit of the Parisian economy.

SQUARES

Few examples of town planning are as visually imposing as the 'square', and in Paris "[n]o one had a greater impact on the appearance of French architecture during the late seventeenth century than . . . Jules Hardouin-Mansart"[21]. In keeping with the tradition established by Louis Métezeau or Claude Chastillon in their development of the Place Royale (now the Place de Vosges), Hardouin-Mansart designed both the Place Victoires and the Place de Vendome. Commissioned by Marschel François d'Aubusson, duc de La Feuillade, the former square was laid out between 1681 and 1685 around an equestrian statue of Louis XIV and was intended to commemorate the Treaty of Nijmegan of 1679 when the king was at the height of his power. Originally the square, with its rounded corners, was surrounded by a rusticated ground floor arcade with giant Ionic columns on its two living floors, and was surmounted by a 'mansard' roof, but in the nineteenth and early-twentieth centuries, the square and surrounding streets were redeveloped stripping away most of the original motifs.

The second square, the Place Vendome, is much larger than the Place Victoires and is one of the great urban spaces in Europe. Commissioned by Minister Louvois in 1686, its shape is rectangular and its principal design attributes consist of bevelled corners, elegant facades with rusticated ground floors and giant coupled Corinthian pilasters on the first and second floors, alternating oval and rectangular windows, and triangular pediments surmounting the centre of each of the façades and each of the bevelled corners. Originally as its

76   *Place Vendome, 1686*

centrepiece, the square contained an equestrian statue of Louis XIV (as in the Place Victoires) but this was replaced in the early nineteenth century by a bronze pillar commemorating the battle exploits of Napoleon in 1805 (see chapter 9).

Though developed in accordance with the same principals as the Place Royale, but built mainly of stone rather than brick, both the Place Victoires and Place Vendome epitomise the *Louis Quatorze* style of architecture and are significantly more elegant and sophisticated than earlier models.

The wealth of Paris had increased enormously during the seventeenth century and the new squares soon became the abode of the "heads of the wealthiest financial houses on which the king depended to fight his wars".[22] But with the shift in political power to Versailles after 1682, and with the unfinished palace competing with the armed forces for funds, it is not altogether surprising that Louis XIV showed comparatively little interest in the further development of Paris. As a result, an unknown number of development schemes in the capital had to be shelved, while work on others had to be delayed, for example the Place Vendome was not completed until 1725.

REFERENCES

1. C. Cook, *A Dictionary of Historical Terms,* (London: Macmillan Press Ltd., 3rd Edition, 1998), p.2
2. B. P. Lenman and T. Anderson, *Dictionary of World History* (Edinburgh: Chambers, 2000), p.4
3. A. Blunt, *Art and Architecture in France, 1500-1700* (London: Yale University Press. 5th Edition.) p.149
4. Ibid
5. R. Furneaux Jordan, *A Concise History of Western Architecture* (London: Thames & Hudson, 1969), p.232
6. C. Jones, *Paris. Biography of a City* (London: Penguin Books, 2006), p.193
7. Ibid
8. A. Horne (B), *Friend or Foe. An Anglo-Saxon History of France,* (London: Phoenix, 2005), p.175
9. A. Blunt, *Art and Architecture in France, 1500-1700,* (London: Yale University Press, 5th Edition.), p.219
10. R. Furneaux Jordan, opt. cit., p.230
11. R. Furneaux Jordan, opt. cit., p.229
12. H. Wischermann, *Paris. An Architectural Guide* (Verona: Arsenale Editrice, 2005), p.63
13. C. Norbert-Shultz, *Baroque Architecture* (London: Faber & Faber, 1986), p.171
14. Ibid, p.171
15. C. Norbert-Shultz, opt. cit., p.172
16. Bill Risebero, *The Story of Western Architecture* (London: Herbert Press, 3rd Edition, 2001)
17. A. Horne (B), opt. cit., p.181
18. R. Price, *A Concise History of France* (Cambridge: Cambridge University Press, 1993), p.58
19. A. Horne (B), opt. cit., pp.167-8
20. C. Jones, opt. cit., p.185
21. Prina, F., E. Demartini, *A 1000 years of World Architecture,* (London: Thames and Hudson, 2005), p.192
22. C. Jones, opt. cit., p.185

CHRONOLOGY

1643-1715	Louis XIV, King of France
1648-53	The Fronde uprising
1653	**St-Roch Paris Church begun**
1659-74	**Cour Carrée of Louvre completed**
1660 onwards	**Hôpital de la Salpêtrière constructed**
1663-91	**Collège des Quatre-Nations built**
1667-72	**Observatory built**
1667 onwards	**Champs Élysées built**
1671-73	**Porte St-Denis constructed**
1671-74	**Hôtel des Invalides/Église des Soldats/St-/Louis-des-Invalides built**
1674	**Porte St-Martin built**
1681-85	**Place de Victoires built**
1686	**Place Vendome**
1701-14	War of the Spanish Succession
1701-40	**St-Roch Paris Church completed**
1704-09	**Hôtel de Soubise constructed**

8

THE EMERGENCE OF PARIS
AS A SUPERPOWER CAPITAL

INTRODUCTION

The development of the Parisian built environment throughout the reign of Louis XV was generally confined to periods of peace: first, from his succession in 1715 to the War of the Polish Succession (1733-8); second, between the War of the Austrian Succession (1740-48) and the Seven Years War (1756-63); and, finally, during the eleven years of Louis's reign prior to his death in 1774.

ARCHITECTURAL EVOLUTION

While there were many examples of Classical architecture in Paris at the start of Louis XV's reign in 1715, as yet it "had not been applied in Paris on a sufficient scale to transform the city,"[1] and thus the French capital still remained essentially medieval. Within this context the Académie Royale d'Architecture attempted to ensure a high standard of urban development, particularly in the case of public buildings, and propagated a distinctly French style of architecture "based on proportion, a very high standard of materials and execution, and on the correct use of classical features."[2] However, one strength of French classicism in the eighteenth century was its flexibility in presentation. Initially, it was marginally transmogrified from the Baroque into the Rococo. Later, in the second half of the century, the Neoclassical tendency emerged as a reaction against the self-indulgence of the Rococo, but which was also linked to the purism of eighteenth-century Enlightenment.

DEMOGRAPHY AND THE BUILT ENVIRONMENT

From 1700 to 1784, despite high rates of mortality, the number of inhabitants of Paris increased steadily from around 600,000 to 660,000 largely as a result of immigration from provincial France. However, although the population of France as a whole escalated from 21 to 28 million, the population of her capital city fell from 2.9 to 2.4 per cent of the national total, while at the same time the overall density of the Parisian population diminished from 44,877 per km² to 15,205 per km³, a decrease in density attributable to the substantial increase in the spatial extent of the French capital in the eighteenth century due to the re-drawing of its official boundaries.[4]

Although the population of Paris as a proportion of the national total had diminished, the French capital was still the largest city in Europe (at least until the mid-eighteenth century) and its importance as the economic and cultural heart of France increased enormously. Throughout the reign of Louis XV, "trade and manufacturing sectors boomed; [Paris's] role as a centre of consumption reached new heights; and its intellectual prowess soared."[5] If this was not enough, Paris became the unofficial capital of the European Enlightenment, the movement of ideas [while its] cultural institutions flourished in ways which the rest of Europe envied and tried to mimic."[6]

Under these circumstances it was to be expected that there would be a surge in the demand for housing among the burgeoning middle classes and nobility. Since there were few sites suitable for the construction of quality housing in the centre of Paris, its new outer suburbs proved particularly attractive for new housing development. To meet high-income demand, the Faubourgs St-Honore (on the Right

Bank) and St-Germain (on the Left Bank) became the most fashionable addresses in eighteenth-century Paris overtaking the once-chic Marais, now increasingly viewed as unfashionable. Notwithstanding their need to be present at Versailles from time to time, little could stop the monarch's courtiers – both 'nobles of the sword' and 'nobles of the robe' – from migrating to Paris in search of a lifestyle that could only be found in the capital, while well-off financiers and merchants relocated to the outer *faubourgs* away from their former residences in the older urban core. Further areas of growth included the fashionable Chaussee d'Antin neighbourhood north of the Rue de Richelieu and its adjacent areas to the west and east.

However, in contrast to the new *faubourgs*, the environment of the Île de Cité and the neighbourhoods around the Hôtel de Ville and Les Halles, were severely blighted by "overpopulated tenements and narrow streets clogged up with waste and detritus"[7]. Within such areas, higher income groups were rapidly moving out, while an increasing proportion of the remaining population consisted of the poor and sick who, to an extent, benefited from an improvement in environmental health arising from the formerly open sewer, the *Grand Égout*, being covered from the 1760s and beyond.

1715-33 A PEACEFUL INTERLUDE: THE EMERGENCE OF NEOCLASSICAL ARCHITECTURE

Born in 1710, Louis XV, the great-grandson of Louis XIV, was a sickly five-year-old when he ascended the throne of France and, under well established procedure, the reins of royal power were passed to a Regent, this time Philippe, duc d'Orléans, the nephew of the former *Roi Soleil*. Philippe, in an attempt to strengthen his hold on the levers of power, replaced bourgeois ministers with councils of leading aristocrats notwithstanding their total lack of expertise, and – disbanding the court at Versailles – continued to live in his Parisian residence, the Palace Royal. Immediately, a light-hearted and some would say profligate lifestyle emerged at court replacing the austerity of the final years of Louis XIV's reign, while peace superseded warfare as the principal aim of foreign policy as was demonstrated when the Quadruple Alliance between Britain, Holland and the Empire was formed in 1719 in an attempt to deter Philip V of Spain from claiming the French crown in the event of Louis XV's early death. With secretaries of state replacing aristocrats at the centre of power in 1718, France enjoyed fifteen years of peace, save for a minor war with Spain in 1719. Despite more stable conditions, the French government was not complacent in matters of defence. To ensure that there would be an adequate supply of arms should a major war break out in the future, the *Regence* commissioned the construction of the Arsenal on the Rue de Sully. Commissioned in 1718, designed by Germain Boffrand and built between 1718 and 1745, the building is remarkable for its austerity. Situated on a former gunpowder and weapons factory built c. 1594 by the Duke of Sully for Henry IV, the Arsenal is a long three-storey block, five storeys in height inclusive of a basement and attic. At the narrow western end of the block, its façade faces the street and is noted only for its rusticated portal and minimal Rococo ornamentation above.

Wars, or even the possibility of a war cost money as well as lives. Wars that were waged by Louis XIV left the Treasury with an enormous

77   *Elysée Palace, 1718–22*

78   *Hôtel Biron, 1728-31*

deficit of around 220 million *livres*[8] at the beginning of the Regency, while a shortage of precious metals and coins in circulation deflated the French economy and heralded massive changes in the banking system . Introduced by John Law (an Edinburgh banker who fled to Paris following a financial scandal at home), the Bank General Priveé (set up in 1716) issued government-backed paper money but this failed to stabilise the value of currency, especially when combined with the speculative trading ventures that Law launched in Louisiana and the West Indies in 1717-19, namely the Compagnie d'Occident and Compagnie Pepetuelles. Since there was not enough specie to cover demand, an edict reduced the value of notes and share certificates by 50 per cent. In 1721 Law, fearing retribution fled to Venice, and the monarchy tottered while "the bourgeoise created and enriched by the Roi Soleil [were] ruined, worse they [became] dangerously disillusioned with a regime that proved itself so flawed."[9]

In these circumstances, it was both surprising and enlightening that Louis XV commissioned the further development of the Bibliothèque Royale (known as the Bibliothèque Nationale de France for the first time in 1792). In 1661, the library had been transferred from cramped premises in the Rue de Harpe on the Left Bank to a more spacious building in the Rue Vivienne, north of the Louvre, where it could accommodate a greater number of publications, and in 1692 it subsequently opened to the public. However, designed by Robert de Cotte, the façade of the building together with its *cour d'honneur* was reconstructed between 1729 and 1735 in a decorative Rococo style.

But the development of royal property, however prestigious, could not disguise the collapse of the financial system and its effects on Parisians of all classes. "Paris seethed: social disorder multiplied, developing into civil disorder, with murders and robberies rampant."[10] However, helped by Controllers-General of Finances, Michel Robert Le Peletier des Forts (1726-30) and more particularly by Philibert Orry (1730-45), Fleury stabilised the French currency in 1726 and even managed to balance the budget in 1738.

Notwithstanding the financial and economic crisis of the latter years of the *Regence*, the demise of permanent court life at Versailles after the death of Louis XIV stimulated *hôtel* construction in Paris particularly but not exclusively in the Faubourg St-Germain on the Left Bank. During the earlier years of Louis XV's reign, *hôtels* in the Baroque style were on the way out and by the middle of the eighteenth century, the Neoclassical style was in the ascendancy, promulgated by a range of patrons and their architects. While the conventional *hôtel* plan that had emerged by the early eighteenth century continued for several more decades,[11] there were some changes in design: mansard roofs were no longer so elevated as hitherto; wider frontages with bays of equal width became more commonplace; windows with full semi-circular arches gave way to simple rectangular windows with segmental lintels being used on only one of the storeys, and ironwork balustrading was much used in the window spacing or as narrow balconies on the *piano nobile*.[12] Among the many *hôtel particuliers* built in Paris during the reign of Louis XV, two are of special interest: the Palais d'Elysée and the Hôtel Biron (see pp. 155–56). Though the former is French classical in style and the latter somewhat Rococo, both are rectangular and two storeys in height, have respectively 11 and 9 axes on their facades and have corner pavilions. Built in 1718-22, since 1874 the *palais* has been the office and residency of the President of the French Republic and the meeting place of the Council of Ministers, while the latter, built in 1728-31 was acquired by Marechal de Biron in 1753 who owned the property until 1788. It became the Musée Rodin in 1909.

TABLE 8.1

PROMINENT *HÔTELS PARTICULIERS* IN THE PARIS OF LOUIS XV

Palais d'Elysee, Rue du Faubourg-St Honore (1718-22), *built for Henri Louis de la Tour d'Auvergne, and designed by Armand Claude Mollet*

Hôtel de Gouffier de Thoix, Rue de Varenne (1719-27), *built for the Marquise de Thoix, and designed by the industrialist Boudouin*

Hôtel Chenizot, Rue St-Louis-en-Île (1719-22). *The original 1610-20 building was redecorated by Pierre de Vigny for the tax collector François Guyot de Chenizot*

Hôtel de Noirmoutier, Rue de Grenelle (1722-23), *built for Antoine- François de la Trémoille, Duc de Noirmoutiers, and designed by Jean Courtonne*

Hôtel de Charoste, Rue du Faubourg-St Honore (1722-25), *built for Duc Paul François de Charoste Béthune, and designed by Antoine Mazin*

Hôtel de Lomenie de Brienne, Rue St Dominique (1724), *built for the Marquise de Prie, and designed by François Debias-Aubry*

Hôtel Biron (now the Musée Rodin), Rue de Varenne (1728-31), *built for the financier Abrahem Peyrene de Moras and designed by Jacques V Gabriel and Jean Aubert*

Hôtel du Grand Veneur, Rue de Turenne (after 1733). *The original 1636 building was expanded for Augustin Vincent Hennequin, Marquis d'Ecquevilly according to a design by Jean-Baptiste Beausire*

Hôtel d'Albret, Rue des Francs-Bourgeois (1740-44), *built for the President de Parlement, Charles de Tillet, Marquis de La Bussière, and designed by Jean-Baptiste Vautrain*

Hôtel de Montmort, Rue de Temple (1751), *built for the financier Jean Habert de Montmore*

Hôtel Alexandre, rue de la Ville-l'Eveque (1763-66), *built for the banker André Alexander, and designed by Étienne Louis Boullée*

Hôtel d'Hallwyl (after 1766), *designed by Claude Nicolas Ledoux*

Hôtel de Cassini, Rue de Babylone (1771-73), *built for the Cassini family and designed by Claude B. Bélisard and Pierre Lemonnier*

Source: Wischermann, H.

The *Regence* came to an end when Philippe d'Orléans died in December 1723, and in the same year Louis XV was not only declared to have reached his majority but moved his court to Versailles where he remained throughout the rest of his life. However, still at the tender age of thirteen he looked to his cousin, the duc de Bourbon (his first minister) for guidance on a range of political matters. Throughout Louis XV's short residency in the Tuileries Palace (1715-23), a number of buildings of distinction in the French capital had been constructed or at least begun. First and foremost was the Palais Bourbon (1722-28) commissioned by Louise Françoise de Bourbon, a daughter of Louis XIV and Mme de Montespan, but this was accompanied by a number of sumptuous *hôtels* designed for the nobility while at the same time there was a continuation in the development of terraced rental housing that had commenced in the late-seventeenth century. Work also continued on the parish church of St-Roch, while a start was made on the façade of the church of St-Sulpice, an enormous parish church on the Left Bank.

Clearly Louis XV's departure to Versailles in 1723 did not stunt the growth of Paris as the capital of France. Indeed, it could be argued that the "kingdom's cultural centre of gravity had returned to the capital city for good"[13] and engendered the further expansion and importance of the city – still the largest in Europe. The rigid etiquette of Court life in Versailles during the reign of Louis Quinze was increasingly an anachronism, reminiscent of the residency of his great-grandfather

79   *Palais Bourbon, 1722-28 (facade built 1806)*

the Roi Soleil. It was being quickly replaced by salons consisting of gatherings at the houses of wealth sponsors (usually a noblewoman) for the purpose of teaching aristocratic manners and how to behave in Court society. By the second decade of the eighteenth century, salons had changed their role dramatically. They were now "serious literary and intellectual forum[s]"[14] and to a significant extent, fountainheads of the Enlightenment hosting such philosophers as Montesquieu, Voltaire and Diderot. Other notable cultural institutions that increasingly replaced the omnipotence of the French Court were the periodic press and the café. The former not only provided news, but also reviews and critical discussion of new books, and the latter gave people "a place to meet and discuss matters of common interest, and also to read the newspapers."[15] One of the first and most famous cafes to fulfil this role was the Café Procope (founded in 1694 and still in existence today). Located on the Left Bank on the Rue des Fossés – Saint-Germain (now the Rue de l'Ancienne-Comédie), it became throughout the eighteenth century the favourite meeting place of philosophers such as Diderot, d'Alembert, Voltaire, Rousseau, Marmonterl, Beaumarchais, Mercier and many others less famous. But the Enlightenment was not just confined to philosophy or politics, it also influenced the development of buildings in Paris and other cities in Europe. It was no accident that the introduction of the Neoclassical style of architecture was an outcome of the writings of Johann Joachim Winckleman (1717-68) who, as one of the founders of scientific archaeology, publicised the essential attributes of architecture in Ancient Rome. In Paris, as a consequence, Baroque and Rococo architecture favoured by royalty and the aristocracy was no longer in vogue. Some would indeed say that the adoption of Neoclassical architecture illuminated the townscape to an extent that – to future generations – Paris became known as the 'City of Light'.

THE WAR OF THE POLISH SUCCESSION (1733-38)

Motivated by the need to produce a royal heir (to nullify any Spanish claim on the French throne should Louis XV meet an early death), the duc de Bourbon – on becoming first minister – immediately arranged the marriage between Louis and Maria Leszczinksa, the daughter of Stanislas, the deposed King of Poland, who reckoned that with French help he could secure his kingdom's independence from the Hasburgs. Notwithstanding his first minister's undoubted diplomacy abroad, Louis was obliged to dismiss de Bourbon in 1726 because of unpopularity at home. Louis therefore asked his former tutor, the seventy-three year old Cardinal de Fleury to hold the reins of government, but although Fleury wished to maintain peace since France could not afford any further wars after those waged by the *Roi Soleil*, Louis XV – prompted by Germain Louis Chauvelin, his secretary of state for foreign affairs – intervened in the War of the Polish Succession in an attempt to reinstate Stanislav as king of Poland. The war, however, was abortive, and at the Treaty of Vienna (1738), the displaced king received the Duchy of Lorraine in compensation, a province that reverted to the French crown after Stanislav's death in 1766.

Though the war had an adverse effect on the development of secular buildings, it did not deter the construction of a few relatively major churches of distinction, in large measure because a significant proportion of funds required for construction derived from monastic coffers rather than from state sources. One of the finest church buildings of the 1730s is the large parish church of St-Roch in the Rue de Honore, a sober masterpiece of Baroque church architecture. Though begun in 1653 according to plans by Jacques Lemercier, the church was largely finished in 1736-38 under the direction of Robert de Cotte who designed the elegant two-storey façade. Although the façade is reminiscent of Sta.Susanna in Rome and the Val de Grace in Paris, it is much more austere and almost devoid of decoration except for its two sets of engaged columns on each storey and a large pediment above.

In contrast to St-Roch, the church of St-Sulpice is located in an elegant part of the Left Bank. The church was begun many years before in 1634 but was the recipient of a new Neoclassical façade constructed between 1736 and 1869, though there was a whiff of Baroque ornamentation. Designed by Giovanni Nicolo Servandoni, a Florentine by birth, and his pupil Jean-François-Therese Chalgrin, the massive western front of the church consisted of a two-storey portico, five central bays and two outer bays in the form of bell towers, quite unlike any other building in France though somewhat reminiscent of St Paul's in London.

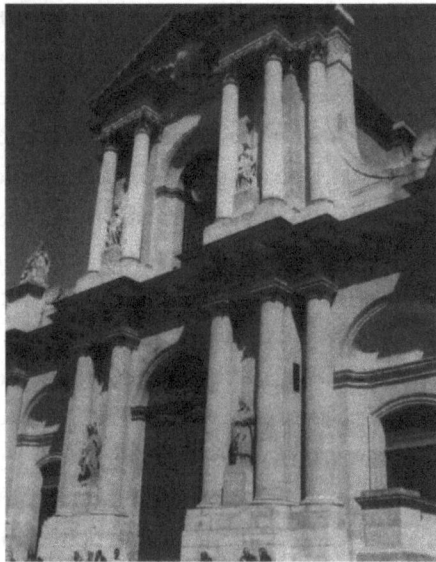

80   *Parish Church of St-Roch, 1736-38*

Notwithstanding short-term peaks and troughs in building activity throughout the eighteenth century, there were severe weaknesses in the wider economy in the long term. To be sure there were benefits resulting from the completion of the St-Quentin canal linking the Oise and Somme rivers in 1738 and the Low Countries a few years later, and also from the extensive network of roads that were established throughout the eighteenth century by *ponts et chausse* engineers aided by labour statutorily obliged to work on the "king's highway", but there were serious fiscal impediments to the free circulation of goods around France. Customs and excise dues and tolls were imposed on domestic trade with harmful effects on industrial efficiency, competition and the creation of wealth. France remained essentially an agricultural country "with manufacturing dispersed in small workshops in both town and

81　　*Parish church of St-Sulpice, façade begun 1736-1869*

country".[16] An industrial revolution was not even on the horizon to the detriment of capital accumulation and the physical development of Paris.

THE WAR OF THE AUSTRIAN SUCCESSION (1740-8)

Peace after the Vienna treaty was short-lived. In 1740 Maria Theresa succeeded to the throne of Austria after the death of her father, Emperor Charles VI. With the prospect of Austria seizing Silesia, Frederick II of Prussia, aided and abetted by France, annexed the province and triggered off a military conflict, the War of the Austrian Succession (1740-48), with Britain, Hanover and the Dutch allying themselves with Austria.

Notwithstanding Britain's defeat of the French at Dettingen (1743) and France's avenging victories over the British forces at Fontenay (1745), Rocourt (1746) and Lauffeld (1747), the war ended in an *impasse*. Louis – despite opposition at home – voluntarily gave up his conquest of the Austrian Netherlands and sought to secure his kingdom within the hexagonal boundaries of France, while the peace of Aix-la-Chapelle (1748) spread the spoils of war fairly evenly. It recognised Frederick II's right to Silesia; installed two branches of the House of Bourbon in Italy, one in Naples, the other in Parma; and recognised the Hanoverians' right to the British crown much to the chagrin of the House of Stuart. At ninety years of age, and still in his official capacity, Fleury had little energy left to oppose the war and died in 1743 before its conclusion. Thereafter Louis dispensed with a First Minister and like Louis XIV during the latter years of his reign, relied at least architecturally upon the advice of mistresses during the eighteenth century: first those exhibiting Rococo attributes and secondly those that were Neoclassical.

The Austrian war constrained large scale construction activity, though there were exceptions between 1739 and 1745. The architect and sculptor Edme Bouchardon – on behalf of the local administration and the business community – presided over the construction of the Fontaine des Quatre-Saisons, a monumental fountain in the narrow Rue de Grenelle on the Left Bank. Though there was a total of 30 fountains built in Paris in the eighteenth century to provide drinking water for the city's residents, Bouchardon's edifice was the largest and most ornate, qualities that were in keeping with its two functions: to provide water for Parisians and to celebrate the benevolence of Louis XV. While it contained only two water spouts, its two-storey structure with its rusticated plinth support curving pilaster walls and niches with Rococo figures of the four seasons, while at the base of a central *aedicula* a goddess representing the city of Paris sits enthroned between two other goddesses representing the rivers Seine and Marne. During the war, church building also took place to a limited extent with the only notable example being the Baroque church of St-Louis in the town of Versailles. Begun in 1742, and designed by Jacques Hardouin Mansart, it is a very late example of the genre and, like St-Roch, is double-storeyed and columned.

Largely because of the war, the budget was in deficit by 100 million *livres* by 1745. Therefore to meet the shortfall as equitably as possible, the king supported the policy of his current Controller of Finances, Machault d'Arnouville to introduce a revised system of fiscal

82   *Fontaine des Quatre-Saissons, 1739-47*

justice. Under the Edict of Marly (1749), Arnoiville therefore created a *vingtieme*, a five per cent tax on the net income of all landowners including – for the first time – those of the privileged classes. However, with intense opposition from aristocrats, ennobled commoners, the clergy and *parlements*, the king directed the new tax at the "third estate", i.e. ordinary commoners, and it became a mere increase in the existing *taille*. After 1745, the effect on the demand for newly built property such as *hôtels*, sumptuous terraced housing, other prestigious buildings and churches was thereby kept to the minimum.

Notwithstanding the late appearance of Baroque at the church of St-Louis, Versailles, its derivate Rococo became the most fashionable means of decorating buildings in Paris from the early-eighteenth century until the 1740s-50s. Terraces, for example, were adorned with balconies that were often continuous on the *piano nobile* and scroll-patterned iron balustrades invariably protected full height windows on the upper floors. Windows on all floors were generally surmounted by segmental lintels "and the space above each lintel was often filled with decorative carvings or panels, or a central carved head or bust".[17]

But from around the 1750s, and particularly during peacetime, comparatively unadorned terraced houses were built in the more favoured central areas of Paris or on its outskirts to meet the demand of the rapidly expanding business and professional community, while the less well-off would "build or rebuild a house of several storeys on a small site in the Halles or another old commercial district, perhaps letting the upper floors as an additional source of income."[18] With the pressure of increased demand, the height of new houses generally rose from up to four storeys on the outskirts to nine or more storeys in the centre, a "trend partly linked to the emergence of the apartment house [fuelled by] a demand for convenient accommodation from single persons, small households and transients."[19]

The Seven Years War (1756-63)

Within seven years of the end of the War of the Austrian Succession, war between France and its adversaries was again imminent, and possibly on a larger scale and more costly than hitherto. Louis XV's favourite mistress and political advisor the Marquise de Pompadour (often referred to as Madame de Pompadour) made it known to Louis that she particularly disliked Frederick II, who had always shown contempt for her, and thus persuaded Louis to see Prussia as a potential enemy, while Louis recognised that the Habsburg Empire was not the power and potential foe it had been in the sixteenth and seventeenth centuries. Thus, new alliances were formed between the different European powers. At the Treaty of Versailles (1756), Louis allied France to its hereditary enemy, Austria, while at the Convention of Westminster in the same year, Great Britain formed an alliance with Prussia. Thus when it seemed apparent that Austria would invade Silesia, Frederick seized Saxony as a protective buffer and triggered off what became the Seven Years War (1756-63). Britain and France were soon in conflict with each other in support of their respective allies, as well as continuing to wage what was previously an undeclared war on each other in India and North America. While Prussia was not rewarded by the subsequent Treaty of Hubertusburg (1763) and at best only retained its territorial integrity, Great Britain greatly benefitted from the Peace of Paris of the same year. France was obliged to cede her possessions in India, Canada and all lands east of the Mississippi to Great Britain but was permitted to retain some of its sugar-growing islands off the West Indies, French Guiana and some small possessions off the coast of eastern Canada. As a consequence, France saw her Empire replaced by that of Britain, while Louis was humbled in the eyes of his subjects, allies and foes.

A PEACEFUL INTERLUDE: THE INFLUENCE OF THE MARQUISE DE POMPADOUR (1748-56)

Whereas Louis gave the Marquise de Pompadour carte blanche in framing foreign policy during the War of the Austrian Succession and the uneasy peace of 1748 to 1756, Louis also responded positively to her attempts to promote the development of royal buildings and public townscapes. Thus under the influence of the Marquise, and sponsored by the financier Joseph Pâris Duvenay, Louis commissioned the construction of the Ecole Militaire in 1751. Influenced by the Val-de-Grace of the 1640s-50s and the great Salpetriere Hospital of 1676 which used porticos "to draw the eye from the middle distance, and a landmark dome or tower to dominate a distant view"[20], the Ecole Militaire was developed according to the plans of Ange-Jacques Gabriel and in its early stages was built between 1751 and 1767. Discontinued between 1768 and 1782, it was completed during the later years of the eighteenth century and early years of the nineteenth. Founded to train disadvantaged cadets to become army officers, the school is situated at the southern end of a military exercise field, the Champs-de-Mars that stretches over 500 metres northwards to the Seine and is in close proximity to the Hôtel des Invalides built around ninety years earlier. Matching the bulk of the Hôtel, but Neo-classical in design rather than Baroque, the school is a rectangular building with its north-facing façade centrally dominated by a portico of eight Corinthian columns in the Italian style and surmounted by a pediment. A low flat sided dome is also centrally placed pierced by *oeils-de-bouef*.[21]

The war, however, did not stop small-scale building projects. In the early days of the Seven Years War, Louis XV ordered the clearance of old housing abutting the church of St-Germain-l'Auxerrois to provide an unrestricted view of the eastern façade of the Louvre possibly to provide a stage for celebration should victory come. He also responded to a vow that he had made during his recovery several years before from a near fatal illness contracted at Metz in 1744 during the Austrian war, and duly funded the reconstruction of the dilapidated Parisian church of Ste-Genevieve, though work on the church would take many years.

Paris was surrounded by a proliferation of seventeenth century *châteaux* and therefore in the eighteenth century there was comparatively little demand among the Parisian social elite for further country retreats within close proximity of the capital. It was the vogue, moreover, for the better off to acquire one of the many *hôtels* in mid-century Paris or at lest an attractive terraced house in the capital. One of the very few rural residences of any quality to be developed in the eighteenth century is the Petit Trianon (begun in 1762). Situated in the grounds of the Palais de Versailles, the charming Palladian villa was designed by Ange-Jacques Gabriel for Louis XV who intended to present it as a gift to the Marquise de Pompadour, though she did not live to see it completed in 1768. The architectural style of the Petit Trianon is

83   *Ecole Militaire, 1751-67*

an example of the transition from the Rococo of the early eighteenth century to the Neoclassical style of the 1750s and beyond. Surmounted with four Corinthian pilasters, while the garden façade is decorated by two detached and two semi-detached Corinthian pillars below which its basement is masked by two staircases from the garden to the *piano nobile*.

THE LAST YEARS OF LOUIS XV'S REIGN

Peaceful conditions prevailed throughout the final years of Louis XV's reign. This gave a stimulus to building work on a major scale. First, though in the ownership of Louis XV between 1756 and 1764, the Palais Bourbon was reconstructed by Louis de Joseph de Bourbon, Prince of Condé between 1764 and 1789 when additional wings, more storeys and integration with the neighbouring Hôtel de Lassay enhanced the size and scale of the building.

Second, the Halle aux Blés (the corn market) was constructed between 1763 and 1767 to facilitate the exchange of grain unloaded

84   *Petit Trianon, Palais de Versailles, begun 1762*

from Seine barges. Designed by Nicolas Le Camus de Mezieres, the two-storey Neoclassical building located on the western edge of Les Halles is an irregular pentagon with a circumference of 122 metres, a diameter of 68 metres and with a courtyard 40 metres wide, and its encasing wall is pierced by 28 arcades with each bay separated by a pilaster. It was not until the early nineteenth century that – after a fire in 1802 – the building – previously open to the sky – was covered by an iron cupola.

Third, Neoclassical church architecture in Paris reached its zenith with the churches of Ste-Marie Madeleine (begun in 1757) and St-Geneviève (started in 1764). St-Marie Madeleine (often referred to as *La Madeleine*) is located close to the Place de la Concorde and situated at the northern end of the Rue Royale. Commissioned by Louis XV, the initial design of Pierre Contant d'Ivry was inspired initially by the Maison Carree at Nimes (an ancient temple) and called for a Latin cross design with a prominent portico and dome. But after the architect's death in 1777, his successor Guillaume decided to demolish what was already built and organise the construction of a Greek cross church inspired by the Pantheon in Rome. However, its construction was temporarily delayed by the French Revolution and was only resumed in 1806 (see chapter 9). Ste-Geneviève, in contrast, is situated on the Mont de Paris on the Left Bank and was designed for Louis XV by Jacques Germain Soufflot who produced an enormous building 100 metres in length and 84 metres wide in the shape of a Greek cross. Its 22-column portico employs the Corinthian order and is surmounted by an enormous pediment, reminiscent of the Roman Pantheon. At the transept crossing, a dome rises to 83m (272 ft), its drum surrounded by 26 freestanding fluted Corinthian pillars that frame a peristyle atop a pedestal.[22]

Funded by the State, property development was partly responsible for the French national debt standing at 2,200 million *livres* in 1763, in real terms a figure comparable to that of 1715[23], and to make matters worse, no brake was put on government expenditure. Though Louis had ordered his Secretary of State for War, the duc de Choiseau, to put an end to the Seven Years War, there were few benefits to the Exchequer since the war secretary was soon instructed to rehabilitate the army and navy in preparation for a war of revenge against England. De Choiseau also purchased the Genoese island of Corsica on behalf of the king, a task he completed at considerable cost. Faced with a budget deficit

85   *Church of Ste-Marie Madeleine begun 1757*

of 63 million *livres* in 1769, and with revenue being spent in advance during the following two years[24], Louis encouraged his Chief Minister, René de Maupeou to reform the country's inefficient and inequitable system of taxation. In 1771, the *parlements*, which had opposed reform, were therefore reorganised and no longer permitted to obstruct royal decrees, while measures were put in place by Joseph Marie Terray, Controller General of Finances, to tax the previously exempt nobility and clergy. (Note: these were reversed after Louis's death at Versailles on May 10, 1774).

It was no wonder that one of the most important public buildings in Paris during the final years of Louis XV's reign was the royal mint,

86   *Church of Ste-Geneviève, started 1764*

the Hôtel des Monnaies, an excellent example of Neoclassism. Built between 1768 and 1775 according to the designs of Jacques Denis Antoine and on the questionable assumption that appropriate premises would improve financial efficiency, the massive austere three-storey building is rectangular and has a façade 117 metres in length containing "27 subtle harmonious axes, a central portico emphasised by six gigantic Ionic columns, and a semi-circular closed-off main courtyard, 35 metres in length and 30 metres wide."[25] An altogether different public building, the Faculté de Médecine was built on the eastern fringe of the Faubourg St-Germain between 1769 and 1786. Situated on the site of the former College de Bourgogne and College des Premontres, the new medical college was commissioned by Louis XV and designed by Jacques Gondouin. On the street side of the Neoclassical building, a lengthy Ionic colonnade is topped by a half storey whose main feature is an elaborately carved plaque above the outer entrance to the building. Behind is a courtyard with three wings, the central one of which is a six-columned portico leading into the main building.

87 *Hôtel des Monnaies, 1768-75*

TOWN PLANNING

In 1715, Paris was already endowed with some quite magnificent buildings and a greatly improved infrastructure, a gift from a succession of monarchs from François I to the Sun King, and a legacy of countless other benefactors eager to display their wealth, power or piety. However, Paris was still essentially a medieval city and as such remained "an uncoordinated and straggling mess."[26] With royal encouragement, the municipal authorities attempted to create order from disorder, and aesthetic appeal from displeasure. A variety of plans were therefore produced to develop new streets and piazzas, and to isolate monuments and grand vistas. The most successful schemes involved the creation of *parvis* outside of the western doors of respectively Notre Dame (completed 1757), St-Sulpice (begun 1752) and St-Eustache (only partly completed in the eighteenth century), and above all the gradual separation of the east end of Louvre from a mass of old houses that was encroaching on it, a process begun in 1758.[27]

After the Peace of Aix-la-Chappelle (1748), the Paris municipality decided to erect a bronze statue in honour of Louis XV to celebrate the

end of an eight-year war with Britain, and in response the king provided a large open site between the Tuileries gardens and the Champs Élysées on which to position the statue, a work created by Edme Bouchardon. The architect Ange-Jacques Gabriel was commissioned not only to oversee the erection of the statue in its correct place but to design a huge eight-sided piazza that would not only link the Tuileries with the Champs Élysées but also provide greater access across the whole of the western Right Bank. The scheme, approved by the king in 1757, also provided for the construction of the Rue Royale that extended northwards from the piazza at right angles to the church of Ste-Marie-Madeleine and for two large three-storey *hôtels* flanking the Rue Royale and facing the piazza. Of these, the Hôtel de Crillon on the west was divided into private properties whereas, on the east, the Hôtel de Coislin was initially a royal storeroom, the Garde-Meuble. Modelled on the east end of the Louvre, the central façade of each building is rusticated and colonnaded at ground level, and its upper floors are set back and adorned above with 12 Corinthian columns and a balustrade.

89 *Place de Louis XV (now the Place de la Concorde) showing the Hôtels de Crillon and de Coislin, separated by the Rue Royale, with the church of Ste-Madeleine in the distance, started 1775*

Large pavilions mark the two extremities of each *hôtel*, each standing on their own rusticated base and having four Corinthian columns above, topped by a pediment. Originally named the Place de Louis XV, the Place de la Concorde as it has been known since the Revolution was the very last large-scale piazza to be built in Paris.

REFERENCES

1. A. Sutcliffe, *Paris. An Architectural History* (London: Yale University Press, 1996), p.148
2. Ibid
3. A. Sutcliffe, opt. cit., p.48
4. Demographia, *Ville de Paris: Population and Density from 1600* (Belleville: II, USA, Wendell Cox Consultancy, 2005)
5. C. Jones. *Paris. Biography of a City* (London: Penguin Books, 2006), p.204
6. Ibid
7. C. Jones, opt. cit., p.232
8. J. Swann, 'Politics. Louis XI' in W. Doyle (Ed.), *Old Regime France 1648-1788* (New York: Oxford University Press, 2001), p.198
9. A. Horne (A), *Seven Ages of Paris. Portrait of a City* (London: Pan Books, 2002), p.166
10. Ibid
11. Sutcliffe, opt. cit., p.55-6
12. Sutcliffe, opt. cit., p.55-6
13. D. A. Bell, 'Culture and Religion' in W. Doyle (Ed.), *Old Regime France* (New York: Oxford University Press, 2001), p.91
14. Ibid, p.92
15. Bell, opt. cit., pp 91-2
16. R. Price, *A Concise History of France* (Cambridge: Cambridge University Press, 1993), p.62
17. Sutcliffe, opt. cit., p.63
18. Sutcliffe, opt. cit., p.63
19. Sutcliffe, opt. cit., pp.64-5
20. Sutcliffe, opt. cit., p.59
21. Ibid

22. H. Wischermann, *Paris. An Architectural Guide* (Verona: Arsenale Editrice, 2005), p.80

23. J. Swann, 'The State and Political Culture' in W. Doyle (Ed.), *Old Regime France* (New York: Oxford University Press, 2001), p.215

24. R. Prince, opt. cit., p.78

25. H. Wischermann, opt. cit., p.120

26. Sutcliffe, opt. cit., p.50

27. Sutcliffe, opt. cit., p.51

CHRONOLOGY

1715-74	Louis XV, King of France
1718-22	**Palais d'Elysèe built**
1718-45	**Arsenale constructed**
1722-28	**Palais Bourbon (Assemblée Nationale) built**
1728-30	**Hôtel Biron built**
1733-8	War of Polish Succession
1739-47	**Fontaine des Quatre-Saisons constructed**
1740-48	War of the Austrian Succession
1751-67	**Ecole Militaire built**
1755 onwards	**Place de la Concorde built**
1756-63	The Seven Years War
1757-64	**Church of Ste-Geneviere**
1763 onwards	**Ste-Madeleine built**

9

REVOLUTIONARY AND IMPERIAL WARS: THE IMPACT ON THE BUILT ENVIRONMENT OF PARIS

INTRODUCTION

While the population of Paris had increased substantially from little more than 150,000 in 1500 to 630,000 in 1789, it decreased to 546,856 in 1801 mainly because there had been a marked reduction in the number of migrants attracted to the capital in the last decade of the eighteenth century, particularly during the escalating violence of the French Revolution. Though there were some major buildings of distinction constructed from 1775-1790 in the first fifteen years of the reign of Louis XVI, the volume of construction activity and the aesthetic quality of new buildings generally diminished, and in contrast to the earlier years of the *Ancien Régime*, town planning played an insignificant role in embellishing the townscape of Paris.

Though there were many improvements to the Parisian urban environment during the reign of Louis XV, the French capital "was still a noisy, smelly city, [among] the largest in Europe, and with her narrow streets still medieval in plan. Jean Jacques Rousseau [d. 1788] found it a city of small, dirty and stinking streets, ugly black houses, an air of filth, poverty, beggars, carters, sewing women, women hawking tisanes and old hats."[1] During the early years of Louis XVI's reign, there was no general improvement in the environment of his capital, and in the most tumultuous period of the Revolution (1790-95), the physical condition of Paris deteriorated still further. However, during the years of the Directory, 1795-1799, and even more after Napoleon's ascendancy, a number of new construction projects were begun which to an extent enhanced the built environment of the city.

THE LAST YEARS OF THE ANCIEN RÉGIME

When Louis XVI inherited the French throne from his grandfather, Louis XV in 1774, the French nation was jubilant. After the absolutism and profligacy of Louis XV's reign, it was thought that harmonious relations would develop between the ruler and the ruled, and that a sizeable proportion of the population would enjoy a period of prosperity. This was indeed true and during the first fifteen years of Louis XVI's reign, Paris witnessed a spate of construction projects both in the private and public sectors.

The provision of new *hôtels* was the first form of property development to take off at the beginning of Louis XVI's reign. The Faubourg St-Germain on the Left Bank, for long the favoured location for the development of prestigious *hôtels*, remained a high-status residential area during the closing years of the *Ancien Régime* and during the Napoleonic era. Designed by Mathurin Cherpitel for the Marquise de Courteille, the Hôtel de Rochechouart in the Rue de Grenelle is stylistically the epitome of the sumptuous town house that had emerged during the reign of Louis XVI. Begun in 1776, the Neoclassical building has an elegant five-storey façade, huge Corinthian pillars, a pilaster décor and buttress wings. Sometimes architects took the lead in the development process. Alexandre Theodore Brongniart, for example, acquired a site in the Rue Monsieur and looked for potential clients for whom he could build custom-made residences. One such client was Louis Joseph de Bourbon-Condé for whom he designed the Hôtel Bourbon-Condé. Begun in 1782, the three-storey, three-wing building was Brongniart's masterpiece,[2] its most attractive features being its bulging middle section with its Ionic pilasters.

90   *Hôtel de Salm, 1782-88*

Designed by Pierre Rousseau and built for Prince Fredrich III of Salm-Kyrburg between 1782-86, the ornate Hôtel de Salm, on its river front, has an elegant one-storey façade with pedimented windows, busts in niches and a centrally situated apsidal bay, and on its opposite side, in the Rue de Lille, has a six column portico projecting into a colonnaded court.[3] The nearby Rue de Grenelle continued to provide an attractive location for high-value residential development when, between 1784-91, the Hôtel de Gallifet was built for Simon Alexandre de Gallifet, president of the Parlement of Provence. Designed by François Étienne Legrand, the most striking features of the building are its six axes and huge Ionic peristyle. Dating from the beginning of the previous century, the Hôtel de Beauharnais on the fashionable Rue de Lille was luxuriously remodelled by Nicolas Betaille for Eugene Rose de Beauharnais soon after he acquired the hotel in 1803. Eclectically, Beteille provided an Egyptian portico, an 'Empire' room with Pompeian frescoes and a Turkish boudoir.[4]

Overshadowing the development of the Parisian built environment in the 1780s was famine and malnutrition with their adverse effects on morbidity and mortality, a situation not helped by a poor transportation infrastructure for bulk foods. To make matters worse, Louis had inherited a nation close to bankruptcy with a national debt amounting to almost two billion livres. This was because France had recently been involved in the Seven Years War and the American War of Independence. The inefficient and antiquated tax system was not only incapable of providing sufficient revenue to meet the cost of large-scale military adventures but was grossly unfair. The clergy and nobility were virtually exempt from taxation and it would have been impossible to have increased the tax burden on the remainder of the population without severely reducing their standard of living. In a country where the distribution of wealth and incomes was very uneven, the risk of public hostility was enormous.

However, among the bourgeoise, incomes were sufficient to maintain a reasonable standard of living, not least with regard to the acquisition of fashionable middle-class housing. In the mid-eighteenth century, developers of middle-class housing were slow to abandon Rococo and adopt the Neoclassical style of architecture, but by the 1780s, virtually all developers had abandoned the former and adopted the latter. But rather than replicating the stylistic exuberance of *hôtel* architecture, developers instead adopted "a Spartan, geometric style with skeletal classical components."[5] Sutcliffe provides three examples of this: First, a giant unadorned nine-storey apartment block on the Rue de Valois constructed around 1780; second, a fairly austere six-storey rental house on the Rue de Bailleul built in 1782 and embellished only by a heavily rusticated arcade and entresol; and third, a house of some size in the Boulevard St-Denis in 1789 adorned only by rusticated first floor or entresol, indifferent window pediments on the piano noble, and an attic with a balcony.[6]

But throughout much of Paris, famine and malnutrition had an adverse impact on the majority of the population (the poor), with the public inevitably pouring scorn on the conspicuous consumption of the nobility, particularly the court of Louis XVI and Queen Marie Antoinette at Versailles. Criticism of royal profligacy rose to a peak in 1785 when the Queen, already tarnished by gossip, was rumoured to have defrauded the crown jewellers, Bohmer and Bassenge, of the cost of a diamond necklace valued at two million livres. Although not proven, the allegation was significant since it marked the beginning of the French populace's disillusionment with the reign of Louis XVI which ultimately culminated in the French Revolution. Not only were the nobility in many cases collecting feudal dues on their estates but the Roman Catholic Church – the largest landowner in the country – levied a tax on crops known as the *dime* (or tithe) exacerbating the plight of the poorest who faced a daily struggle to avert starvation, while the government erected *barriers* (customs barriers) around Paris that worsened food shortages among its poor. It was in this doom and gloom scenario that the seeds of the impending Revolution were beginning to sprout.

The introduction of a more equitable system of taxation was essential if revolution was to be averted. Since the Controller General of Finance Anne Robert Jacques Turgot was unable to produce acceptable changes to the tax system, he was dismissed in May 1776, and replaced the following year by Jacques Necker, a citizen of Geneva, who not only proposed that the clergy and nobility should no longer be exempt from taxation but that borrowing should be relied upon to solve any remaining fiscal problems of the kingdom. However, his credibility was soon undermined since he seriously underestimated the size of the budget deficit by roughly 36,000 livres and suggested that the spending power of the *parlements* should be reduced to offset the deficit, a solution that found disfavour among the king's ministers, and like Turgot he too was sacked. Necker was replaced by Charles Alexandre Calonne who initially spent liberally but soon recognised the severity of the fiscal deficit and thus proposed the introduction of a new tax code, a notable feature of which would be a land tax that would fall particularly on the clergy and nobility. Faced with opposition from the nobility, Calonne organised the summoning of the Assembly of Notables (unelected advisors of public esteem) to endorse or reject his proposals, but unfortunately for the finance minister, the Assembly could not support his proposed tax code. As a way out of the *denouement*, the Parlement of Paris in 1787 demanded the convening of the Estates General which had not met since 1614. The king responded positively and summoned the Estates General to begin its proceedings on 5 May 1789. To help arrive at a solution to the fiscal *impasse*, he also re-appointed Necker as his Controller of Finance.

Meeting at Versailles on 5 May 1789, the Estates General was organised into three groupings: The First Estate comprising 300 clergy, the Second Estate consisting of 291 nobles and the Third Estate made up of 610 representatives of the *Communes* (i.e. the bourgeoisie). It had been customary in the past for each estate to have one vote, and two estates could outvote the third, for example it was usual for the clergy and nobles to outvote the bourgeoisie. However, inspired by the Abbe Sieves publication *Qu 'est-ce que le tiers etat? (What is the Third Estate?)* the Third Estate advanced the view that no decision of the Estates General should be reached in separate chambers, but instead should be made by all deputies in a merged single assembly. In this way, the Third Estate with sympathisers from the clergy and nobles could expect to gain a majority of votes. On the 10 June, the *Communes* invited the other two estates to join them, but since they did not immediately accept the invitation, the Third Estate declared itself the National Assembly. To prevent the Assembly from convening, Louis XVI ordered the closure of the Salle des États where the Estates General met, causing the Assembly to relocate in the nearby real tennis court from where they swore an oath on 20 June 1789 (the Tennis Court Oath) not to depart until they had given France a constitution. Meanwhile, a majority of representatives from the clergy and nobility had joined the Assembly which from the summer of 1789 until September 1791 was known as the National Constituent Assembly. An early casualty in the proceedings of the Assembly was Necker who was considered by many members of the French court to be too supportive of the interests of the Third Estate. Thus, following his suggestion that the royal family reduce its expenditure to conserve funds, the king relieved Necker of his post, and completely reorganised his finance ministry to render it difficult for the Assembly to exert its influence over financial matters.

In parallel to the proceedings of the Assembly, dramatic events occurred beyond Versailles that shook the very foundations of the kingdom of France, despite the establishment of a so-called Committee of Public Safety on 13 July 1789. Insurgents tore down the hated *barriers* and ransacked the monastery of St Lazare. In the evening of the same day, the writer and orator Camile Desmoulins (close friend and political ally of the revolutionary George Danton) called upon an increasingly agitated crowd in the garden of the Palais Royal to head towards the Bastille. Merging with the disaffected inhabitants of the eastern Faubourg St-Antoine, the assembled Paris mob stormed and torched the prison, released its prisoners and executed its governor,

Marquis Bernard de Launay, and then proceeded to the Hôtel de Ville and inflicted the same fate on the mayor of Paris, Jacques de Flesselles. Meanwhile, the Marquis de Lafayette, whose distinguished military record was earned during the American War of Independence, became commander of the National Guard. Thinking that his safety was assured, Louis XVI drove from Versailles to Paris on 17 July under the protection of the National Guard in an attempt to reconcile himself with the people, but it was probably too late. Insurrection – known as 'La grande Peur' (the Great Fear) – was already spreading throughout France, a prelude to what was to come in Paris in the near future. Predicting the worse, French royalists began to emigrate, some to Switzerland, most to the Rhineland.

Before the Revolution had had an adverse effect on property development, a plethora of public buildings were developed across Paris. It is interesting to note that whereas the construction of theatres in London was privately financed, in France their provision was seen very much a governmental responsibility. Thus, to provide the frequently itinerate state-owned Comedie Francaise with a permanent home, Louis XVI acquired a site close to the Palais du Luxembourg c.

91   *Theatre de l'Odeon, 1797 (formerly the Théatre Comedie Francaise, 1770)*

1770 for the construction of the Theatre Comedie Francaise. Funded by the royal household and the Municipality of Paris and under the direction of Pierre Louis Moreau, work started in 1774 but his plans were modified in 1780 to correspond to the more appropriate designs of Marie-Joseph Peyre and Charles de Wailly. A superb Neoclassical building emerged, but since the Comedie had a preference for locating closer to the centre of royal power near the Louvre, the new building was renamed the Theatre de l'Odeon in 1797. Facing a semi-circular piazza, known since its inception as the Place de l'Odeon, the rectangular 1,900 seat theatre is imposingly adorned by a huge Doric portico with an arcaded entrance on the ground floor, while the remaining three sides of the building are, by comparison, elegantly austere. After a very short interlude, another state theatre, the 2,000 seat Theatre-Francais was built between 1786-90 and it immediately became the home of the Comedie Francaise. Commissioned by the Duke of Chartres, Victor Louis designed the building on a site shared with the Palais Royale to its east. Its Neoclassical façade was marked by a ground floor colonnade, supported by 16 Ionic columns, though together with its four upper floors, most of it was projected outwards onto the Place Colette in 1863.

92   *Theatre-Francais, 1786-90 (became home of the Théatre Comedie Francaise)*

Broadly at the same time as the state-owned theatres were being constructed disproportionately for aristocratic and bourgeois audiences, the Enceinte des Fermiers Generaux (the 'Wall of the Farmers General') was being erected around Paris to compel consumers to pay a customs duty on produce brought into the capital. The stone-built wall was 24 kilometres in circumference and 3.24 metres high, and was pierced at intervals by 62 tax-collecting *barriers* (or toll-houses) but since the incidence of a duty on food is highly regressive, the erection of the wall was seen by many to have been one of the causes of the Revolution. It is remarkable that in the circumstances it was considered necessary for each tollhouse to be designed in the most advanced Neoclassical style. Claude Nicolas Ledoux, in particular, produced a number of toll houses "that became temples and pavilions of funeral grandeur, combining an obsessive concern with geometric forms and a somewhat grotesque taste in classical detail."[7] They included the Rotonda de Chartres of c. 1780 on the edge of the Parc de Monceau that boasts a cylindrical core, circular colonnade and Doric columns, and with a drum and cupola added in 1861 virtually replicating Bramante's Tempietto of S.Pietro in Montorio in Rome; the Barriere d'Enfer of 1784-7 on the Place Denfert-Rochereau

93   *Rotonda de Chartres, Parc de Monceau, 1780*

94   *Toll houses in the Place de la Nation, 1780s*

95   *Rotonde de la Villette, 1786-92*

that consists of two rectangular pavilions with arcaded openings on their ground floors; a pair of toll houses of 1785-87 together with two gigantic columns in the Place de la Nation; and the Rotonde de la Villette of 1786-92 in the Place de Stalingrad, a massive Greek cross with four identical porticos surmounted by a rotonda with Doric columns.

Financial resources, however, did not extend to hospital-building, partly because the need for new hospitals was declining (the city's population decreased from 630,000 in 1789 to 546,856 in 1801), and partly because a commission established by Louis XVI in 1774 to investigate the whole subject of hospitals in the capital recommended that future hospital-building should prioritise the provision of smaller health facilities. This was remarkable since the enormous Hôtel Dieu near Notre Dame was burnt down in 1772, and despite plans drawn up by Charles François Viel and Antoine Petit in 1773-4 to rebuild it on the edge of Paris, their proposals were rejected and instead relatively small hospitals were developed around the city such as the hospital designed by C-F Viel for the Abbe Cochin in the parish of St-Jacques-du-haut-pas and begun in 1780, and the Hôpital Beaujon in the Rue du Faubourg St-Honore designed by J-D Antoine and started in 1784.

THE FRENCH REVOLUTION

Under the presidency of Mirabeau, the work of the Assembly proceeded rapidly. Opting for a single chamber, it abolished the French feudal system on 4 August 1789, introduced the Declaration of the Rights of Man and the Citizen on 27 August, and subsequently issued *assignats* (paper money) and nationalised church property. Though popularly accepted, Parisians were concerned about the harsh economic situations they faced, particularly bread shortages, and they also feared that the king would block the measures introduced by the National Constituent Assembly. Thus on the 5 October, 7,000 women joined the march of dissenters to Versailles in an attempt to persuade Louis XVI and Marie Antoinette to return to Paris. Though the palace was stormed, the royal family managed to vacate the building unscathed and under the protection of La Fayette and his National Guard, travelled to Paris on 6 October and resettled in the Tuileries palace.

Immediately fearful of the way in which the Revolution was being conducted in Paris, Louis XVI accepted an offer from General Bouille to provide him with a safe refuge at his camp at Montmedy in north-eastern France. Therefore, on the night of 20 June 1791, the King and his family fled the Tuileries in disguise, but on the following day were recognised and arrested at Varennes in the Meuse *departement* en route to General Bouille's camp. The royal family was duly brought back to Paris under guard, but while the Assembly permitted the royal family to resume residence in the Tuileries, Louis was provisionally suspended as king. Despite the flight to Montmedy, most of the Assembly still favoured a constitutional monarchy as opposed to a republic and persuaded the king to swear an oath to the constitution. However, there was considerable opposition to the continuation of the monarch, even though Louis was by now little more than a figurehead. A petition drafted by Jacque Pierre Brissot demanded that Louis be deposed as king, but at the Champs de Mars – where a large crowd gathered to sign the petition – a breakdown in public order provoked the National Guard under LaFayette to fire into the crowd, killing between 15 and 50 people. But neither the petition nor the 'Massacre of the Champs de Mars' had any effect on the role of the monarchy. Louis unequivocally accepted the constitution and, after elaborating on his intent to support it by all the means at his disposal, drew enthusiastic applause when addressing the Assembly. It must be recognised, however, that the constitution of 1791 was a middle-class creation for the benefit of that class. The poor, by far the largest segment of the population, exercised no power at all.

Despite this weakness, the Constitution of 1791 enabled France – for the first time – to function as a constitutional monarchy. While the king had to share power with an elected Legislative Assembly, he retained the royal veto and was able to exercise his right to appoint ministers. Meeting for the first time on 1 October 1791, the Assembly lasted for less than a year. Though it was broadly based – consisted of 330 Girondists (liberal republicans) and Jacobins (radical revolutionaries) on the left, 165 Feuillants (constitutional monarchists) on the right, and 250 independent representatives – it was a complete failure particularly since its expenditure greatly exceeded its revenue. It left behind an undisciplined army and navy and it presided over a breakdown in law and order. Therefore, on the night of 10 August 1792, insurgents broke into the Tuileries, the royal family were taken as prisoners to the Temple Tower, and a rump of the Legislative Assembly suspended the monarchy. On 20 September 1792 a National Convention was charged with the responsibility of writing a new constitution, and henceforth it became the new *de facto* government of France. On 21 September it abolished the monarchy and declared a republic.

It was during this tumultuous time that an attempt was made to start work on the construction of the church of Ste-Marie Madeleine in 1798 but because of political events and anti-religious antagonism, work ceased in 1791 and was not resumed until 1816 at the beginning of the Bourbon Restoration and not completed until 1842. Constructed according to the plans of Pierre de Vignon (d. 1828), the temple-like church was 108 metres in length, 43 metres in width and 30 metres in height. Built on a plinth of 4 metres in height, the imposing building boasts a single row of 52 Corinthian columns, each 15 metres high, surrounding the church, while a giant pediment dominates the south end of the building overlooking the Rue Royale.

The lack of respect for organised religion also resulted in the church of St-Geneviève (built in 1764) being converted from a place of Christian worship into a 'Pantheon' for the great late-eighteenth century exponents of liberty. With construction work directed by Antoine Chrysostome Quatremère de Quincy in 1790, 42 of the massive windows around the church were closed and replaced by masonry, and entrances in the transepts were sealed. The building which had formerly been a well-lit classical hall "was converted into a cool, enclosed grave building, a church changed into a monumental mausoleum of Revolutionary architecture."[8] Despite several subsequent attempts to convert the building back into a church in the nineteenth century, the building was officially established as the Pantheon in 1881.

The year 1790 saw the Val de Grace become a military hospital and the Louvre changed its use from a royal palace to a national museum in 1793, and a substantial amount of property owned particularly by the church or *émigré* members of the nobility either fell out of use or was confiscated by the Commune.

But military matters, as well as religious or political, were overshadowing architecture. On 25 July 1792, the Brunswick Manifesto had committed the armies of Austria and Prussia to retaliate against the

French people if they refused to reinstate Louis XVI as King of France. The French would not comply with this ultimatum and in response, a Prussian army swept across eastern France until checked at the Battle of Valmy on 20 September 1792 where they were forced to withdraw. The new-born French Republic subsequently defeated the Austrian forces at the Battle of Jemappes on 6 November and soon absorbed the Austrian Netherlands which brought France into conflict with Great Britain and the Dutch Republic who both had a vested interest in maintaining the independence of the southern Netherlands. The aforementioned commitment by Austria and Prussia was to prove counterproductive. It made Louis XVI appear to be conspiring with the enemies of France against public liberty and the general safety of the French people and thus led – following his trial on 17 January 1793 – to his execution by guillotine in the Place de la Revolution on 21 January. Across Europe, royalty was horrified at this outcome, and many countries including Great Britain, the Netherlands, Spain and Portugal soon joined Austria and Prussia in the War of the First Coalition against revolutionary France. French forces faced defeat almost immediately on several fronts, but by the autumn of 1793, the republican regime had halted but not reversed the allied advance into France. From the beginning, the war had proved to be an economic disaster for France. Prices rose substantially generating on the one hand rioting in the streets by the *sans-culottes* (poor labourers) and the Jacobins and, on the other, counter-revolutionary activity. In an attempt to quell economic and political instability, the Jacobins seized power through a parliamentary *coup*, and together with the *sans-culottes*, became the centre of the new government. Policy immediately became more radical. Price control on basic foodstuffs was introduced and offenders were executed, but with the rise to power of the Committee of Public Safety, price control was extended to all foodstuffs and a lengthy list of other goods as well. Since farmers and other producers no longer found it profitable to put their goods on the market, widespread shortages resulted.

On 10 June 1793 the Revolution entered its most extreme stage. The Committee of Public Safety came under the control of the Jacobins and their most influential member, Maximilien Robespierre. It not only installed a revolutionary dictatorship but in response to Robespierre's direction, unleased the Reign of Terror (1793-94) during which time at least 2,800 people in Paris died under the guillotine. On 24 June, the Convention adopted the first republican constitution of France, notable for embracing universal male suffrage, a provision that did not take effect due to subsequent political change during the latter years of the Revolution. The Reign of Terror was also notable for enabling the revolutionary government to avoid military defeat, for example it threw back the Austrians, Prussians, British and Spanish. This was in part attributable to the French army being dramatically increased in size, and in part due to the army now being under the command of young officers who had demonstrated their ability and patriotism in battle rather than being under aristocrat commanders who owed their positions purely to their privileged background. The Reign of Terror effectively came to an end on 27 July 1794 when the Thermodorian Reaction led to the arrest and execution of Robespierre. The new government with a large Girondist majority soon took revenge on their former foes, the Jacobins, by executing many of its former members in what was known as the White Terror.

Of all the times in Parisian history when the development of new buildings was constrained or abandoned by political conflict, the terror of 1793 was the worst, but there was soon 'some light at the end of the tunnel.' During the summer of 1794, with French victories against allied forces, the War of the First Coalition was largely abandoned, with only Britain and Austria remaining at war with France. Domestically, there was also the potential for a peace. In the aftermath of the excesses of the Terrors, the Convention approved the new 'Constitution of the Year 111' on 22 August 1795, an arrangement that was ratified by a plebiscite by the franchised and came into being on 27 September 1795. Established by the new constitution, the *Directoire* (Directory) was the first bicameral legislature in French history. Though it comprised 500 elected representatives and 250 non-elected senators, executive power was vested in only five directors chosen by the senators from a list supplied by the representatives. Popular government was also eroded since universal suffrage was superseded by limited representation based on property. Despite these shortcomings, the populace welcomed the new arrangements since they heralded a period of stability and peace. Conditions were now conducive to a resumption of property development, particularly on the Right Bank, for example, an impressive arcaded street, the Rue des Colonnes (near the

Palais-Royal) was constructed in 1797-98, while sumptuous residences were developed along the Rue du Faubourg St-Honore, around the Chaussee d'Antin, and in the Roule district. However, notwithstanding these additions to the Parisian townscape, more buildings were destroyed in the capital in the 1790s than were built,[9] but the extent of destruction should not be exaggerated. Fewer buildings were laid waste in Paris during the Revolution than the number destroyed in London during the Gordon Riots of 1780. Though the population of Paris decreased to 546,856 in 1801 or less than 20 percent lower than it had been in 1784, this was due more to out-migration resulting from the fear of violence, the confiscation of properties, food shortages and uncertainty about the future rather than the destruction of housing.

96   *Rue des Colonnes, 1797-98*

Political optimism among Parisians in the last decade of the eighteenth century quickly turned to pessimism. It was soon apparent that elections were being rigged, and the terms of the constitution were being disregarded, while draconian measures were used to quell dissent. Far from advocating peace, the Directory was sympathetic to war since it knew that without plunder and the tribute of foreign countries, it would have been impossible for a government to ameliorate the public debt that had accumulated during the early years of the Revolution. Inevitably, the Directory met opposition from both Jacobins and Royalists, and consequently had to rely upon the army to suppress riots and counter-revolutionary activity.

It was within this context that the popular general, Napoleon Bonaparte, ultimately gained power. Having already established a reputation as an outstanding commander of republic forces in Toulon, the Vendee, northern Italy and Egypt between 1793 and 1798, Napoleon staged a *coup d'état* against the Directory on 9 November 1799 (18 Brumaire of Year III) and established a three-man provisional consulate (or rump legislature) which included himself and two former members of the Directory: Emmanuel Sieyès and Roger Ducos. By drafting the Constitution of Year VIII, Napoleon immediately outmanoeuvred his two fellow consuls and secured his own election as First Consul.

NAPOLEONIC RULE

Napoleon's new role commenced just after the start of the War of the Second Coalition (1799-1802) in which France was in conflict with Britain, Austria, Russia, Turkey, Naples and Portugal. However, following the Treaty of Luneville (9 February 1801) and Treaty of Amiens (27 March 1802), a fragile peace ensued for three years. In 1802 Napoleon not only produced the Constitution of Year X that made him Consul for Life, giving him even greater powers to wage war, but annexed the state of Piedmont, while in 1803 – with the intention of invading England – he assembled the 'Armee de Angleterre' at Boulogne. In March 1804, the Code Napoleon – concerning civil law – was promulgated throughout France and her territorial possessions, present and future, and on 2 December 1804, Napoleon – in the presence of the Pope – crowned himself Emperor in the Cathedral of Notre Dame and the French Empire was duly created. In May 1805, Napoleon was subsequently crowned King of Italy and from August to December of the same year, France was engaged in the War of the Third Coalition against Britain, Austria, Russia, Prussia, Naples and Sweden, a conflict marked by the land battles of Ulm (20 October) and Austerlitz (2 December) in which, on both occasions, France was victorious, and the sea battle of Trafalgar (21 October) which she lost. The war was concluded by the Treaties of Schonbrunn (12 December) and Pressburg (26 December), the latter settlement leading to the dissolution of the Holy Roman Empire, its replacement by the Austrian Empire and the establishment of the Confederation of the Rhine with Napoleon named as its *Protector*.

In Napoleonic Paris, the Neoclassical style of architecture continued to be dominant in the development of new buildings, its foremost exponents being Jean-François Therese Chalgrin (1739-1811), François-Joseph Belanger (1744-1818), Pierre- François-Leonard Fontaine (1762-1853), Charles Percier (1764-1838), Jean-Antoine Alavoine (1778-1834) and Louis-Hippolyte Lebas (1782-1867). From his rise to power from First Consul to his early years as Emperor, Napoleon attempted to make Paris the 'most beautiful city in the world'. He was only too aware his capital was a "worn, wrecked and exhausted city. [It] smelt more of filthy mud and sewage than she had at the worst moments of the Middle Ages. There had been [in Sainte-Beuve's words] 'ten years of anarchy, sedition and laxity, during which no useful work had been undertaken, not a street had been cleared, not a residence repaired, nothing improved or cleansed.'"[10]

Thus, as well as encouraging the Commune and the private sector to rectify these deficiencies, Napoleon commissioned five major projects in the French capital: the construction of the Quai d'Orsay in 1802 which – on the Left Bank – was to eventually stretch from the Pont Royal to the Pont de la Concorde; the Place du Chatelet (started 1802); the development of the Rue de Rivoli (begun 1802) together with its main offshoot the Rue de Castiglione that runs northwards to the Place de Vendome, and the Rue de Napoleon (called the Rue de

97   *Place de Chatelet, 1802-1810*

la Paix after his abdication) that connects the Place de Vendome to the (later) Palace de l'Opera; the refashioning of the north façade of the Assemblee Nationale (1803-07); and – designed to resemble Trajan's column in Rome – the Colonne de la Grande Armee (1806-10) in the Place Vendome. Meanwhile, Napoleon ordered the construction of the city's first vaulted sewer network, 30 kilometres long, while his stepson Eugene Rose de Beauharnais began to remodel his Parisian residence in 1803, a building that subsequently became known as the Hôtel de Beauharnais.

The early years of the nineteenth century also witnessed large-scale private development, mainly on former church land on the Left Bank and largely residential, a reflection of the greater prosperity of the bourgeoisie. Following the building paralysis that occurred during the French Revolution, the Spartan style of the 1780s was rejected in favour

98   *Colonne de la Grand Armee, Place Vendome, 1806-10*

of a partial reversion to Classicism during the Empire notwithstanding the constraints of the 1783-4 building regulations that remained in force. Several apartment blocks of this period are still extant such as a four-storey Italianate building in the Rue Duphot dated 1807, and countless others followed throughout the century, a legacy of Napoleonic urban design largely absent in Britain though common throughout much of the Continent.

It was during this period of relative calm and tranquillity that Napoleon began to consolidate his empire still further by making his elder brother, Joseph, King of Naples, and from September 1806 to July 1807, he led France to victories in the War of the Fourth Coalition against the armies of Britain, Prussia, Saxony and Russia, most notably against Prussia at the battle of Jena – Aurerstedt (14 October 1806) and against Russia at the battles of Eylau (6 February 1807) and Friedland

(14 June 1807). Only with the Treaties of Posan (December 1806) and Tilsit (7-9 June 1807) were hostilities suspended, but only partly and only for a short while. The effects of the war were numerous. Through the Berlin Decree of 21 November 1806, the so-called Continental System was introduced whereby countries under Napoleon's control agreed to impose an embargo on the import of British goods. In 1807 Napoleon's younger brother, Jerome, became King of Westphalia, and in the same year the Duchy of Warsaw was established and ceded to Saxony, a French ally. France also occupied Portugal in 1807 because of her unwillingness to cooperate with Napoleon over the operation of the Continental System. In a strategic move, Napoleon subsequently invaded Spain and, after discarding the Spanish monarch, Charles IV, handed the Spanish throne to his brother Joseph who was transferred from his Neapolitan kingdom. With Napoleon returning to France in 1809 to combat a military threat from Austria, the French army in Spain without his leadership was embroiled in the Peninsular War until 1814 in an unsuccessful attempt to quell Spanish resistance and defeat British and Portuguese forces under the command of Arthur Wellesley, 1st Duke of Wellington.

99   *Place de la Bourse, 1808*

100 *Halle aux Blés reconstructed, 1809-13 – with Doric
column from the former Hôtel de Soisson, 1572*

During his periods of office as Emperor, Napoleon attempted to
enhance the grandeur of the French capital and duly ordered that the
old stock exchange of 1724 be rehoused in a new building located to the
north of the Palais Royal on a site eponymously called the Place de la
Bourse. Begun in 1808 by Alexandre Theodore Brongniart and worked
on by Eloi E. De Labarre from 1821-26, the new Bourse resembled
a Roman temple, with an imposing Corinthian peristyle. North and
south wings and an extended peristyle were added to the building in
1903 by J. B. Cavel increasing the total number of columns from 48 to
64, each of which are over ten metres in height. At the same time as the
new bourse was being rebuilt, the Halle aux Blés (the corn exchange)
was being restored after its wooden roof was damaged by fire in 1802.
Between 1809-13, François Joseph Bélanger provided the building

101   *Passage des Panorames,*

with a cast iron and glass cupola, a prelude to its further development later in the century when a pedimented portico supported by four giant Corinthian columns were built on its western edge in 1886-90.

The development of commercial buildings, however, was not confided to stock – or produce exchange. Retail markets and shopping arcades were also important, and these were developed in the Napoleonic period and its aftermath. Thus, after a history dating back to the twelfth century, including being burnt down in 1762, the Marche de St-Germain (essentially a food market) was rebuilt in 1811 in the manner of the Italian Renaissance with a roofed colonnade around an open square; and in the 1820s-40s a plethora of new shopping arcades were developed in the vicinity of the Bourse, such as the passages Jouffroy, du Caire, des Panorames, Verdeau and du Grand-Cerf, and the galleries Colbert, Vivienne and Vero-Dodat. Their new steel-framed structures not only sheltered shoppers and browsers from the vagaries of the weather and the traffic and dirt from the streets, but possibly afforded shopkeepers some protection from theft and burglary.[11]

102   *Galerie Vivienne, 1820-40*

During the last six years of Napoleon's rule, several notable buildings were left unfinished and very few others were commissioned. Only a very limited supply of resources could be allocated to building work because of the cost of conducting large scale warfare across the width of Europe. Coinciding with the early stages of the Peninsular War, the War of the Fifth Coalition took place in 1809 and in contrast to earlier coalition wars involved only three belligerents: France, Austria and Britain. With Austria resuming its war against France in April 1809, Napoleon assumed command of forces on the Danube and German fronts. Although French forces suffered a defeat at the Battle of Aspern-Essling on 22 May, they secured a victory at Wagram on 5 July and negotiated a peace treaty with Austria at Schonbrunn on 14 October. The French were also at war with Britain but although her troops found difficulty in combating Wellesley's forces in the Iberian Peninsula, she easily defeated Britain in a poorly conducted Walcheran Campaign aimed at seizing Antwerp. French territorial ambitions continued unabated. In 1810, France annexed Holland and North Germany, and in 1812 set its sights on Russia to enable the Duchy of Warsaw to absorb the eastern part of Poland that had fallen into Russian hands. Deploying his *Grande Armée* of more than 450,000 men, Napoleon's eastward invasion commenced on 23 June 1812. Although the Russians offered some resistance at Smolensk, on 18 August their strategy was to withdraw deep into Russia where the French found it increasingly difficult to forage food for themselves and their horses. Eventually, on 7 September, the Russians became engaged in battle with the French at Borodino on the outskirts of Moscow. Although this left about 44,000 Russians and 35,000 French dead, wounded or captured, the outcome was by no means as decisive as Napoleon had hoped. While the remains of the Russian army retreated eastward past Moscow, Napoleon entered the Russian capital intending to negotiate a peace treaty with Tsar Alexander I, but the people of Moscow were determined not to host a capitulation and, on orders from its mayor, burnt the city down. Napoleon had little alternative but to return to France but, in so doing, the *Armée* was decimated by 40,000 of his men (out of an original force of over 400,000 frontline troops) retreating across the Berezina River (in present day Belarus) on 26-28 November 1812.

During the Revolution, Consulate and Empire, a series of public buildings were either reconstructed or extended, examples of which include the Palais Bourbon that was confiscated in 1792 and rebuilt as the Assemblee Nationale, a temple-like edifice with a twelve column peristyle added in 1803-07; the Louvre that became the Musee de la Republique in 1793 and, in an extended form designed by Charles Percier and Pierre-François-Leonard Fontaine, the Musee Napoleon in 1806-11. Bridge-building was also a feature of the period: the Pont de la Concorde – linking the Place de la Concorde with the (then) Palais Bourbon – was constructed by J. Rodolphe Perronet in 1788-91; the cast iron pedestrian Pont des Arts, with its nine arches, was built across the Seine from the Louvre to the College de Quatre Nations in 1801-03 under the direction of Louis-Alexandre Cessart and Jacques Dillon (Napoleon changed the name of the college to the Institut de France in 1805); the Pont d'Austerlitz traversed the Seine from the Right Bank to the Jardin des Plantes in 1802-07, while the Pont d'Iena was built over the river from the Right Bank to the Champs de Mars in 1806-13. As well as ensuring that the Seine was adequately bridged, Napoleon was also interested in securing an adequate supply of drinking water for the citizens of Paris. He thus commissioned the construction of the Canal de l'Ourcq in 1802 to bring fresh water from woodlands, 180 kilometres north east of Paris.

To many people during the Revolution and its aftermath, any bellicose images of the royal presence were repugnant, and thus an equestrian statue of Henry IV on the Pont Neuf was destroyed in 1792, and in the same year equestrian statues of Louis XIV in the Place des Victoires and Place Vendome were both damaged beyond repair. However, it was considered not only necessary to safeguard the Revolution from a resurgence of royal support, but also to protect the state from belligerent Bourbon allies abroad. Thus, between 1802-06, Napoleon extended the Quai d'Orsay to the Pont de la Concorde to facilitate the construction of barges that could be used in an invasion of England, and from 1808-15, the quay further lengthened to the Pont d'Iena.

TOWN PLANNING

From a sound base in the seventeenth and early eighteenth centuries, town planning in Paris during the final years of the *Ancien Régime* and later during the Consulate and Empire achieved a degree of sophistication unsurpassed until Haussmann redrew the map of the capital in the mid-nineteenth century (see chapter 11). Under Napoleon's orders, a plethora of prestige monuments were constructed to celebrate his victories abroad. Firstly, he demolished the Grand Chatelet between 1802-10 and replaced it with the 'Fontaine du Palmier', and Nicholas Bralle's victory column of 1806-08.[12] Secondly, in 1806 he ordered work to begin on the Arc de Triomphe du Carrousel to celebrate his victory against Austria and Russia at the Battle of Austerlitz in 1805. Built in the courtyard of the Tuileries, according to the design of Charles Percier and Pierre François Leonard Fontaine, and completed in 1808, the Parisian arch replicates the Arch of Septimus Severus in Rome, but on a smaller scale. It was enhanced by pink and white Corinthian columns, adorned by marble bas-reliefs on all four sides depicting Napoleon's victories, and is surmounted by statues of Imperial soldiers (and later by a bronze chariot group sculptured by François-Joseph Bosio in 1828 to represent the Restored Bourbon monarchy). The third major monument begun in 1806 was the grandest of all, the Arc de Triomphe. Commissioned by Napoleon and designed by Jean-François-Therese Chalgrin as a monument to the French army, the arch was constructed at the highest point of the Champs Élysées on a site which later became the vertex of twelve streets. At 50 metres in height and 45 metres in width, the massive simple *arc* is without columnar formations or a *quadriga*, but because of the immensity of its scale and because of political changes brought about by Napoleon's demise and the Restoration, the arch was not completed until 1832.

Probably influenced by Joseph Benard's largely unadorned Rue des Colonnes – a short arcade of Doric pillars surmounted by four residential floors built between 1797-98, and possibly inspired by the many arcades and colonnades of Italy, Napoleon sold some of the

103   *Arc de Triomphe du Carrousel, begun 1806*

104   *Arc de Triomphe, 1806-32*

republic's land on the edge of the Jardin des Tuileries in 1802 with the intention of building a lengthy arcaded street to link the Place de la Concorde in the west to the Marais in the east. With plans produced by Charles Percier and Pierre-François-Leonard Fontaine, the Rue de Rivoli was constructed between 1811-56 and named in celebration of Napoleon's victory over the Austrians at the Battle of Rivoli in January 1797. Its refined arcaded section, with a string of balconies, extends no further east than the Place du Palais-Royal, and beyond it, individual properties were developed as far as the seventeenth century church of St-Paul-St-Louis. Leading northwards at 90 degrees from the arcaded Rue de Rivoli, a similar street, the Rue Castiglione joins the seventeenth century Place de Vendome.

105   *Rue de Rivoli, 1802-56*

NAPOLEON'S DEMISE

Before Napoleon's plans for the redevelopment of Paris could be completed, the War of the Sixth Coalition broke out and postponed construction activity. Russia and Prussia (from March 1813), Britain (from June 1813) and Austria (from August 1813) were again in conflict with France. At first, Napoleon focused his attention on Germany and gained several victories over the Coalition, most notably at the Battle of Dresden in August 1813, but on 16-19 October, French forces lost the Battle of Leipzig, the largest single battle of the Napoleonic Wars, costing a total of 90,000 casualties. Though his army decreased in size from 350,000 men at the beginning of the war to only 70,000 troops after Leipzig, Napoleon had been able to win a series of victories against his enemies but these were not enough to prevent Coalition forces from capturing and occupying Paris on 31 March 1814, with a large number of Russian troops camping in the Jardin des Tuileries on the very edge of Napoleon's Paris residence. With his army being unwilling to march on the capital, Napoleon had no choice but to abdicate. By the subsequent Treaty of Fontainebleau, the Coalition exiled him to Elba on 6 April 1814, but this was not the end of the matter. Napoleon was unvanquished. He still craved power and therefore a year of uncertainty passed before the next legitimate head of the French state, Louis XVIII, settled down to rule.

REFERENCES

1. A. Horne (A), *Seven Ages of Paris* (London: Pan Books, 2002), p.170
2. H. Wischermann, *Paris. An Architectural Guide* (Verona: Arsenale Editrice, 2005), p.92
3. J. Summerson, *The Architecture of the Eighteenth Century* (London: Thames & Hudson, 1996), p.88
4. H. Wischermann, *Paris. An Architectural Guide* (Verona: Arsenale Editrice, 2005), p.139
5. A. Sutcliffe, *Paris. An Architectural History* (London: Yale University Press, 1996), p.63
6. Ibid
7. J. Summerson, opt. cit., p.86
8. H. Wischermann, opt. cit., p.81
9. C. Jones, *Paris. Biography of a City* (London: Penguin, 2006), p.287
10. Ibid, p.289
11. A. Horne (A), opt. cit., p.185
12. M. Padberg, *Art & Architecture, Paris* (Potsdam: A. F. Ullmann, 2012), pp.188-91

CHRONOLOGY

1789	The beginning of the French Revolution with the fall of the Bastille
1792-99	The First Republic
1797-98	**Rue des Colonnes built**
1799-1804	Napoleon Bonaparte, First Consul
1802 onwards	**Rue de Rivoli constructed**
1802-10	**Place de Chatelet built**
1803 onwards	**Hôtel de Beauharnais (begun 1713-15) completed**

1804-15	Napoleon I, Emperor of the French
1806-08	**Arc de Triomphe du Carrousel constructed**
1806-10	**Place de Vendôme built**
1806-30	**Arc de Triomphe constructed**
1808 and 1821-26	**Paris Bourse de Commerce built**
1809-13	**Paris Bourse (stock exchange) constructed**
1814	**Gas street lights installed**
1815	Napoleon I, defeated at Waterloo and exiled to St-Helena

10

THE RESTORATION OF THE BOURBON MONARCHY AND ITS EFFECT ON THE GROWTH OF PARIS

INTRODUCTION

Though the population of Paris had grown slowly during the Revolutionary and Imperial wars, from around 650,000 in 1789 to only 700,000 in 1815, by 1850 the population of the capital had soared to well over a million. The distribution of social classes throughout Paris in the first half of the nineteenth century was broadly the same as in the eighteenth. The working poor were crammed into high density housing in areas criss-crossed by narrow, ill-paved and filthy streets such as those in the Butte de Montmartre and the Faubourg St-Antoine; bohemians (for example social rebels, artists and academics) settled in the Latin Quarter in the vicinity of the Pantheon and Sorbonne; the *petit bourgeoisie* continued to live in the Marais close to the Place des Vosges or in the square itself; the *haut bourgeoisie* and the Napoleonic nobility were attracted to the Faubourg St-Honoré and the Chausée d'Antin; and the old pre-revolutionary aristocracy had a preference for residing in the Faubourg St-Germain.[1]

In an attempt to satisfy the demand for housing from the more affluent segment of the capital's growing population, privately-funded developers built 21,000 apartments and laid-out 65 new or restructured streets between 1815 and 1830[2], though there remained a considerable shortfall of housing for the poor that was only partly overcome by outward migration to the fringes of Paris later in the century.

LOUIS XVIII (R. 1814-24)

On 24 April 1814 a Bourbon was returned to power. Napoleon's Imperial Councillor, Charles de Talleyrand-Perigord, had persuaded the Coalition powers to invite Louis XVI's brother to become king of France under the name of Louis XVIII (the immediate heir to the throne would have been Louis XVI's son, Louis XVII, had he not died in the Temple prison in 1795). On 30 May the Peace of Paris reinstated the French frontiers of 1792, and on 4 June it was confirmed by a constitutional charter that Louis XVIII would reign as a constitutional monarch. The charter, on the one hand, proclaimed that 'the person of the king is sacred and inviolable' and that 'executive power belongs to the king alone' giving him the sole right to initiate legislation and to dissolve parliament at will, but on the other hand it set up a two-chamber assembly: an upper chamber of peers consisting of lords and dignitaries from pre-revolutionary France, and a lower chamber of deputies elected by a land-based suffrage of some 90,000 landowners. Ministers were given the responsibility of countersigning royal acts, while parliament was given powers to approve or block changes in taxation. The charter also promised equality before the law, and re-established status and property rights "including those to land confiscated from the Church and former émigrés during the Revolution.[3]

The system of constitutional monarchy adopted in France under the Revolution was of course notably different from that practised in England, and even more advantageous to the king than that on offer in 1792. The French king was far more than a figurehead with very limited rights of intervention. He both governed as well as reigned and showed little empathy to the former supporters of the Revolution and replaced the tricolour with the white and gold standard of the Bourbons. In September 1814 the Congress of Vienna was convened in September 1814 by the Coalition powers to decide upon the break-up of the former Napoleonic empire much to the disgust of an antagonistic Napoleon exiled in Elba. Determined to regain his authority as emperor, Napoleon escaped from the island on 26 February 1815 and landed in the Golfe Juan near Cannes two days later. At Grenoble en route to Paris, the former Emperor was able to encourage the 5th Regiment that was sent to intercept him to change sides, and together they marched to Paris, prompting Louis XVIII to flee the capital and take refuge in Ghent. On the 17 March, Britain, the Netherlands, Russia, Austria and Prussia agreed at Vienna to deploy 150,000 troops in the field to end his rule, but Napoleon arrived in Paris three days later, and from the Tuileries – governed for a period now called 'the Hundred Days'. By the beginning of June 1815, Napoleon had assembled an army of 200,000 men and went on the offensive in an attempt to drive a wedge between the British and Prussian armies. On the 18 June, however, he was defeated in Belgium at the Battle of Waterloo by the armies of Wellington and von Blücher, though in the words of Wellington, it 'was the nearest-run thing you ever saw.' The Coalition forces quickly made their way to Paris. Occupying the capital and with Russian forces camped in the Jardin des Tuileries, they restored Louis XVIII to the French throne. Napoleon was imprisoned and then exiled on 9 July to the British island of Saint Helena in the South Atlantic, where he died in 1821.

However, in the wake of Waterloo, a Second Peace of Paris was signed in November 1815 once again redrawing the boundaries of France and returning them to their 1790 configuration, a less generous settlement than that concluded at the first Peace of Paris eighteen months earlier. But although France forfeited Belgium and the Left Bank of the Rhine, the peace ensured that France lost none of its own territory. However, the maintenance of the *status quo* was not confined to geographical boundaries. Earlier in August, 78 percent of the 50,900 voters who elected the 402 deputies to the first parliament of the regime were clearly very conservative (the 'Ultras'), and working through their semi-secret organisation, the *Chevaliers de la Foi*, they attempted to revert to the *status quo* of pre-Revolutionary France by conducting a campaign of violence against former Jacobins. Through the so-called 'White Reign of Terror', the Ultras conducted a series of massacres against their foes, removed Republican officials from their posts and seized property previously requisitioned by the State during the Revolution. However, when Napoleon's leading general, Marshal Ney, was sentenced to death by the Chamber of Peers and executed by firing squad, Louis XVIII denounced further violence and in September 1816 dissolved the unmanageable Chamber of Deputies on the advice of his first minister, Armand Emmanuel, duc de Richelieu.

Through the use of government influence and an increase in the size of the electorate to 100,000, Louis XVIII secured a more liberal Chamber, paving the way for a moderate policy of reforms under the new first minister, Elie, 1st comte Decazes.[4] However, following the assassination of the duc de Berry, the Ultras demanded and achieved the minister's dismissal since they blamed his liberal attitude for the death of the duke. From then onwards, the Ultras and allied factions soon influenced policymaking, for example a law was introduced that suspended individual liberties and the freedom of the press was curtailed.

Though Louis XVIII reigned for ten years, his influence on the built environment of Paris was negligible. Except for the development of a number of apartment blocks, some with interesting features, such as a four-storey apartment house with modified Palladian windows in the Rue Lamartine dating from 1824, very few secular buildings of note were constructed during his reign. However, three ecclesiastical buildings required consideration. The Madeleine, begun in the reign of Louis XV, was still being built, but two other churches of note were constructed during the early years of the Restoration. The first is the Chapelle Expiatoire that was built for Louis XVIII in 1816-26 close to the Place Louis XV and on the site of the Cimetiere de la Madeleine where many of the victims of the Revolution were buried or had been buried later such as his brother Louis XVI and aunt Marie Antoinette whose remains were transferred to the Abbey Church of St Denis in 1815. Designed by Hippolyte Lebas and Pierre François Leonard Fontaine, the church has a flight of steps leading to a square nave and three apses and is surmounted by a modest cupola. The second is the church of Notre-Dame-de-Lorette in the Rue de Chateaudun. Designed by Lebas and built between 1823-26, the basilica has a portico with Corinthian columns and a pediment, a nave with a flat roof, four domed side chapels and a domed apse.

Some attention, however, was paid to the restoration of royal monuments iconoclastically destroyed during the Revolution. A new bronze equestrian statue of Henri IV was put in place on the Pont-Neuf, and the destroyed statues of Louis XIII and Louis XIV were restored respectively in the Place de Vosges and Place des Victoires. Perhaps more importantly, Parisians benefitted from the introduction of gas-lighting, provided first in the Place Vendôme in 1825 but rapidly attracting 1,500 subscribers by 1828. Around the same time, pavements were beginning to be laid along the principal thoroughfares of the capital to the obvious convenience of pedestrians and a public horse-drawn bus line was opened along the *grand boulevards* from the Place de la Bastille to the Madeleine.

CHARLES X (R. 1824-30)

Louis XVIII's death in 1824 heralded the reign of the last Bourbon king of France, Charles X, the last surviving brother of Louis XVI. He decided to be crowned in Rheims, anachronistically recalling the coronations of the *Ancien Régime* and a precursor to the Ultras dominating government until his demise in 1830 at the age of 72. In 1825, a large Ultra majority in government, under Jean Baptiste comte de Villèle, brought in legislation that provided indemnities for former émigrés whose property had been requisitioned during the Revolution, enabled the Church to regain its position within the State through its control of education, and imposed capital punishment on anyone found guilty of stealing a liturgical artefact. But such was the opposition to these measures among the populace at large, that Villèle was forced to resign.

He was succeeded as first minister by Jean Baptiste comte de Martignac who attempted to introduce more liberal policies, but such was Charles X's preference for severe authoritarian policies, Martignac was replaced in August 1829 by Prince Jules de Polignac, a firm supporter of absolute monarchy. However, oppression at home and the failure of Charles's declared aim to conquer Algeria reduced support for the Ultras at the election of 1830. Hoping to strengthen his hold on the levers of power, the king published four ordinances on 26 July

1830 to suspend the freedom of the press and re-establish censorship, to dissolve the new chamber of deputies, to modify electoral law and to schedule new elections for September.

In angry response to Charles's proposal to gag the press, Adolphe Thiers of *Le National* and fellow journalists decided that newspapers would be published on the following day (the 27 July), but this provoked the *gendarmerie* into destroying the printing presses with the result that a hostile public rioted in support of a free press. On the 28 July Marshal Marmont's small detachment was unable to put down the riots and on the 29 July barricades were built across the streets of the capital and the Louvre and Tuileries were pillaged. In fear, the government fled to Saint-Cloud, 9.6 kilometres to the west of central Paris. The three days in which the king was defied have been referred to as the *Trois Glorieuses*, a prelude to Charles's abdication, his flight to England and a complete change in government.

During Charles's tempestuous reign, very few buildings of any note were commissioned by the monarchy, the church or the public. Charles X recognised that since a number of major projects started by Napoleon earlier in the century needed to be completed such as Rue de Tivoli, the Madeleine, the Bourse and the Arc de Triomphe, there was little desire to embark upon further public development, while in the private sector political and economic instability deterred the development of anything worthy of note.

LOUIS PHILIPPE (R. 1830-48)

In Paris on 30 July 1830, a group of liberal politicians established the so-called 'July Monarchy'. With the assistance of an aged Lafayette and a reconstituted National Guard, they ended the power vacuum left by the political demise of Charles X by offering the throne to Louis Philippe, the Duke of Orléans, son of Philippe Égalité and a descendent of Philippe, the first Duke of Orléans and younger son of Louis XIII. The offer was on condition that the new king guaranteed the constitution and – in response to a proclamation written by the political activist and writer, Adolphe Thiers – would empathise with the continuing revolution as a 'citizen king'. He even chose the title

106   *Part of the north end of the connecting gallery of the Palais Royal, 1830*

107   *Colonne de Juillet, 1831-40*

108   *Luxor Column, Place de la Concorde. 1836*

'King of the French' rather than 'King of France' linking the monarchy to a people rather than a territory, dispensed with the white flag of the Bourbons and replaced it with the tricolour of the Revolution, and revived the *Marseillaise* as the national anthem. However, in keeping with his new role, Louis Philippe abandoned his ancestral home, the Palais Royale, where he had been residing since 1815 and established himself in the Tuileries.

During the first few days of his reign, Louis Philippe formed a government and on 8 August, the Chamber of Deputies revised the constitution to firmly tilt the balance of power in parliament's favour, though it was still dominated by the king.[5] However, the political situation was far from being trouble-free. Though a new electoral law reduced the tax qualification from 300 francs to 200 effectively reducing the weight of the nobles, country landowners (including farmers), professionals, businessmen and the more prosperous artisans increased in importance. But by far the largest segment of the total population – the lower-middle class, urban workers and peasants – remained disenfranchised[6] and at this time in history, the electorate still excluded women of whatever class.

Soon after the 'Citizen King' ascended the throne, Parisians witnessed the start of major building projects on the western and eastern edges of the capital. In 1830, Louis Philippe commissioned Pierre François Leonard Fontaine to build a glass-covered connecting gallery across the north of the garden of the Palais Royal for the enjoyment of the king and his court, and in the same year the church of Ste-Geneviève reverted to a Pantheon for France's great men. From 1831-40 the Colonne de Juillet – some 50 metres high – was constructed to commemorate the 540 lives that were lost during the three-day July Revolution of 1830[7], and in 1836 the Place de la Concorde was remodelled, placing the Luxor column on the site of Louis XV's old equestrian statue, while in the same year the Arc de Triomphe de Étoile was eventually completed commemorating the end of Early Modern Paris and heralding the Modern Age.

Though the development or completion of major building projects by the State might have been intended to enhance the legitimacy of his regime, Louis Philippe was soon confronted by a series of militant reactions against his government motivated by the belief among republicans that Louis Philippe far from being egalitarian had 'sold-out' to the interests of the wealthy *bourgeoisie*. Demonstrations occurred in February and October 1831, in 1832 and particularly in 1834 when all the people living in an apartment block in the Marais' Rue Transnonian were massacred by troops allegedly on the orders of Marshal Bugeaud. However, throughout the early 1830s, as 'Citizen King' Louis Philippe habitually walked around the streets of the capital carrying his 'trademark' green umbrella and shaking hands with passing Parisians, he did not fear for his life. That is until July 1835 when opposition to his reign was marked by a failed assassination attempt by Giuseppe Maria Fieschi, a Corsican immigrant and extreme republican.

As a friend of businessmen, bankers, investors and industrialists, Louis Philippe was a vigorous supporter of a *laisser-faire* economy particularly in the labour market. This was at a time when the bargaining strength of industrial workers was particularly weak. Paris industrialised slowly in the first-half of the nineteenth century, but manufacturing was mainly workshop- rather than factory-based, in contrast to Britain.[8] Although by 1848, the capital had as many as 65,000 industrial enterprises, including a disproportionate percentage of textile firms, only 7,000 of the total number employed a workforce of more than ten.[9] By 1848, a third of all workers in Paris were employed in the textile and clothing trades, one in ten in the furniture industry and the same number were in metallurgy, all largely workshop-based, while only one in nine workers were in the building and construction industries.[10]

With the population of Paris increasing by 25 percent between 1830 and 1848, largely because of migration from the countryside, the supply of labour greatly exceeded demand, and this together with the absence of large firms and collective bargaining exerted a downward pressure on wages. Within this scenario, Louis-Philippe's government was able to adopt an antagonistic stance against the development of organised labour, its quest for higher wages and improved working conditions and its demands for a widening of the franchise. In an indirect attempt to weaken the labour movement, a major law on primary education was introduced in 1833 to 'moralise' the lower working class in the vain hope that it would not become dependent on collective action.[11] But in response, small groups of enfranchised middle class republicans politicised disenfranchised workers through the formation of clandestine organisations such as the *Société des Droits de l'Homme*, but fearful of an alliance between republicans and workers, the regime brought in a law to ban the formation of such organisations.

Despite the militant opposition to this law and the brutal repression that ensued, the political peace that followed was in part attributed to strong authoritarian government and in part due to its attempt to increase prosperity through public-private infrastructural projects within an otherwise untrammelled free market economy. Although a rail network was duly developed throughout France, most main lines centred on Paris enhancing its economy and increasing the importance of the French capital. Begun in the 1830s, but opened in 1840, the Gare de l'Ouest – later renamed the Gare Montparnesse – provided rail services from Paris to the west and south west of France, and eventually linked the capital to Tours, Bordeaux, Rennes and Nantes. Under its original name, the Gare d'Orléans, the Gare d'Austerlitz was completed in 1840 and thenceforth provided services from the capital to Orléans and Bordeaux with a connection to Toulouse. The Gare Saint-Lazare was built in the 1840s, though an earlier station, the Embarcadère des Batignolles – opened by Marie-Amélie, wife of Louis Philippe in 1837 – was situated 150 metres north-west of its present site. Since the mid-nineteenth century the Gare Saint-Lazare has provided services from Paris to Normandy and particularly to Le Havre. Perhaps most famous of all, the Gare de Nord was inaugurated in 1846 and was connected to Amiens and Lille by the Chemin de Fer du Nord.

Infrastructural projects were not confined to railways, the redevelopment of the streets of Paris, albeit on a limited scale, also attracted government involvement. During his tenure as Louise Philippe's *préfet* of the Seine *département*, Claude Philibert Barthelot, comte de Rambuteau (1833-48) implemented policy, first introduced earlier in the Restoration, to improve "house alignments in Parisian streets and by strictly maintaining building regulations which allowed new construction to integrate harmoniously within the existing built environment."[12] Of at least equal importance, Rambuteau recognised that there was a causal relationship between a squalid built environment and the poor state of public health and, through his influence, legislation in 1841 empowered the prefect to expropriate private property where the health of a community was a concern. In this regard, the prefect's greatest achievement was the construction of the Rue Rambuteau: a straight 13 metre wide street that was driven through a labyrinth of medieval streets from the church of St-Eustache in Les Halles to the Rue des Francs-Bourgeois in the Marais.[13] Rambuteau also attempted to improve the environment of the Île-de-la-Cité, constructing a number of new streets on the island, notably the Rue d'Arcole (1834) and the Boulevard Morland (1843), in addition to extending the Rue de Lutèce (1838) and building the Pont du Carrousel (1833-4).

Church-building also laid outside of a free market economy, and among the more imposing churches built entirely during the Restoration is the church of St-Vincent-de-Paul in the Place Franz-Liszt. Constructed between 1831-44 under the direction of Jakob Ignaz Hittorf, the church – at the top of a long flight of steps – boasts a large portico with six Ionic columns and a giant pediment in front of a twin towered façade, while internally its layout is that of a basilica with a nave and four aisles. Of comparable interest is the church of St-

109   *Church of St-Vincent-de-Paul, 1831-34*

Denis-du-St-Sacrement in the Rue de Turenne. Designed by Étienne-Hippolyte Godde in a neo-Grecian style, and begun in 1835, the main feature of this generally unadorned church is its sculptured tympanum supported by four sturdy Doric columns. But the most imposing church of the period, the Madeleine, was eventually completed in 1842 after many years of interrupted construction dating back to the reign of Louis XV in 1781. The church was an enormous building 100 metres in length and 84 metres wide in the shape of a Greek cross. Its 22-column portico employs the Corinthian order and is surmounted by an enormous pediment, reminiscent of the Roman Pantheon. At the transept crossing, a dome rises to 83 metres, its drum surrounded by 26 free-standing fluted Corinthian pillars that frame a peristyle atop a pedestal.[14]

110   *An extended Hôtel de Ville, 1837-49 (rebuilt 1873-82)*

Louis Philippe's regime funded a plethora of public projects in the 1840s, most notably the updating of the Palais Bourbon that accommodated the Chamber of Deputies, the Palais du Luxembourg that housed the Senate, the Hôtel de Ville that tripled its size, and the Palais de Justice on the Île-de-la-Cité,[15] while the university sector was largely or entirely immune from market forces when it developed the library of Ste-Geneviève (1844-50). Situated close to the Pantheon and designed by Henri Labrouste, the edifice was originally intended to accommodate the treasures of the neighbouring cloister. Using long ashlar blocks, its exterior – with a centrally positioned entrance – was built in a neo-Renaissance style, but its interior encloses a slender two-storey reading room on the upper floor, 85 metres in length and 21 metres in width, with book stacks and administrative space at ground level. The library is one of the earliest buildings in Paris to employ steel in its construction. Its "18 light-cast columns and ornamental trusses bearing the decoratively painting vaulting, with the books on the long walls."[16]

Though 150 new streets were built in Paris from 1815 to 1848 – latterly under Rambuteau's stewardship – the increase in the number of houses in the capital increased by a third from 24,000 to 31,000 over the

111   *Library of Ste-Geneviève, 1844-50*

same 33 year period resulting in a massive housing shortage throughout much of Louis Philippe's reign.[17] This was not only attributable to the population of Paris virtually doubling over the same period, but also due to the malfunctioning of the housing market. Market failure was caused, first, by the reciprocal decline in 'vertical stratification' in which the poor lived at street and roof level, and the rich on the floors in between, and the increase in 'horizontal stratification' where the poor moved out of housing in the central and western areas of Paris to seek housing – often unsuccessfully – in the city's eastern areas or on its outer fringe; second by the allocation of resources – through the medium of public-private partnership schemes – to build houses for the social elite in newly prestigious environs such as the Chaussée d'Antin and the Rues Malesherbes and Lafayette rather than for the public in general. Much of this housing, moreover, was unaffordable and remained empty or difficult to let.

In 1841, the government cautiously decided to construct a wall around the outer edge of Paris, 34 kilometres in length and employing 25,000 workers in its construction. Prudently commissioned by Louis Philippe on the advice of his powerful minister Adolph Thiers, the wall was built at a time of troubled international relations and was intended to protect the capital from foreign invasion, something the 2 metre high Farmers-General Wall (built between 1784 and 1791) would be unable to do. The Thiers Wall and a series of paved *boulevards des maréchaux* encircled Paris and defined its outer boundary. It was to this circular belt of low value land that, in accordance with municipal regulation, noxious industries were relocated from the centre of Paris, while – within the belt – market forces led to the development of dense levels of poor working class housing, though there were some instances of housebuilding for the *bourgeoisie* particularly in the west. As a result of these developments, the population of Paris on the inner edge of the wall increased from 75,000 in 1831 to 173,000 in 1856.

After ten or more years of economic growth, attributable in no small measure to a building boom across Paris, a severe downturn in the economic cycle in 1845-46 provoked widespread opposition to the regime particularly in the capital. To circumvent the laws against political meetings, a 'banquet' campaign emerged to debate popular grievances and to demand an extension of the franchise at the very least by means of a reduction in the tax qualification to 100 francs, or far more radically through the introduction of complete manhood suffrage. With the banquet campaign attracting widespread support across northern and eastern France, it was decided by its participants to hold a mass banquet in Paris but, afraid of the breakdown of law and order, the government banned the gathering much to the relief of moderate politicians. In the context of intensive political and economic discontent, the response was inevitable. On 22 February 1848, mass demonstrations by students and workers took place in front of the Madeleine and in the Place de la Concorde, and on the following day elements of the predominantly middle-class National Guard gave their support to the protesters since they recognised that the regime solely represented the interests of the upper classes (the *grande bourgeoisie*) rather than electorate as a whole, let alone the population at large. Louis Philippe responded immediately to the crisis facing his government. He replaced the intransigent first minister François Guizot with the more liberal comte de Molé, but it was too late.[18]

By the morning of 24 February, 1,500 barricades were erected across the narrow and twisting streets of central Paris, but when the demonstrators attacked a guard post, shots were fired, and 16 people killed. In the absence of clear orders, an attempt of Marshal Bugeaud and his royalist troops to clear the streets proved unsuccessful, and he withdrew his men towards the Tuileries to protect the king and his family. In the early evening of the same day, a Provisional Government comprising of well-known republican politicians was proclaimed by the crowds at the Hôtel de Ville, ironically the same location where Louis Philippe accepted the throne eighteen and a half years earlier. It is also ironic that, like his predecessor Charles X, on abdicating he fled to England, a nation much further along the path to democracy than that of his mother country, France.

REFERENCES

1. R. Cole. *Paris* (London: Phoenix, 2005), pp.150-151
2. Ibid, p.151
3. R. Price, *A Concise History of France* (Cambridge: Cambridge University Press, 1993), p.158
4. Ibid, p.159
5. R. Price, opt. cit., p.165
6. R. Price, opt. cit., p.166
7. D. Gray-Durant, *Paris and Versailles* (London: A & C Black, 2001), p.259
8. C. Jones, *Paris. Biography of a City* (London: Penguin Books, 2006), p.325
9. R. Cole, opt. cit., p.157
10. R. Jones, opt. cit., p.326
11. R. Price, opt. cit., p.127
12. R. Jones, opt. cit., p.328
13. Ibid
14. H. Wischermann, *Paris. An Architectural Guide* (Verona: Arsenale Editrice, 2005), p.14
15. R. Jones, opt. cit., p.312
16. H. Wischermann, opt. cit., p.102
17. R. Jones, opt. cit., p.329
18. R. Price, opt. cit., p.170

CHRONOLOGY

1814-24	Beginning of the Bourbon Restoration. Louis XVIII, King of France
1824-30	Charles X, King of France
1830	Revolution in Paris
1830-48	End of the Bourbon Restoration. Louis Philippe, King of France
1831-40	**Place de la Bastille built**
1839	**National Bank of Paris built**
1844-50	**Ste-Geneviève Library built**

11

NAPOLEON III'S PARIS
– THE CITY OF LIGHT

INTRODUCTION

After Louis Philippe, the 'Citizen King', had been deposed by the revolution of February 1848, a provisional government, dominated by a minority of socialists, took over. Its most prominent members included the reformer Louis Blanc, the historian and poet Lamartine, the republican advocate Ledru-Rollin and, representing the working class, Albert Martin who was customarily known as 'Albert'. But most importantly, the nephew of the Emperor Napoleon I, Louis Napoleon entered the centre of the political arena and in April ran for, and won, a seat in the Constituent Assembly elected to draft a new constitution.

Louis Napoleon had attempted to enter French politics for a number of years before his electoral victory. Encouraged by a Bonapartists movement that wanted to restore a Bonaparte to the throne, Louis Napoleon initiated a coup in Strasbourg in October 1836, but was arrested by local troops and escaped in exile in Switzerland and thence to England where he resided in London and Leamington Spa in 1838-39, and again in London to August 1840 where he travelled to Lille in the hope of conducting a more successful coup than hitherto, but again he met with failure and was subsequently imprisoned in a fortress in

Ham in the Somme *département*. He escaped yet again and returned to England where he stayed briefly in London and then for two years in Southport, Lancashire, until the political demise of the 'Citizen King' Louis Philippe enabled him to return safely to France and ultimately to participate legitimately in government.

Following his election to the National Assembly in April 1848, Louis Napoleon was far from satisfied with the events that ensued. To be sure, the introduction of manhood suffrage at a stroke increased the size of the electorate from 250,000 to close on 10 million – a realised dream for radicals, and that for the first time in history the entire male population of a major state was qualified to vote (84 percent did so in the April election) but this did not mean that progressive policies would be adopted by the newly constituted assembly. Through their superior organisation and propaganda, particularly in rural areas, conservative candidates won the day much to the great dissatisfaction of radicals.[1] On 22 June the assembly, against much external opposition, provocatively closed down the National Workshops that had been set up the previous February to provide employment for 80,000 workers. As many as 40,000 to 50,000 demonstrators consequently assembled in the Poissonnièr, Temple, St-Antoine, Marais, Quartier Latin and Montmartre working-class areas of Paris on 23 June to protest both against the move and the limited outcome of the revolution. Despite the erection of barricades, the demonstrations were brutally crushed by the 30,000 regular troops brought into Paris by train at the instigation of the Defence Minister, General Louis Eugène Cavaignac, causing the death of 914 soldiers and 1,435 protestors.[2] As a reflection of anti-socialist feeling in government, the assembly 'rewarded' Cavaignac by appointing him head of government. However, his moment of glory was short-lived.

LOUIS NAPOLEON AS PRESIDENT

On 10 December 1848, despite his poor skills as an orator, Louis Napoleon stood in the Presidential election and won a massive landslide victory against his main opponent Cavaignac by 74 percent to 19 percent of the vote. His platform was based on the restoration of order, strong government, social consolidation and national greatness and was supported by the Monarchist right, much of the aristocracy, and by a large portion of the industrial class because of Napoleon's progressive economic views. Above all, his overwhelming victory was due to the support of the biggest class in France: the peasants to whom the name of Bonaparte conjured up memories of Napoleon I who was credited with raising the nation to the pinnacle of military greatness and establishing social stability after the upheaval of the French Revolution. During his term as President, from 20 December 1848 to 2 December 1852, Louis Napoleon styled himself *Le Prince Président*.

Though Louis Napoleon owed a debt of gratitude to the monarchists for their support at the Presidential election, he recognised that their allegiance was ephemeral since they saw his government only as a half-way house to the restoration of either the House of Bourbon or House of Orléans. Therefore, during his first year in office he shrewdly chose his ministers from among the 'centre-right' Orléanist *Parti de l'Ordre*, and avoided conflict with the predominantly conservative assembly. The *Prince Président* also had to tread a tightrope in his dealings with the Catholic majority in the assembly. While he assisted the restoration of the Pope's temporal rule in Rome (formerly under the control of Mazzini), he also attempted to please secularist opinion in the assembly by peremptory demands on the Pope to introduce liberal changes to his government of the Papal States, a stance that antagonised the Catholic members of the assembly. In an attempt to ameliorate their hostility, Napoleon approved the *Loi Falloux* in 1851 which restored a greater role for the Catholic Church in the French educational system, a role abolished during the reign of Napoleon I.

The constitution of 1848 required future French presidents to stand down after four years in office, but by mid-term Louis Napoleon was concerned that this restriction on his presidency would prevent him from fully implementing his political and economic programme. The National Assembly, moreover, dominated by monarchists, not only wished to restore the Bourbon dynasty and refused to amend the Constitution in favour of longer presidential terms, but it also restricted universal male suffrage by imposing a 3-year residency requirement preventing a large proportion of the lower classes from voting. Louis Napoleon responded by breaking with the Assembly and surrounding himself with prominent figures loyal to him, such as Charles de Morney (Louis Napoleon's half-brother) and Jean-Gilbert Victor Fialin, secured the support of the army, toured the country seeking populist support and presented himself as the protector of universal male suffrage.

Helped financially by his mistress Harriet Howard, Louis Napoleon staged a *coup d'état*, arrested prominent opponents, and seized dictatorial powers on 2 December 1851, ironically the 47th anniversary of Napoleon I's crowning as Emperor. Approved by the French people in a referendum (by 7,500,000 votes to 640,000 with 1,500,000 abstentions) the coup alienated the reactionary elements in the Assembly. Subsequently, "A second plebiscite on 21-22 November 1852 approved the re-establishment of the hereditary empire . . . its constitution [being] based on that of the first empire, arrogating immense authority to the prince-president then the emperor."[3]

As Prince-President, Louis Napoleon set up a personal dictatorship. He had command of the army, made war and peace, appointed people to every conceivable post and ensured that justice was meted out in his name. Although universal male suffrage was re-established, the legislative body, whose members were elected, had only a consultative role. At election time, Napoleon proposed official candidates and gave them his full support. It was the Council of State which drafted laws. All public liberties were suspended. The freedom to meet, the freedom to associate and the freedom of the press no longer existed. Finally, the slide towards an Empire was completed with the senates-consult of 7 November proclaiming: "Louis Napoleon Bonaparte is Emperor of the French people under the name of Napoleon III".[4] For the very last time, Paris became a royal capital.

THE SECOND EMPIRE

By far the greatest legacy that France inherited from Napoleon III after his demise in 1870 was the modernisation of Paris. Together with the chief administrator of the city, George-Eugène Haussmann, he turned Paris into one of the greatest and most enchanting capitals in the world and all within an amazingly short period of twenty years. Accompanying this very great achievement was the resurgence of

France as a major player in international politics (a role that had greatly diminished after the demise of his illustrious uncle and during the dying years of the Bourbon dynasty). He also presided over economic matters that helped propel France into a new industrial age, while during the latter half of his reign – after a period of authoritarianism – he gradually introduced a raft of liberal measures designed to enhance social welfare. To generalise, it probably would have been politically inept for Napoleon to have rebuilt his capital at considerable expense, while at the same time allowing the international standing of France to deteriorate through the neglect of economic matters, foreign policy and political divisions at home. Alternatively, it would have been highly incongruous and politically hazardous to have embarked on economic development, a bold foreign policy and the settlement of political differences domestically while at the same time allowing both the medieval fabric of much of Paris and the welfare of its citizens to deteriorate further. Perhaps more than at any other time in history, the French monarch recognised that economic issues, foreign affairs, domestic politics and urban planning were inextricably linked.

ECONOMIC DEVELOPMENT IN MID-CENTURY PARIS

From 1840 to 1860, both the Parisian and national economy benefited from the development of the railways, the electric telegraph, the organisation of commerce, and the growth of the textile, metallurgical and engineering industries. In total, these developments "represented a transition from a civilisation based upon wood and water to one built upon coal and the steam engine as the primary sources of heat and energy."[5] Whereas the economy had grown slowly from 1815 to 1851, during the Second Empire (1852-70) the pace of industrialisation accelerated. There was a transport revolution, rapid urban growth and increased migration from the countryside and living standards improved.[6] The booming economy was lavishly celebrated by the Paris Exposition Universelle of 1855 held mainly in the Palais de l'Industrie on the Champs-Élysées. The palais, inspired by London's Crystal Palace erected four years earlier, was a Gallic example of how iron and glass could be used in the construction of a grandiose building, though it was not as impressive as its London equivalent and like the Crystal Palace, remained on its site only temporarily.

The increase in banking was no less important than the development of industry. The Paris Bourse became the biggest capital market on the continent, and mighty banking concerns like the Crédit Foncier were established, the latter designed to underwrite the emperor's vast building programme.[7] However, some of Napoleon's main backers were Saint-Simonians, who applauded him for being – in their view – a 'socialist emperor'. Saint-Simonians at this time founded a new type of business institution, the *Crédit Mobilier*, which sold stock to the public and then used the money raised to invest in industrial enterprises across France.

Napoleon's Empire has been said to be the first regime in France to give 'distinct priority to economic objectives.' Napoleon sought to advance his belief in free trade, cheap credit and the need to develop infrastructure as ways of ensuring progress and prosperity through government policy. Napoleon, as well as Haussmann and Jean-Gilbert-Victor Fialin (Minister of the Interior, 1852-4 and 1860-62) believed that the budget deficits that the state incurred due to high expenditure would be offset by future profits. As it turned out, the 1850s-60s were favourable for industrial expansion since the gold rushes in both California and Australia increased the European money supply. In the early years of the Empire, the economy also benefited from the coming of age of those born during the baby boom of the Restoration period. The steady rise of prices caused by the increase in the money supply encouraged company promotion and investment of capital. Rail mileage in France increased from 3,000 to 16,000 kilometres during the 1850s, and its growth allowed mines and factories to operate at higher production rates. The 90 kilometre short rail lines of France were merged into 6 major lines, while new iron steamships replaced wooden ships facilitating a substantial increase in maritime trade. Asian and East African markets and sources of food and materials became more accessible after the Suez Canal was constructed between 1856 and 1869 by the Compagnie Universelle du Canal Maritime de Suez and under the direction of Ferdinand de Lessops.

FOREIGN POLICY

Napoleon III's foreign policy was motivated by his ambition to make France, once again, a major world power. He not only attempted to strengthen France as a colonial power by making Senegal a French possession in the late 1840s, but also attempted to improve his country's standing in North Africa by adopting a liberal policy towards Algeria that allowed Algerian Muslims to migrate to France, granted French citizenship to Algerians if they accepted the French civil code, and gained favour with the majority of Algerians by restricting French settlement to their coastal zone. Under Napoleon's leadership, France also participated with some success in the Crimean War against Russia and in alliance with Britain and the Ottoman Empire (1854-6), a prelude to more interventionist policies from then on. Closer to home, he took France into a war in Italy 1859 to help the Italians expel the Austrians from Lombardy and Piedmont, and in return encouraged the Piedmontese prime minister, Cavour, to cede Savoy and Nice to France, adding quite substantially to the area of south-east France.

Though he had an ambition to intervene on the side of the Confederates during the American Civil War (1860-64), he recognised that this would not have been feasible without the assistance of Britain, but this was not forthcoming. Instead he intervened in Mexico since he was determined to stamp his mark on the politics of North America. Unfortunately for Napoleon, with French forces he supported the installation of the Austrian Archduke Maximillian as emperor of Mexico in 1863 but, together with the Mexican monarchists, Napoleon's troops were defeated by Republican forces under Benito Juárez and he consequently withdrew his troops from Mexico in 1866. Napoleon had also set his sights on furthering French interests in East Asia. His forces invaded Vietnam in 1861 in a successful attempt to open three ports for French trade, Cambodia became a French possession in 1863, and together with Britain waged an Opium War in China and forced the Chinese to concede more trading rights to the European allies. In addition, France sent a military mission to Japan in 1867 in support of the Shogun Tokugawa Yoshinobu, and sent troops to fight alongside the Shogun's army against Imperial forces during the Boshin war. But colonial and foreign policy should not be examined in isolation. It fulfilled just part of Napoleon's ambition to raise the status of France in world affairs. An accompanying and probably more important aim was to make Paris a truly world city, the most important capital city in the world and aesthetically a 'city of light', and in this he largely succeeded deploying, in turn, authoritarean and liberal administrations.

DOMESTIC POLICY

In the 1850s, Napoleon exercised supreme power in domestic policy with his ministers merely rubber-stamping his diktats. He repressed his political opponents and allied himself to clerical and reactionary forces, while his regime became dependent on aristocrats and bourgeois civil servants. Most of his ministers were ex-Orléanists, conservatives who believed that the cooperation of the upper classes was essential. He remained in power because of strong government, political stability and economic prosperity, his greatest supporters being urban property-owners and much of the rural population "who were attracted by the Bonaparte legend and the emperor's show of sympathy for the poor."[8] Nationally, the Second Empire was more popular than its predecessors as was demonstrated when government candidates received 80 percent of the votes cast at the 1857 election.

But with political stability, there were calls from liberals and republicans for the re-establishment of a parliamentary system "as a means by which they could participate more fully in political decision-making and protect their own vital interests."[9] But such calls were of no avail. Until about 1861, Napoleon's regime remained authoritarian by using press censorship, manipulating elections and depriving Parliament of the right to free debate or any real power.

URBAN POLICY

Economic growth, a strident and largely successful foreign policy, and the establishment of dictatorial powers at home encouraged Napoleon III to embark upon a policy of transforming Paris into one of the most magnificent cities in the world. His task was not easy. Whereas in 1851 only 3 percent of the French population (of 35.8 million) lived in the capital and its suburbs, by 1911 – when Napoleon's economy had matured – this had risen to as much as 10 percent (of 39.9 million), and over the same period the population of Paris rose from 1.74 to 3.9 million. But the economic structure of the city had become increasingly complex. Whereas in the early decades of the nineteenth century artisan forms of production had been dominant, subsequently heavy industry had developed, particularly engineering and chemicals on the northern and eastern outskirts, while central Paris – although continuing to shelter the artisanal trades – proved attractive to the development of administrative, financial and commercial activity that often squeezed-out lower-income households. Thus the cost of housing and continuing in-migration tended increasingly to force most low-wage earners to reside in the more peripheral *quartiers*, aided later by the development of suburban railways, trams, omnibuses and the Paris Metro.

It was against this background that Haussmann came to prominence in the early 1850s. Though his parents were from Alsace, he was born in Paris in 1800, educated at Collège Henri IV and subsequently studied law. He then pursued a career in the French civil service and rapidly became *sous préfet* of Nérac in 1830. After a successful career in the provinces, he was chosen by the Minister of the Interior Jean-Gilbert Victor Fialin in 1853 to be *préfet* of the Saone department, and together with Napoleon transformed Paris – still a largely medieval city – into a modern capital, Haussmann holding the post of chief administrator and planner until 1870. It is often claimed that Napoleon III had a considerable influence on Haussmann's achievements, but this view must be treated with a degree of scepticism. It is true that, during his repeated exiles in England in the 1830s-40s, he was undoubtedly impressed by a number of recently completed development schemes such as John Nash's 'Royal Mile' in the west end of London and Lord Street, a wide and elegant tree-lined avenue, 1.6 kilometres in length in Southport, Lancashire, but this did not necessarily mean that he considered it feasible to develop broadly similar thoroughfares in Paris. He hardly knew the French capital before he arrived there in 1848 to begin his rise to power, and therefore it is highly probable that the extensive development of thoroughfares across Paris is attributable to Haussmann who was very familiar with its built environment. If the thoroughfares were inspired by earlier development, this was more likely to have been the city's tree-lined Grand Boulevards, built two centuries earlier, rather than recent developments in England. However, Napoleon's fondness for St James's Park and other open spaces adjacent to his former London residences inspired the opening up of the Bois de Boulogne and Bois de Vincennes for public use, and being impressed by London's relatively modern sewage system, he ordered the redevelopment of the capital's very inadequate sewers in 1855, Haussmann extending the length of the total system to 600 kilometres by 1878.

HAUSSMANN'S PARIS: 1853-59

THE PLANNING OF THOROUGHFARES

When Haussmann took up his appointment as *préfet* of the Seine *département*, he not only became, as the chief administrative officer of Paris, Napoleon III's representative in the capital but he was also obliged to work either in close cooperation if possible, or by *diktat* if necessary, with the directly elected members of the twelve *arrondissements* (municipal authorities) and with those members of the *arrondissements* who were selected to sit on the Council of Paris located at the city's Hôtel de Ville. Whereas Haussmann was given considerable powers by Napoleon, particularly within the field of city planning and development, the *arrondissements* and the Council were concerned with more day-to-day matters such as local taxation and the provision of services such as street cleaning and local public utilities. However, with the rapid and uneven growth of Paris, it soon became clear that arrondissement boundaries enclosed areas with different populations and different amenities, while much of outer Paris was excluded from the capital's system of local government. Therefore, with the need to improve efficiency and extend representative government to a higher proportion of the Parisian population, twenty new *arrondissements* each with its local *mairie* (town hall), were designated throughout the capital replacing the original seven established in 1795 and adding a further thirteen. In Central Paris the boundaries of *arrondissements* 1-4 and 8-12 on the Right Bank and 5-7 on the Left Bank were redrawn, while the less densely built-up areas skirting the centre and extending out as far as the Thierre's fortifications of 1846 were now incorporated into *arrondissements* 16-20 on the Right Bank and 13-15 on the Left Bank.

Within this governmental context, Haussmann's plan for Paris comprised a wide range of initiatives ranging from the construction or re-structuring of boulevards, avenues, streets and bridges, the creation of *rond-points* (roundabouts), *places* and vistas, the imposition of regulations on the façades of buildings, to the provision of public parks and the building of water works and sewers. The French capital in the middle of the nineteenth century was in dire need of modernisation. With the exception of some notable buildings and public places developed from the late-sixteenth century to the early-nineteenth, the centre of Paris was very largely medieval with its cramped buildings and narrow alleys and streets, restricting the penetration of daylight, the flow of traffic and circulation of fresh air. Partly because its population density was as high as 100,000 persons/ km², and partly because of an inadequate system of water provision and sewage disposal, central Paris suffered disproportionately badly during the cholera epidemic of 1832 (which killed a total of 20,000 persons in Paris out of a total population of 650,000), but this was but one of the many outbreaks of disease that inflicted the population of the nation's capital after the 1789 Revolution.

It was, however, during the French Revolution that the need to restructure much of the physical fabric of Paris was first acknowledged. A 'Commission of Artists' was formed to advise on planning and development within the city. It suggested the widening of avenues across Paris and particularly the construction of a street from the Place de la Nation (known later as the Place de la Concorde) to the Louvre. Napoleon I subsequently embraced his recommendation and ordered the construction of the Rue de Rivoli that was to extend eastwards along the northern edge of the Jardin des Tuileries. By the late 1830s, the Préfet of the Département of the Seine, Claude-Philibert Barthelot, comte de Rambuteau, believing that the cholera epidemic of 1832 was an outcome of poor air circulation, proposed the cutting of 13 metre-wide streets through the centre of the city, but because of a shortage of funds, problems of land expropriation and the political upheaval of the period only succeeded in building one such street, the eponymous though somewhat diminutive Rue de Rambuteau that stretches west to east across the medieval core.

In appointing Haussmann as the new *préfet* of the Seine department in 1853, in succession to Jean Jacques Berger who was hesitant about incurring the vast costs involved in the redevelopment of Paris, Napoleon III knew that he found a man who could plan the large-scale reconstruction of Paris along the lines that he had envisaged when, from exile, he arrived in the French capital in 1848. However, Napoleon recognised that he also needed to employ other notable collaborators. Fialin, the Minister of the Interior, and the investment bankers Émile and Isaac Péreire were given responsibility for financial matters, Jean-Charles Alphand was commissioned to deal with the parks and plantations, while Paris Map Services were employed to ensure that geometry and graphic design determined the configuration of the new boulevards, avenues and streets, and to enforce newly formulated construction rules. The design of the buildings themselves was the responsibility of a host of architects including Théodore Ballu, Victor Baltard, Gabriel Davioud and Jacques Ignace Hittorff. Napoleon III almost certainly believed that only with a strong or even authoritarian regime, such as his own, would capitalists and professionals discount risk and be motivated to implement projects that would benefit society as a whole, including the poor.

THE FIRST NETWORK OF ROADS

Haussmann was fortunate to have taken up his appointment one year after a decree of 26 March 1852 had introduced new regulations regarding the reconstruction of the capital's thoroughfares. Henceforth, "property adjacent to the street and affected by [municipal] plans should also be subject to compulsory purchase and made available for development. This allowed chaotically complicated street- and house-plans to be almost surgically replaced by rectilinear roadways. It also permitted the construction of new buildings in replacements of what was torn down."[10] The city was also given powers to level streets, align buildings and regulate connections to the sewer, while owners of buildings were obliged to clean and, where necessary, repair and renovate the façades every ten years.

With finance assured and with the introduction of new regulations in 1852, Haussmann was able to take full advantage of the most authoritarian period of Napoleon III's rule to begin transforming much of Paris from a relic of a bygone era to a modern capital city of the industrial age. The early stages of his plan, based on the blueprint that the emperor had produced, called for the reconstruction of the centre of the old city from the inside out. This initially required the development of two great axes, a new North-South routeway from the Boulevard de Sebastopol (begun in 1854) on the Right Bank to the Boulevard St-Michel (1855) on the Left (the two boulevards later connected to each other by the Boulevard du Palais on the Île de Cité in 1858), and a West-East thoroughfare formed by Napoleon I's Rue de Rivoli being extended from the Tuileries to the ancient Rue St Antoine (by 1859), completing the much longer axial roadway from the Arc de Triomphe to the Place de la Bastille and beyond. The focal point of the whole scheme was Place du Châtelet, the centre of the *grande croisée* where the north-south and west-east thoroughfares intersected. Haussmann relentlessly implemented this scheme in the face of much opposition from critics who, although supportive of a west-east routeway, argued that "Paris had perfectly serviceable north-south arteries, namely the Rues St-Denis and St-Martin on the Right Bank and Rue St-Jacques on the Left."[11]

Though Parisians "endured years of flying dust, noise and falling plaster and beams"[12], they witnessed the transformation of the fabric of central Paris by the construction or deconstruction of boulevards, avenues and streets to ensure a better circulation of air around the capital and ostensibly to enhance hygiene; to improve communications to the benefit of commercial development; and to produce a capital city worthy of a great power. On the Right Bank, a major project involved the redevelopment of the *Grands Boulevards*, a ribbon of tree-lined thoroughfares established during the reign of Louis XIV along the extent of the demolished Charles V wall of the late-fourteenth century that had outlived its defensive role. Thus across the pre-1870 *arrondissements* of 1, 2, 3, 5, 6 and 8, Haussmann began to redevelop the boulevards Madeleine, Capucine, des Italiens, Monmartre, Poisonniers, Bonne Nouvelle, St-Martin, Temple, Filles-du Calvaire and Beaumarchais.

112   *Boulevard Sebastopol, 1854*

Also on the Right Bank, across the pre-1870 *arrondissements* 1-9, Haussmann carved through more recent areas of Paris as well as much of the old city by the construction of new carriageways, notably the Boulevard Strasbourg (started in 1852), followed by boulevards Diderot (1853), Pereire (1853), Sebastopol (1854), Magenta (1855), Haussmann (1857), Prince Eugène (now Voltaire)(1857) and Lenoir (1859); the avenues Carnot (started 1854), l'Impératrice (now Foch) (1854), Essling (now MacMahon)(1854), Malakoff (1854), Wagram (1854), D. Iena (1858), Victoria (1858) and Daumesnil (1859); and by the Rues de LaFayette (started 1823 but improved in the 1850s). Rivoli (extended 1852-59, St-Antoine (extended 1854-59), Reaumur (1854), Turbigo (1854) and Étienne Marcel (1858).

On the Left Bank, across the pre-1860 *arrondissements* 10-12, the lengthy and imposing Boulevard du Montparnasse (begun in 1768) pre-dated Haussmann's thoroughfares, namely his boulevards St-Germain (1852), St-Michel (1855), Arago (1857) and St-Marcel (1860), his extension to the Avenue Gobelins (begun in 1850); and his rues de Rennes (1853), des Écoles (1852 and 1855), and Monge (1859).

Not only did railways disgorge their passengers close to the centre of Paris but also provided a speedy transport mode to other areas of

113   *Gare de l'Est, 1849-54 (reconstructed 1885 and 1900)*

114   *Gare St-Lazare, 1837-54*

France. Since Paris was at the heart of the national railway network, train passengers needed to travel to the capital if their journeys were from one provincial region to another. Haussmann therefore realised that it was necessary not only to provide easy access from the capital's rail terminals to the centre of the city but also, wherever possible, from one terminal to another. Haussmann therefore recognised that railway termini as well as circuses, hexagons and other open spaces could also act as hubs of boulevard development.

Thus on the Right Bank, the Embarcadère de Belgique (completed 1846), accommodating rail services to and from Lille, was not only connected to central Paris by the Boulevards de Magenta, Strasbourg and Sebastopol, but was also conveniently close to the Gare de l'Est (1849 and 1854) which, apart from being linked to the capital's centre by the Boulevards de Strasbourg and Sebastopol, ran rail services to and from Strasbourg and Mulhouse. To the west, the Gare St-Lazare (1837

115   *Gare du Lyon, 1849-55 (reconstructed 1900)*

and 1854), with services to and from Normandy, was connected both to central Paris by the Boulevard Haussmann and a succession of other boulevards to the Boulevard de Sebastopol and the *grande croisée* at the centre of Paris, and to the Embarcadère de Belgique and Gare d l'Est by the Rue LaFayette. To the south-east, the Gare du Lyon (1849 and 1855), with services to and from Dijon, Lyon and eventually Marseilles, was connected to the Place de Bastille by the newly constructed Rue de Lyon and thence either by way of the Rue St-Antoine and Rue de Rivoli to the *grande croisée* or via the Boulevards Beaumarchais, Filles du Calvaire and Temple to the Place de la République and thence to the Gare de l'Est and Gare du Nord.

On the Left Bank, the Gare Montparnasse (1840), with its rail services to and from cities such as Tours, Bordeaux, Rennes, is not directly connected at street level to other Parisian rail terminals, but is partly linked to central Paris by the Rue de Rennes, though this particular street (contrary to Haussmann's intentions) was never extended north of St-Germain de Pres, only 600 metres south of the Seine.

SOME PROMINENT BUILDINGS: 1848-58

Extensive residential development across much of Paris was accompanied by the construction of a number of individual buildings of diverse uses both during the Second Republic and Napoleon's subsequent authoritarian years. The first two developments were train stations, built on the outer edge of central Paris. Located on the Left Bank in arrondissement 15, the Gare de l'Ouest of 1840 was transformed into the Gare Montparnesse in 1848-52 and henceforth provided services to the west and south-west of France. From its completion in 1849 the Gare d l'Est, on the Right Bank in arrondissement 10, began to provide a rail service to Strasbourg and by 1854 the line was extended to Mulhouse. After a number of years of construction, in accordance to a design by François Duquesnay, its main hall provides a testimony to emerging steel and glass architecture of the age.

However, during his early years as emperor, Napoleon III was not content with improving public transportation in and out of his capital, he also wished to provide a new venue for public entertainment. He

116 *Winter Circus, 1852*

therefore commissioned Jacob Ignaz Hittorff to construct a heated circus as a gift to French citizens. Completed in 1852, the twenty-sided Winter Circus – whose interior dimensions were 48 metres in diameter and 28 metres in height, accommodated 6,000 spectators. Its exterior was equally impressive, but in terms of its decoration rather than its capacity. Its richly coloured "foundation is really a plinth supporting columns, which in turn bear the light roof. Decorations include amazons (by James Pradier) near the entrance, figured relief bars with scenes of mythological horses, a line of windows and beams."[13]

By 1853, and partly because of the influence of the design of the Gare de l'Est, iron and glass construction became the vogue although there was still some opposition to the use of these materials. In producing plans for the reconstruction of Les Halles Central, the capital's principle food markets (or the 'Belly of Paris' as it was coined by Émile Zola in his novel, *Le Ventre de Paris*), Victor Baltard (1805-74), City Architect of Paris, at first proposed a fortress-like stone-built market. But Haussmann had other ideas and accepting the advice of the engineer Hector Horeau persuaded Baltard to construct "six individual structures with large glass windows and partly glazed roofs"[14], a structure that was fit for purpose until it was demolished in 1971.

117   *Les Halles, 1852*

Early in the Second Empire, work began on the largest commission in nineteenth-century France, the completion of the Louvre at an eventual cost of two million francs. Initiated by Napoleon III in 1852, building work began under the direction of the architect L.T.J. Visconti in collaboration with Hector Martin Lefuel from 1854. Essentially, the task of the architects was to extend the Louvre towards the Tuileries mainly by means of six new sumptuous blocks, the Pavilions Mollien, Denon and Daru on the southern side of the contemporary Cour Napoleon, and the Pavilions Turgot, Richelieu and Colbert on the northern side together with the Pavilion Bibliothèque flanking the Rue de Tivoli. Napoleon's aim was to turn the Louvre "into the greatest palace in the world, larger even than Philip II's sombre vast pile of the Escorial,"[15] and in this he succeeded.

Designed in a mixed Renaissance and Baroque style, the high pavilion roofs and richly sculptured surfaces of the Louvre "set an influential pattern in France and the United States".[16] At the same time that the palace was being completed, the Orangerie (originally built by André Le Nôtre in 1664) was reconstructed under the supervision of the architects Pascal Cribier and Louis Bénech. Located at the western

118   *Pavilions Turgot, Richelieu and Colbert at the Louvre, begun 1854*

end of the Jardin des Tuileries, it looked onto the Place de la Concorde to the west and the Seine to the south.

As with train stations and market halls, iron and glass also became the principal materials in the construction of churches. Initially funded by Marie-Dominique-Auguste, the Archbishop of Paris, St-Eugène-St-Cécile is the first of several churches to be built during the Second Empire. Located on the north-western fringe of the centre in arrondissement 9 and built in 1854-5 as the parish church of the Faubourg Poissonnière, it was designed by the architect Louis Auguste Boileau working in collaboration with engineer Louis Adrien Lusson. Though externally the building appears to be a quite ordinary rectangular neo-Gothic box (950 x 20m), its interior is essentially a "three-aisled basilica, with four 23 metre-high double bays (rounded windows and 6 ribbed vaults), 4-part vaulting in the side aisles, continuous chapels with low roofs beneath elevations with pointed barrel vaulting, and three polygonal apses."[17] Built in only 20 months, the church is the first in France to have a largely cast and wrought iron structure, except for its main walls which are built of masonry. Its metallic content not only reduced the costs of construction but enabled its internal columns and walls to be thinner thereby providing a sense of spaciousness and facilitating the penetration of external light, while externally eliminating the need for flying buttresses. However, because of the ecclesiastical financial difficulties, the City of Paris purchased the building on 28 April 1859 to ensure its proper maintenance. But this did not stop iron and glass being used in the construction of Parisian churches in the 1860s (see below).

During the Second Empire comparative few *hôtels particuliers* were constructed in Paris, the period not being one in which the affluent wished to flaunt their wealth or position in society. However, an exception was the Hôtel Païva, a refined mansion built in a mixed Franco-Italian style in 1856-66 "with a forecourt [that] once accommodated [the] famous soirees of the Marquise Païva y Araujo, a beautiful courtesan.[18] Since 1904 the building has housed the Travellers' Club.

In the heart of Paris, in *arrondissement* 1 on the Île de Cité, the Palais de Justice (built 1857-68) majestically occupies part of the site of the former royal palace of St-Louis and is adjacent to the Sainte Chapelle. The rest of the site contains, parallel to the Seine, the ancient structure of the Conciergerie. Since medieval times the royal palace had dispensed justice, and from the sixteenth century to the French

119   *Palais de Justice, 1857-68*

Revolution, the palace was the seat of the Parlement of Paris (the city's high court). Designed by Joseph-Louis Duc and Honoré Daumet, the Palais de Justice of the Second Empire boasts a monumental east-facing façade with a massive stepped four-columned portico surmounted by an oval dome and much of the exterior exhibits sculptural work by Jean-Marie Bonnassieux.

Located in the Bibliothèque National on the centrally-located Rue de Richelieu in arrondissement 2, the spacious rectangular reading room designed by Henri Labrouste is "one of the most important early achievements in iron architecture[19] and presents a synthesis between engineering and architect."[20] Built between 1858-68, it seats 259 readers and its notable attributes include extradas, terracotta clad cupolas supported by 16 fine cast iron columns, a glass partition between reading rooms and the book stacks.

THE DOMESTIC POLITICS OF LIBERALISM: 1860-70

By 1860 it was apparent that Napoleon III, unlike his uncle 50 or more years earlier, was not going to prolong the life of an authoritarian form of government. Instead, he gradually created a constitutional regime that was less dependent on himself as head of state, and more dependent on *parlement*. By a decree of 24 November 1860, the *Corps legislative* was granted the right to debate Napoleon's address from the throne at the beginning of each parliamentary session; and when appropriate to nominate ministers without portfolio to explain, debate and defend government policy before the elected assembly. With anxiety about the escalating national debt, Napoleon granted *parlement* greater control over the budget in December 1861, "a vital means of enhancing the influence of the representative assembly."[21] Throughout the decade, the press was also given greater freedom to hold the government to account.

Napoleon was also anxious to reconcile the stance of liberals and republicans towards his regime. However, there were major differences of view concerning the 1860 commercial treaty with Britain designed to intensify competitive pressures and to force the pace of modernisation; an alliance with Piedmont against Austria in support of a 'Europe of the nationalities'; a loosening of the alliance between Church and state established during the Second Republic to further the development of mass primary education as a means of social control; the enhanced role of *parlement*; and the legislation of strikes; and an amnesty for republicans.[22] There was manifestly concern among liberals about the economic dislocation which might result from free trade and especially its impact on agricultural prices and on the metallurgical and textile industries, while clerics were anxious about the threat posed by Italian nationalism to the papacy's temporal power, and it was not altogether surprising that both liberals and clerics demanded greater parliamentary control to protect the interests of farmers, industrialists and the custodian of the Papal States.[23]

It was evident that by the early 1860s Napoleon had failed to engineer a national reconciliation between himself, the Republicans and the Liberals. To counteract this *denouement*, he "began by taking initiatives in the social field [by attempting] to modernise and develop the education system. The Emperor also tried to win the confidence of the working classes by granting the workers the right to strike in 1864. This daring 'social' policy met with little success and caused very few to rally to the Emperor."[24]

Not gaining the support from the Republicans and Liberals that he thought he deserved, he looked elsewhere for support. Conciliatory overtures were made to workers through a discussion group established in 1861 by the emperor's nephew, the republican prince Napoleon-Jérôme in 1861. It dispatched a workers' delegation to the London International Exposition in 1862 which led indirectly to the legalisation of strikes in 1864 and a growing toleration towards illegal union activity. After the elections of May 1863, an extremely heterogeneous but increasingly effective parliamentary opposition was formed with the aim of defending the interests of the Church, while ignoring Bourbon supporters, irreconcilable Orléanist notables, and independent liberals and republicans. Although only thirty-two outright opponents of the regime were successful at the polls, they combined with some of the liberal dissidents to constitute a Third Party.[25] This decisively changed the political context. Acts of political opposition now became far less risky than hitherto, and renewed prosperity was – as in 1855 – again flaunted by an international exhibition, the Great Exposition of 1867 held on the Champs de Mars where Napoleon I had paraded his troops before departing to Waterloo, and close to where the Eiffel Tower stands today. In 1868, a law partly re-established the freedom of the press, and immediately there was a spectacular revival of newspapers and political meetings, most of them hostile to the government. The circulation of Parisian newspapers which had been around 50,000 in 1830 rose to over 700,000 in 1869 reflecting rising literacy and falling production costs as well as the political situation. Interest in politics was being renewed, bringing to an end the widespread indifference of the previous two decades.[26] In a plebiscite of 8 May 1870, 7,350,000 votes resoundly approved the liberal reforms that had been introduced since 1860, compared with only 1,538,000 who disapproved and 1,900,000 who abstained. This suggested that nationwide voters believed that the liberal empire offered both greater political liberty, order and prosperity. However, in Paris 59 percent of the votes were negative and in its predominantly worker *arrondissements* of the north east over 70 percent of voters were disenchanted with the reforms, almost certainly since they gained little or nothing from Napoleon's policies.[27]

HAUSSMANN'S PARIS, 1859-70

Paris is often called 'The City of Light' (*La Ville Lumière*) not only because of its leading role during the Age of Enlightenment – including its adoption of neo-classical architecture – but because of the effects of Haussmann's improvements to the built environment of the French capital. During the 1860s, Paris became one of the first cities in the world to adopt gas lighting, its streets and monuments being illuminated by 56,000 gas lamps, but during day-light, the inner *arrondissements* lost much of their medieval squalor and many of their dark and gloomy streets as an outcome of Haussmann's road programmes.

Haussmann introduced new regulations in 1859 that were to prove particularly influential in determining the future physical fabric of Paris. With the aim of improving health and enhancing townscape, a lighting-angle of 45 degrees was established so that on streets wider than 20 metres "a maximum height of 20 metres was now permitted, allowing the insertion of another storey to provide six or seven floors."[28] In addition, the ground floor and basement of each residential block was to be parallel to the street and encased within thick load-bearing walls; the mezzanine floor would have low ceilings; the *l'étage noble* (second floor) would be balconied; the third and fourth floors would be in the same style though with less decorative stonework and might not have balconies; the fifth floor would have a continuously undecorated balcony; and the very top floor would accommodate garret rooms with dormer windows. Each block or succession of blocks was designed as a homogeneous whole, providing a unified townscape over much of central Paris. Fairly uniform façades, where cornices and balconies are perfectly aligned, are further outcomes of the 1859 regulations, and so to – though indirectly – was the use of massive stone blocks instead of stone cladding, a practice facilitated by stone-sawing and the introduction of rail transportation.

Remarkably, to this day, very few buildings across the *arrondissements* of Paris are more than 20 metres in height, not least along the boulevards. High buildings, of course, require deep foundations to support their weight, but building work of this sort has been impracticable since as many as 650 kilometres of tunnels had been dug over the centuries just below street level to facilitate the mining of limestone, sand, clay and other minerals and from the late eighteenth century Parisians used many of the tunnels as catacombs to reduce the pressure on the city's cemeteries. The inhabitants of Haussmann's Paris were of course fully aware of the impact of these tunnels on street development since there had been several disasters in the past when rows of buildings collapsed into a subterranean void.

Until 1859, the larger apartment blocks (albeit no more than seven floors in height) normally accommodated a cross section of society, "shops on the ground floor, their owners on the first, the rich bourgeoisie on the second, lower middle classes on the third and fourth, workers on the fifth, and servants, students and the miscellaneous poor on the top."[29] However, in the 1860s and beyond, whole areas became gentrified and, although apartment blocks still accommodated shops and other businesses on the ground floor, most of the other floors housed well-off middle class people with the top floor providing *chambers de bonne* or maids rooms. A further effect of the gentrification was that "because of rocketing ground values, deep sites were avoided which meant that, unlike housing in Victorian London, Haussmann's apartments had few gardens, the streets few leafy squares."[30] This might partly explain why a 'café society' developed in the central residential streets of Paris and not in London, with cultural ramifications unique to the French capital. Poorer households, meanwhile, were increasingly displaced from their homes and familiar surroundings and sought housing in the new slums and ghettos on the fringes of Paris.

Whereas many of the new carriageways developed in the 1850s cut through the built-up areas of old Paris, during the subsequent ten years, most of the new thoroughfares stretched outwards across the newly established *arrondissements* where existing housing densities were markedly lower than in the centre of the capital. New and, to an extent, more flexible regulations were introduced in 1859 to control the dimensions of buildings and to enhance the aesthetic aspects of their frontages (see below). Under these regulations development proceeded apace. On the Right Bank work that had commenced in the 1850s was continued well into the late nineteenth century and beyond, while in the 1860s Haussmann oversaw the development of boulevards Malesherbes located in *arrondissements* 8 and 17, Clichy in 9 and 18, Rochechouart in 9, de la Chapelle in 19 and 18, de Belleville in 19 and 20, and Barbes and Ornano in 18. Only Boulevard Henry IV is centrally-located in *arrondissement* 4. Newly-developed avenues on the Right Bank also tend to be located on the edge of central Paris. For example, Avenue Beaujon (now Avenue Friedland) is in *arrondissement* 8 while Avenue Kleber is in 16. Likewise Rue Faubourg – St-Antoine is on the periphery, in *arrondissement* 12.

On the Left Bank, apart from continuing work in the inner *arrondissements*, it is again the fringe areas of Paris that provide the locations for the new thoroughfares of the 1860s, The Boulevards Raspail is located in *arrondissement* 6 and 14, and the boulevard de Grenelle is in *arrondissement* 15, Massena and Kellermann are both in 13 and Jourdan is in 14. Avenue de l'Observatoire extends outward from *arrondissements* 5 and 6 to *arrondissement* 13, whilst the Rue Gay-Lussac, located in *arrondissement* 5, occupies a fairly central location.

Over the whole period of Haussmann's role as chief administrative officer of Paris, 1853-70, the total length of the city's streets doubled from 424 to 850km, while major improvements were made to the surfacing of new thoroughfares enhancing the mobility of pedestrians and horse-drawn vehicles across the capital.[31] Cobble stones were eschewed since these could be easily ripped up by street protesters, sandstone was known to crumble, tar macadam was muddy and smelly when wet and dusty when dry, and asphalt by itself was slippery. However, when mixed with small stones, asphalt was problem-free and was selected by Haussmann when surfacing began to increase in momentum in 1867.[32]

HUBS, PLACES, VISTAS AND BRIDGES

One very notable aspect of planning in Paris in the 1850s was that, with the duel aims of easing the traffic flow and enhancing townscape, Haussmann ensured that when appropriate, both new and existing carriageways would focus on, or stem from, newly developed or adapted *ronds points* (roundabouts or circuses), like the spokes of a wheel attached to a hub. Most but not all of his hubs were constructed on the Right Bank. Without them, new and improved carriageways would have crossed each other at hazardous and unsightly intersections. Some attention was also paid to clearing congested areas to provide public spaces, and creating boulevard vistas in an attempt to provide unrestricted views of notable buildings or monuments across the centre of Paris.

The most famous of all hubs in Paris is the Place de L'Étoile (now the Place Charles de Gaulle) with the Arc de Triomphe, completed in 1836, at its centre. Located on the western edge of the old city, the star-shaped *cirque* (circus) dating from 1777 initially provided a hub for five thoroughfares (see Appendix 3) but from the 1850s-60s a further seven were constructed by Haussmann, in clockwise sequence the Avenue d'Essling (now Avenue MacMahon), the Boulevard de l'Étoile (now Avenue Wagram), Avenue Joséphine (now Avenue Marceau), the Avenue l'Iena, the Avenue Roi de Rome (the Avenue Kleber), the Avenue l'Impératrice (the Avenue Foch) and Avenue Carnot.

Dating from July 1789, following the storming and subsequent demolition of the Bastille prison and the clearance of rubble, the *place* was laid out as a hexagon. The aptly named Place de la Bastille eventually became the main traffic hub on the eastern edge of the old city from which no fewer than nine carriageways were built anew or redeveloped, mostly by Haussmann. Radiating from the *place* are the Boulevard Beaumarchais, the Boulevard Richard Lenoir, the Rue de Roquette, the Rue du Faubourg St-Antoine, the Rue de Lyon leading into the Avenue Daumesnil, the Boulevard de la Bastille, the Boulevard Bourdon, the Boulevard Henri IV and the Rue St-Antoine. Situated in the centre of the hexagon, the Colonne de Juillet (the July Column) erected in 1840 commemorates the victims of the *Trots Glorieues* (three days of street fighting) of July 1830.[33]

Initially laid-out as the Place de la Trône-Renvensé in 1792, the Place de la Nation as it has been known since 1880 is located some 1.9 metres east of the Place de Bastille, and as a *cirque* is the hub to five principal carriageways developed or redeveloped by Haussmann: the Avenue Philippe Auguste, the Avenue Trône, Avenue du Bel Air, Boulevard Diderot, the Faubourg St-Antoine and the Boulevard Prince Eugene (later renamed Boulevard Voltaire). Immediately east of the *cirque* are two pavilions built in 1788 each acting as a plinth for two Doric columns 30.5m high, one for a statue of Philippe Auguste and the other of Louis IV.[34]

The Place de Châtelet fortress, a stronghold constructed at the northern end of the Pont du Change in 1130 that soon became both the offices of the prévôt of Paris and a number of prisons. However, by the beginning of the nineteenth century, the area abutting the northern edge of the fortress had become dangerously notorious as a centre of crime, and therefore under Napoleon I the Grand Châtelet was demolished in 1802-10 and its site and northern peripheral was cleared and redeveloped as the Place de Châtelet. Since the mid-nineteenth century, it has often been thought that the small square-shaped Place de Châtelet provides a major crossing point for the north-south Boulevard de Sebastopol and the west-east Rue de Rivoli, the latter carriageway by-passes the square some 50m to the north. What in fact leads into the square from the west and east is the Avenue Victoria while the Boulevard Sebastopol reaches its most southerly point on the northern edge of the square while the north-south carriageway continues southwards over the Pont du Change and onwards as the Boulevard du Palais on the Île de Cité.

Located on the site of the medieval Porte du Temple, the Place de Château d'Eau (known as the Place de la République since 1879) was laid out in 1856-65 by Haussmann, and as a lengthy rectangle, it is the hub of seven principal thoroughfares: the Boulevard de Magenta, the Rue de Faubourg de Temple, the Avenue de la Republique, the Boulevard Prince Eugene (now Boulevard Voltaire), the Boulevard de Temple, the Rue de Temple and the Boulevard St-Martin. The centre of the *place* is adorned by the 25m high *Monument de la République* erected in 1883.

The Place de l'Opera, to the north west of the old city, was the last of Haussmann's hubs. Laid out in the 1860s, the rectangular-shaped *place* is connected to the Rue Auber, the Rue Halevy, the Boulevard des Capucines (which cuts through the *place*), the Rue du Quatre Septembre, the Avenue de l'Opera and the Rue de la Paix. Because of the magnificent façade of l'Opera Garnier across its northern edge of the place, there was little need to build a statue, monument or fountain in the hub itself. Such an aesthetic gesture would have paled into insignificance.

There are only two notable hubs on the Left Bank. Most notable is the Place de Italie, built to the south-east of the old city in 1850. Like the Place de L'Étoile and Place de la Nation, the Place de Italie is a *cirque* and it acts as a hub for six main carriageways built under the direction of Haussmann, namely: the Boulevard Auguste Blanqui, the Boulevard de la Gare (now the Boulevard Vincent Auriol), the Boulevard d l'Hôpital, the Avenue de Choisy, the Avenue des Gobelins and the Avenue d'Italie. Unlike the principal *places* of the Right Bank, the Place de Italie is not adorned by a column or statue. There is also the Place d'Enfer, a rectangular node now known as the Place Denfert-Rochereau. Located to the south of central Paris in 1863, its spokes comprise the Boulevard Raspail, the Avenue Denfert-Rochereau, the Boulevards Arago and St-Jacques, the Avenue Montsouris (now the Avenue René Coty) and Avenue d'Orléans (now the Avenue General Leclerc), and the Rue Protovaux.

As with the provision of new carriageways and hubs, Haussmann recognised that the decongestion of certain central areas was also an important aim of urban development. Thus under his direction, by 1870 the Île de la Cité was transformed from an overcrowded and rundown residential area into an administrative zone with its population falling from 15,000 to 5,000 during the 1860s. Most housing on the island had been demolished, while Notre Dame, the Sainte-Chapelle and the Palais de Justice were left intact. The medieval Hôtel-Dieu on the south side of the Île de la Cité was demolished and relocated in a much larger building on the north side, while the Parvis de Notre Dame abutting the west front of the cathedral was cleared of slum housing and greatly increased in size. On a completely different scale and occupying a small garden square off the Rue de Rivoli between the Place de Châtelet and Hôtel de Ville, the medieval tower of what remained of St-Jacques-de-la-Boucherie was renovated to provide a place of tranquillity in an otherwise busy part of the capital.

Haussmann was also interested in creating vistas, of which five were particularly notable. First, in 1858 the Fontaine du Palmier with its obelisk in the Place du Châtelet was shifted 12m to the west of its original site so that it would now be in the centre of the redeveloped square and visible southward from the Boulevard de Sebastopol; second between 1860-71 the Italo-Byzantine church of St-Augustin was constructed by its architect Victor Baltard on an awkward triangular plot so as to provide a focal point of interest north-westward from the southern end of the Boulevard Malesherbes; third by 1866 a vista was opened up from the Place de Bastille and the Boulevard Henri IV south-westward to the Pantheon but this eventually necessitated building two new bridges in 1875 – the Ponts du Sully – obliquely across the Seine at the Île St-Louis, and the construction of a junction with the Boulevard St-Germain and finally, while l'Opera Garnier provides an impressive vista in terms of its scale, the view of the building from the south loses some of its majesty by being overshadowed by the insistent perspective of the six and seven storey apartment blocks on either side of the Avenue de l'Opera.[35]

SOME PROMINENT BUILDINGS OF THE 1860S

As if to tidy up the southern end of the Boulevard Sebastopol, Haussmann commissioned the construction of the Théâtre de Châtelet and the Théâtre de Ville to respectively demarcate the western and eastern edges of the Place du Châtelet. The former theatre, the largest of the two, was built in 1860-2, and the latter was completed ten years later. Both are typically mid-nineteenth century buildings "with their balconies and arched windows, [and] are almost indistinguishable except for the differences in their size and decoration."[36] In their early years, they staged mainly operettas, particularly by Offenbach.

On the Île de la Cité and looking onto the Boulevard du Palais to the east and the Seine to the south, the Tribunal de Commerce was one of Haussmann's projects to facilitate government. Designed by Antoine-Nicholas Bailly and constructed in 1860-5, this building with its immense staircase and dome was constructed to accommodate the administrative trade courts, though it is interesting to note that the dome which was initial situated in the centre of the building was reconstructed near its east end to align with the new Boulevard Sebastopol to the north.

During the 1860s, Haussmann presided over the construction of a number of remarkable churches within his newly laid-out pattern of boulevards. Located in the Place St-Augustin midway along the Boulevard Malesherbes, the enormous church of St-Augustin epitomises the mood of the Second Empire by exhibiting a mélange

120   *Théâtre de Chatelet, 1860-2*

121   *Théâtre de Ville, 1870-2*

122   *Tribune de Commerce, 1857-68*

of styles – Gothic, Romanesque, Byzantine and French Renaissance. Designed by Victor Baltard, the architect of the iron-and-glass Les Halles market pavilions, St-Augustin is the second church in Paris to use this mode of construction. Despite being 100 metres in length, the building had to be squeezed into a narrow plot of land, necessitating the elimination of braces and flying buttresses and requiring the positioning of its huge 80 metres dome above the altar. St-Augustin's façade displays the four evangelists above its three entry doors, and higher still there is a frieze showing Christ and the twelve apostles, surmounted by a rosette window. The church almost inevitably provokes some criticism since its altar faced north-westward whilst its main entrance faces south-westward, contrary to the normal Christian practice of locating the altar at the eastern end of a church and the entrance at the western end.

Like the church of St-Augustin, the Église de la Trinité built by Théodore Ballu in the style of the sixteenth century Parisian church of St-Eustace, part neo-Gothic and part French Renaissance. Built in 1861-67, Ballu's new parish church has a monumental porch with three openings, three statues personifying Faith, Hope and Charity and a 65

123   *Church of St-Augustin, 1860-71*

metre-high central tower. Its interior is 90 metres long and is 30 metres high, and has 4 double bays flanked by narrow side rows and chapels, barrel vaulting and a raised choir above the crypt with a colonnade and polygonal apses.[37]

Also begun in 1861 but not completed until 1874, the Église St-François Xavier is situated on the Boulevard Invalides at an angle pointing toward a planned thoroughfare which would have gone through the Left Bank in a straight line to join the River Seine at the Pont de Carousel. But since the thoroughfare was never built, the

124   *Église St-François Xavier, 1861-74*

church looks incongruous. Designed by Adrien Lusson, and finished long after his death in 1864 by Joseph Uchard who undertook a design change, the church exhibits a mixture of styles: Classical for the nave and French Renaissance for the façade which is similar to the Trinité church. It features a central section flanked by two square towers, and has five aisles, a transept, a triple-aisle choir with elevations, chapel rows and apses. Since its shell is iron framed, the vault directly rests upon the lateral walls, without side aisles or flying buttresses. Some critics argue that from the outside, the church might just be the ugliest in Paris, but although this view is inevitably controversial, a legitimate criticism is that the church lies along a south-west, north-east, axis with the altar at the south-west extremity of the building and the entrance at north-east end, and like the church of St-Augustin, flies in the face of traditional Christian practice.

After a succession of churches, Haussmann presided over the development of a number of notable secular buildings. The first of these, commissioned by Napoleon III in 1861, was the Jeu de Paume. It is located opposite the Orangerie at the western end of the Jardins des Tuileries and looks onto the Place de la Concorde to the west and Rue

125   *Jeu de Paume, Jardin des Tuileries, 1861*

de Rivoli to the north. Used initially as a court for playing the ancient sport of real tennis, it was later reclaimed by the state and subsequently used as an exhibition hall and an art gallery. But the construction of the Jeu de Paume was but a small scale activity. Much larger and imposing secular buildings were to come. One of the most spectacular of these was the Gare du Nord in the 10th *arrondissement*. Funded by the chairman of the Chemin de Fer du Nord railway company, James Mayer de Rothschild in 1857, designed by Jakob Ignaz Hittorff and constructed in 1861-5, the new train station replaced the old Embarcadère de Belgique built in 1846 which in size and facilities had not kept pace with the increase in rail travel (the original station's façade was removed and transferred to Lille). Constructed of large slabs of stone with an ample use of glass, the new station's 180 metre long façade is dominated by a centrally-positioned triumphal arch encased by double Ionic pilasters, and each flank of the façade consists of a corner pavilion similarly arched. To indicate the extent to which the station is of international and national importance, the whole façade is decorated with the statues of nine European cities, as well as 12 northern French destinations. The interior of the station is no less impressive. It consists of a large hall of metal and glass, 200 metres in length and 70 metres wide, and is supported by two rows of cast iron columns 38 metres in height. [38]

Within a year of building work starting on the Gare du Nord, Haussmann oversaw the construction of the Préfecture de Police in 1862-5. Like the Tribunal de Commerce, it was built on the Île de la Cité (1862-65) but looked westward onto the Boulevard de Palais. Until 1879, the prefecture contained two barracks, but thereafter it had four blocks surrounding a central court. The police headquarters marked the end of Haussmann's massive reconstruction plan to turn most of the Île de Cité into an administrative centre for the city of Paris.[39]

To a large extent, Napoleon III regarded the development of buildings to promulgate the arts as a means of glorifying his reign, and possibly of equal importance to constructing imposing public places and administrative buildings. However, what inspired Napoleon to embark on the development of the enormous purpose-built opera house was, in a sense, fortuitous. The idea was born after he had just escaped an assassination attempt in front of the opera's former home (see below).

126 *Gare du Nord, 1861-5*

In response, Haussmann held a competition to design an opera house for central Paris, and following the submission of plans from as many as 171 architects, the contract to design the building was awarded to Charles Garnier, a 35 year old unknown architect from humble origins and formerly a scholar of the École des Beaux Arts.

Begun in 1862 and finished in 1875 after the Franco-Prussian War, the Opéra Garnier stands on a hexagonal site in the centre of the new business district, the Quartier Vendome. Its main façade looks southward onto the Place de l'Opera, its rear faces the Place Diaghilev, its western walls are parallel to the Rues Auber and Scribe and its eastern flank borders the Rues Gluck and Halevy. On a larger canvas, it occupies a central location within a triangle formed by the Boulevards des Capucines and Italiens, the Boulevard Haussmann and Boulevard Malesherbes, while the Avenue de l'Opera leads southwards from the Place de l'Opera. In its totality, the Opéra and its environs was of utmost value to the development of the townscape of central Paris, and a major component of Haussmann's plan for creating a modern capital for the French nation.

The Paris Opéra is unquestionably a masterpiece, a building of undoubted imperial magnificence and an early example of the neo-

127 *Opéra Garnier (the Paris Opéra), 1862-75*

Baroque style. However, its detractors thought that Garnier's designs would produce little more than a 'giant wedding cake', while the Empress Eugenie complained that the proposed building had no discernible style, to which Garnier retorted "C'est le style Napoléon III."

The functions performed by each part of the iron-framed Opéra are reflected in the structure. Above a flight of steps, the ground floor of the main façade is composed of an entrance arcade with seven outer openings. Above it, the first floor is divided up by a series of composite monumental columns, pierced by five French doors with balconies, and flanked by projecting colonnaded bays each also with a French door and balcony; the first floor is capped by sculptured relief and dome lucarnes, and at both ends has two segmental pediments with sculptured relief on the left and right of façade. The first floor is surmounted by an exuberantly sculptured attic. Deeper into the building, a low dome sits above the auditorium and a large triangular pediment marks the front of the stage area.

Though the opera house was intended to be a jewel in Napoleon's Paris, its design was to a small extent influenced by foreign affairs, particularly in relation to his policy in Italy. Many Italians objected to his support of the Papal States, and one aggrieved nationalist, Felice Orsini, attempted to assassinate Napoleon outside the old Paris opera house in the Rue Le Peletier on 14 January 1858. Thus for the Emperor's safety, Garnier included a pavilion on the east side of his new opera house with a double ramp leading up to it so that the sovereign could securely step out of his carriage into the suite of rooms adjoining the royal box. Though Napoleon fell from power in 1870, and his pavilion is no longer required, it has never been completed. The question of safety also affected the aristocracy and wealthier bourgeoisie, and similarly found its expression in the design of the Opéra, for example, lanterns carried by sculptured women, and designed by Carrier-Belleuse, illuminate the courtyard and the side entrances, originally to the benefit of wealthier opera-goers arriving by carriages.

The Opéra is particularly noted for its decoration. Its main façade exhibits a series of sculptured figures that Garnier commissioned from Carpeaux, while the unique appearance of much of the exterior is due to the mixture of materials (including stone, bronze and multi-coloured marble from different parts of France) enriched by the lavish use of gold mosaic and gilded ornamental detail.

With a total area of 11,237m², the Opéra is the largest theatre in

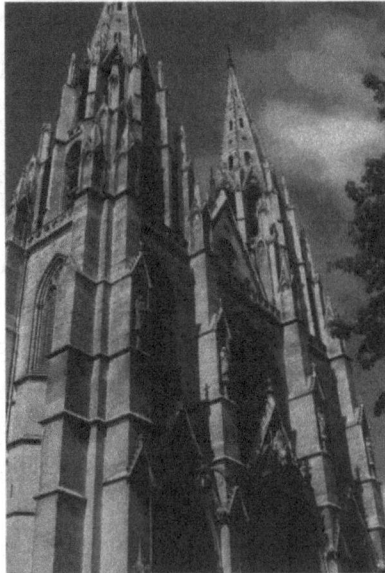

128 *Church of St-Ambrose, 1863-69*

the world. However, its auditorium is only about the size as that of the much smaller Theatre Royal, Covent Garden, London, accommodating an audience of 2,200 compared to 2,255 at the British equivalent or in contrast to 3,600 at La Scale, Milan. Since an extravagantly large amount of space in the Opéra was allocated in the wings for stage changes, the theatre's foyer, sumptuously decorated corridors and rooms, and the grand staircase to the auditorium, the capacity of the theatre has been somewhat constrained.

Started one year after the Opéra, and located in the Boulevard Voltaire in *arrondissement* 11, St-Ambroise was built in 1863-69 using traditional materials rather than the fashionable employment of iron and glass. Like Église de la Trinité, it was designed by Théodore Ballu and alludes to a mixture of Romanesque and Gothic styles, especially the latter. Its façade incorporates a Gothic entrance with three arches supporting a balustrade, while a rose window pierces the western end of the gabled nave.[40]

Very few buildings of note were built after work commenced on the Opéra, in part because financial and other resources were being fully employed on existing schemes. Thus, whereas in the 1850s, the

129   *Hôtel Dieu, 1867-78*

construction of Les Halles was a major project, the Marché du Temple in the Marais was built on a much smaller scale altogether, but like Les Halles, it was constructed mainly of iron, glass and brick. Designed by Jules de Mérindol and Ernest Legrand, the Marché de Temple is situated on the demolished twelfth century Temple complex and initially had six pavilions (in 1906 reduced to two), and its construction could only proceed after Napoleon III demolished both the rotunda and the Temple towers in 1863. The reconstruction of the Hôtel-Dieu and the Gare d'Austerlitz were the last two venues of any importance that were begun during the last six years of Napoleon's reign, and both were the product of Haussmann's continuing role as city planner. The former building located on the southern side of the Place de Parvis Notre Dame, and dating from medieval times, was demolished and rebuilt on a much larger scale on the northern side of the *parvis*, and the latter building, dating from 1840, was substantially modernised and extended in 1865-68 under the direction of the architect Pierre-Louis Renaud.

130   *Gare d'Austerlitz, 1867*

ENVIRONMENTAL HEALTH AND GREEN SPACE

From the beginning of his term in office, Haussmann recognised that water supply was an important component of urban planning. But following a warning from the municipal engineers Alphand and Belgrand that water supply in Paris was qualitatively and quantitatively inadequate to meet the needs of a rapidly expanding city, he both restricted its public consumption from the heavily polluted Seine and Oureq and began building a series of aqueducts at considerable cost from other sources across the Île de France. By this means, freshwater was discharged into newly-built reservoirs within Paris, one of which – the largest in the world – received water from the River Vanne. However, although Parisians by the 1870s were using ten times the amount of water than that consumed by an earlier generation in the 1830s,[41] and while two thirds of housing had running water, the remaining one-third were reluctant to pay a water rate for a product that they regarded as an unnecessary luxury.[42]

Throughout most of the 1850s-60s, and under Haussmann's direction, a new underground network of sewers was also built across much of Paris, with its large mains being harmoniously constructed beneath the development of boulevards, avenues and streets. Haussmann was only too aware that with the recent cholera epidemics of 1832 and 1848-9, and with the streets of central Paris often being polluted with raw sewage in its sluggish journey to the Seine, there was much public concern about the abysmal lack of hygiene across the capital. Thus, by 1870, and with the increased installation of water closets particularly in the richer Parisian districts, nearly every street in the centre was connected to the newly-built mains by an underground drain. But despite the Parisian sewage system expanding more than five-fold from 143 to 773 kilometres between 1850-70, there was a serious downside in sewage development on such a scale. The Seine, an exceptionally slow-flowing river, simply could not cope with the massive increase in the discharge of raw sewage which reached 450,000 kg a day by 1874, and it took until the end of the century to introduce, downstream, an adequate method of using liquefied sewage as an agricultural fertilizer.[43]

In response to Napoleon III's declared appreciation of London's

Hyde Park and Green Park, Haussmann was only too willing to increase the amount of green space in Paris. Although the Grand Boulevards and some of their later equivalent across Paris were lined with horse chestnut trees, and whilst the Jardin du Luxembourg and the Jardin du Tuileries had provided Parisians with green space for well over a century, this was considered insufficient to meet the health and leisure needs of a rapidly growing population. Thus, respectively in 1852 and 1860, Napoleon donated the state-owned Bois de Boulogne (in the outer-west of Paris) and the Bois de Vincennes (in the peripheral east) to the city for the enjoyment of the public. Modelled on Hyde Park, and under the supervision of the municipal engineer Alphand, the Bois de Boulogne was enhanced by the addition of 95 kilometres of pathways, two lakes and countless flowerbeds. The Bois de Vicennes was similarly landscaped some years later. Within the bounds of the city, Napoleon modernised both the Jardins du Luxembourg and Tuileries and gave the royal-owned Parc Monceau (in *arrondissement* 13) and Buttes-Chaumont (in *arrondissement* 19) to the public. Thus, whereas in 1848 there were only 19 hectares of parks in Paris, by 1870 there were as many as 1,800 hectares.

THE ECONOMIC COSTS AND BENEFITS OF HAUSSMANNISATION

The cost of redeveloping Paris was enormous. From 1853 to 1870, Haussmann spent a total of 2.5 billion francs on rebuilding the capital, a sum that staggered his critics, for example Jules Ferry in a publication of 1868, entitled *Les Comptes Fantastiques d'Haussmann* (The Fantastic Tales of Haussmann), alleged that Haussmann had recklessly squandered money and implemented ill-thought-out planning projects, criticism that intensified after he was elected as a Republican deputy for Paris in 1869. Because of such criticism, Haussmann thus abandoned work on Napoleon's plans to extend the boundaries of Paris further outward to the east and west.

Ironically, the bourgeoisie had benefited from many of Haussmann's projects, but with the depression of the late 1860s and its effect on living standards, they turned against any further development. Thus, for reasons of political expediency, Napoleon, in collaboration with the liberal Republic government of Émile Ollivier, dismissed Haussmann on January 5, 1870.

However, from the beginning, Napoleon was convinced that the cost of modernising his capital was affordable, notwithstanding the conviction of *préfet* Jean-Jacques Berger and countless other conservative luminaries that governments should at all times balance their books. Both Napoleon and Berger's successor, Haussmann, were both advocates of deficit financing since only this would produce the necessary funds for the large-scale redevelopment of Paris. It would then be easy "to siphon off part of the surplus wealth, notably in the form of indirect taxes on consumption (the major item in the city's budget). The development logic meant that the government renovated Paris on the cheap, comparatively speaking: the state Treasury bore only around 10 percent of the total cost of public works undertaken [in the 1850s-60s]. Virtually all the rest of the money came from loans, permission for which Haussmann was able to force through the municipal authorities by a combination of bullying, finagling and optimistic accounting."[44]

Loans not only came from the banking sector but also from central government. For example, the municipality borrowed over twenty-six million francs in January 1852 (only two weeks after Napoleon's coup) for the clearance of slums between the Louvre and the Tuileries. Thus when Haussmann was appointed *Préfet* of the Seine *department* in 1853, the system of finance that he subsequently exploited to the full was already in place.

It could be argued that, at the end of the day, the expense of restructuring the built environment of the French capital was worthwhile. Though the French industrial revolution still lagged behind that of Britain, the Exposition Universelle de 1867 in the Champs de Mars – even more than Exposition Universelle of 1855 – "proclaimed to the world that France was successful and that Paris was its shining face."[45]

THE SOCIAL COSTS AND BENEFITS OF HAUSSMANNISATION

It has often been claimed that development of housing in the central areas of Paris benefitted the bourgeoisie who – by the 1860s –

"represented a greater percentage of the inner-city population than ever before."[46] Since this was a direct result of public policy, some would argue that between them, Napoleon III and Haussmann had – either deliberately or inadvertently – adopted a process of 'social cleansing'. It is also claimed that as a result of planning policy, escalating rents and the huge reduction in affordable housing in the central areas of Paris drove a high proportion of the *classes labourieuses* "eastwards and outwards . . . to crowded ghettos that were every bit as evil as those demolished in the centre"[47], while artists, musicians and intellectuals were displaced from their medieval surroundings in the Latin Quarter of the Left Bank and resettled in Montmartre.

It might be difficult to refute these criticisms of public policy since between 1861 and 1901, "there was a 20 percent reduction in the population of the classy first and second *arrondissements*, and over the same period the population of the outer *arrondissements*, from the eighth in the south-west clockwise through to the seventeenth in the north east, doubled".[48] It has been estimated that from 1861 to the beginning of the twentieth century, some 350,000 persons were displaced across Paris *as a whole* through the implementation of Haussmann's plans.[49]

However, the effects of in-migration on available housing in Paris at the end of the *siècle* should not be discounted. The growth in the population of Paris and most major cities across Europe during and immediately after the Industrial Revolution was not due to birth rates greatly exceeding mortality rates, but attributable to migration from the countryside and smaller towns to cities with the greatest economic growth potential, and Paris had that potential. Thus, it can be suggested that the substantial increase in population in the outer *arrondissements* cannot be blamed solely on Haussmann's policy of slum clearance in the core of Paris and subsequent out-migration, but in no small measure on in-migration *per se*.

REFERENCES

1. R. Price, *A Concise History of France* (Cambridge: Cambridge University Press, 1993), p.172-3
2. A. Horne (B), *Friend or Foe. An Anglo-Saxon History of France* (London: Weidenfeld & Nicolson, 2004), p.276
3. Price, op. cit., p.179
4. L. Bély, *The History of France* (Paris: Editions Jean-Paul Gisserot, 2001), p.94
5. Price, op. cit., p.143
6. Price, op. cit., p.153
7. Horne, op. cit., p.281
8. Price, op. cit., p.180
9. Price, op. cit., p.180
10. Jones, op. cit., p.353
11. Jones, op. cit., p.355
12. R. Cole, *A Traveller's History of Paris* (London: The Windrush Press, 2002), p.168
13. H. Wischermann, *Paris. An Architectural Guide* (Verona: Arsenale Editrice, 2005), p.100
14. J Glancey, *Architecture* (London: Dorling Kindersley, 2006), p.388
15. A. Horne (A), *Seven Ages of Paris. Portrait of a City* (London: Pan Books, 2002), p.266
16. Horne, op. cit., p.283
17. Watkins, op. cit., p.454
18. Wischermann, op. cit., p.85
19. Wischermann, op. cit., p.102
20. Wischermann, op. cit., p.59
21. F. Prina and E. Demartini, *1000 Years of World Architecture* (London: Thames & Hudson, 2006), p.272
22. Price, op. cit., p.182
23. Price, op. cit., p.183
24. Price, op. cit., p.183
25. L. Bély, op. cit., p.95
26. Price, op. cit., p.184-5
27. Price, op. cit., p.184
28. Price, op. cit., p.188

29. Horne (A), op. cit., p.271
30. S. Clarke *Paris Revealed. The Secret Life of a City* (London: Transworld Publishers, 2012), p.144
31. Horne (A), op. cit., p.271
32. R. Cole, *A Traveller's History of Paris* (London: The Windrush Press, 2002), p.168
33. D. Gray Durrant, *Paris and Versailles* (London: A & C Black, 2001), p.330
34. Ibid, p.330
35. C. Moughtin, *Urban Design. Street and Square* (Oxford: Elsevier Science, 3rd Edt., 2003), p.137
36. K. Borrus, *Five Hundred Buildings of Paris* (New York: Black Dog & Leventhal Publishers, 2010), p.558
37. Wischermann, op. cit., p.87
38. Wischermann, op. cit., p.103
39. Borrus, op. cit., p.555
40. Borrus, op. cit., p.614
41. Jones, op. cit., p.363
42. Cole, op. cit., p.171
43. J. Reader, *Cities* (London: Vintage, 2005), pp.214-215
44. Jones, op. cit., pp.353-4
45. C. Jenkins, *France. People, History, Culture* (London: Constable & Robinson, 2001), p.141
46. Horne (A), op. cit., pp.272-3
47. Jones, op. cit., p.366

CHRONOLOGY

1848	Revolution in Paris
1848-52	The Second Republic under Louis Napoleon
1852-70	The Second Empire. Louis Napoleon reigns as Napoleon III
1852-70	**The Haussmannisation of Paris's thoroughfares, parks and sewage system Neo-Baroque architecture in vogue**
1852	**Winter Circus constructed**

1855	Paris International Exposition
1861-65	Gare du Nord built
1862-75	Théâtre Nationale de l'Opera constructed
1867	Paris International Exposition

12

AN INTERLUDE FROM REVOLT TO WORLD WAR: 1871 – 1914

INTRODUCTION

Thirty years before the end of the nineteenth century, there was great concern in France that the cousin of Wilhelm I of Prussia, Prince Leopold von Hohenzollern, might succeed to the Spanish throne and squeeze France between two potentially belligerent Germanic states. With his unprepared army, the French emperor therefore declared war on Prussia on 19 July 1870 and was quickly and resoundingly defeated by Otto von Bismarck's better trained and better equipped war machine under the command of General Helmuth von Moltke at Sedan by 2 September. Louis Napoleon and his head of army, Marshal Patrice MacMahon, were duly taken prisoners but were released some six month later on 19 March 1871. Henceforth, Louis Napoleon decided to spend the rest of his life in exile in England and met his death following an unsuccessful operation in January 1873. However, his constitutional role had come to an end nearly two years before, when on 4 September 1870, and encouraged by demonstrating Parisian crowds, the Third Republic was declared from a balcony of the Hôtel de Ville by the Interior Minister, Léon Gambetta.

At this time, Paris was well fortified (a new encircling wall had been built by Adolphe Thiers in the 1840s), even though its 350,000 strong National Guard was poorly organised and inadequately armed. The surrounding Prussian army therefore chose to starve Parisians into submission rather than to take the city by force of arms. Paris was soon short of conventional food supplies, and many of its citizens had little choice but to adopt an unappetising diet of cats, dogs, rats and zoo animals in order to survive.

THE PRUSSIANS BESIEGE PARIS

In north-eastern France – outside of the capital – the Prussian army made substantial advances capturing Metz on 16 October, but Parisian resistance continued. Bismarck, increasingly impatient, therefore ordered his generals to bomb the French capital, and for twenty-three nights from 5 January 1871 "some 12,000 Prussian shells rained down on the city, resulting in more than 400 casualties" and severe damage to over a thousand dwellings and to a number of public buildings such as the Palace de Luxembourg and the Pantheon."[1] Resistance to the onslaught stiffened, while Bismarck frustratingly recognised that it was impossible to negotiate a peaceful settlement without an elected French government, the Provisional Government of 1870 being unrepresentative.

No less than in the Hall of Mirrors at the Palais de Versailles on 11 January 1871, German princes assembled to proclaim the Prussian king, Wilheim I, Emperor of Germany and in consequence the formation of the German nation. Thus with the humiliating establishment of a new and powerful neighbouring state on the eastern flank of France, the Provisional Government agreed to an armistice on 28 January 1871 and the election of a new National Assembly in early February. The outcome was the emergence of a conservative, mainly bourgeois, government under the leadership of Adolfe Thiers (as the recently elected President) and Jules Favre (as Vice President and Foreign Affairs minister). Jointly they negotiated a peace settlement with Bismarck with its terms ratified by the Treaty of Versailles, signed on 16 February 1871. But with the new government being in a weak negotiating position, Parisians and the French in general paid a heavy price. Not only was the capital humiliated by 30,000 Prussian troops marching triumphantly down the Champs Élysées two days before their departure on 2-3 March, but under the Treaty of Frankfurt on 10 May, France was obliged to pay crippling war reparations of five billion francs to Germany, and agree to the transfer of Alsace-Lorraine to her more powerful eastern neighbour. Thus, in less than a year from the downfall of Louis Napoleon, France was immeasurably weakened on the international stage, and Paris was both impoverished and physically severely scarred.

FRENCH REPUBLICAN TROOPS LAY SIEGE TO PARIS

But Bismarck's victory was only the beginning of the Parisian disaster of the early 1870s. Far worse was to come. The establishment of the newly formed Thiers government was unacceptable to the Paris Commune. It therefore decided to send five battalions of the National Guard based in the capital to Versailles to overthrow the new administration, but on 2 April they were quickly repulsed by a 20,000 strong republican army recently released from Prussian prison camps but located at Versailles under the command of Marshal Patrice MacMahon. On the following day, a second attempt was made by a force of 27,000 national guards to overthrow the Thiers government at Versailles, but this too was unsuccessful.

On 10 May, two battalions of republican troops brought the conflict to Paris. Their aim was to seize 200 canons situated on the heights of Montmartre; weapons that had been recently used to defend the capital from the Prussians. But a crowd of Parisians including some members of the National Guard attempted to defend the guns since they had been paid-for by popular subscription and were owned *de facto* by the Paris-based National Guard. A serious scuffle between republican troops and the National Guard resulted in the former being repelled and two of their generals being lynched. It was all too clear to the Thiers government that Paris would not welcome their presence as the legitimate government of France, and for its own safety alone, it was essential to remain in Versailles, at least for the time being. Though many wealthy Parisians left the turbulent capital to be with the government, most of its population remained in Paris and elected a Commune to govern the city. From the outset the Commune set about removing the symbols of previous regimes, for example it dismantled the Vendôme column erected by Napoleon I, as it was a symbol of militarism and wars of conquest.

From 21-28 May, Parisians endured the full terror of *'semaine sanglante'* (Bloody Week) as republican troops from Versailles (disparagingly called the Versaillais) entered Paris and conducted an orgy of violence. From the outset, the Communards motivated by their antagonism to bourgoise and right-wing values and by the fear of their eventual annihilation burnt down the Tuileries Palace on 23-24 May, and attempted unsuccessfully to torch the Palais Royal, the Louvre, the Palais de Justice and the Préfecture of Police. Although they failed to torch Notre Dame and Sainte-Chapelle, they did succeed in burning down much of the Hôtel de Ville and whole streets of residential buildings. In total, the Communards probably wreaked "more damage on Paris than the city had experienced since the age of the Vikings."[2]

However, faced with the surge of republican troops across Paris, many of the Communards retreated to Belleville, Montmartre and Mélinmontant and elsewhere in the outer *arrondissements* that contained a disproportionate number of "radical workers whom Haussmann had displaced from the centre."[3] Even so, among communards, there were as many as "20,000-25,000 fatalities during 'Bloody Week' in contrast to 1,000 government troops"[4]. 'Bloodletting' continued to 28 May when 147 guardsmen were shot against a wall, the *Mur des Fédérés* at the Cemetery of Père Lachaise. In addition, at the end of the conflict, around 43,000 Communards "were arrested of which 10,000 were tried in military tribunals over the next five years."[5] Penalties ranged from execution (often by firing squads in the previously tranquil Parc Monceau or the Luxembourg Gardens), hard labour for life and fixed term imprisonment, while nearly 5,000 were deported to New Caledonia in the Pacific. It was tragic that the "total number of killings during the 'Bloody Week' of 21-28 May 1871 dwarfed the number of fatalities accruing from the Saint Bartholomew's Day

Massacre of 1573 (2,000 dead), the Great Terror of 1793-4 (2,600 victims of the Revolutionary Tribunal) and the 1848 June Days (4,000 dead)."[6]

THE DELUSION OF POST-COMMUNE YEARS

The forty or more years after the collapse of the Paris Commune are often referred to as *La Belle Époque*, a term first used nostalgically after the horror and devastation of the First World War. The epoch was regarded by many people as one of the most fruitful periods in French and particularly Parisian history possessing many of the underlying attributes of the Renaissance of the sixteenth century or the French Enlightenment of the seventeenth. Without any doubt it was a period when the arts flourished with innovative masterpieces in painting and sculpture, music, the theatre, literature and not least, architecture. But the term 'beautiful epoch' was very much a misnomer. It disregarded the very many interconnected and important issues in politics, economics and demography that affected the majority of the population.

Therefore, in the development of the arts, only architecture is considered in this chapter since, more than other forms of artistic activity, it had a major impact on how people live and work in an urban context. But as has been demonstrated throughout most of this book, architecture is not solely an abstract outcome of design. It is to a varying degree a reflection of the political, social and economic attributes of the day.

FROM THE POLITICAL RIGHT TO THE LEFT OF CENTRE

After the demise of the Commune, the future of France and its capital was being formulated by both Monarchist and Republican parliamentarians. Many of the former supported the claim by the Comte de Chambord, Charles X's grandson, to become the next king, until he unwisely insisted that the French flag, the Tricolour, be replaced by a white flag, the Bourbon standard of Henry IV and

Louis XIV. This was found unacceptable across the political divide and, since there was no immediately available royal successor, Adolphe Thiers, formerly Prime Minister and Foreign Minister under Louis Philippe, was designated president of the Republic on 31 August 1871. However, the influence of the Monarchists in government was unquenchable forcing Thiers to resign on 24 May 1873 to be replaced by a monarchist sympathiser, Marshal MacMahon, who as the incoming president, was – through a revised constitution – granted the right to rule for seven years (since 2000 it has been reduced to five years). But MacMahon's term in office was nothing if not controversial. Not only did his presidency coincide with the Long Depression, marked in France by reparations being paid to Germany in consequence of the Franco Prussian War, the collapse of the Paris Bourse in 1873, and a policy of deflation, but at the same time, MacMahon – true to his unwise predilections – favoured the return of the monarchy, but the elections of October 1877 confirmed a Republican majority, forcing MacMahon to resign in January 1879.[7] He was replaced, as president, by Jules Grévy who immediately appointed a government composed largely of Opportunist Republicans which focussed on a wide range of constitutional reforms. As far as Paris was concerned, and unlike the rest of France where mayors were to be elected by universal suffrage, a *Préfet* would be appointed by central government to exercise the functions of Mayor whose policies would need to be broadly in keeping with those applicable to the nation as a whole.

THE RENEWED DEVELOPMENT OF THE PARISIAN BUILT ENVIRONMENT

Following the resignation of the first president of the Third Republic, Adolphe Thiers, the new incumbent, Marshal MacMahon – still essentially a moderate Monarchist – found himself involved in the creation of a new constitution to formalise the functioning of the Third Republic. He also had to preside over a lengthy period of economic depression which from 1873 to 1879 considerably slowed down the growth of the French gross national product and he was unable to continue immediately with the Haussmannisation of Paris because of the shortage of funds, Paris had been 2,500 million francs in debt in 1871. At first there was no immediate solution to this development constraint. Though many Parisians wished to preserve, at minimal expense, the heritage of their city as far as possible, others including architects, engineers, bureaucrats and above all Haussmann officials, were in favour of modernising the capital's infrastructure and increasing its stock of buildings. The outcome of this dichotomy was that reconstruction and new development would be funded by private investors while construction would be managed by former Haussmann officials, many of whom were soon to be employed in a new radical council that inherited Haussmann's plan in 1874.

131   *Basilica of the Sacré Coeur, 1875-1919*

Under the plan, and across the Pont du Sully, the eastern end of the Boulevard Saint-Germain on the Left Bank was connected to the Boulevard Henry IV on the Right Bank, a relatively inexpensive project since the latter part of the routeway ran through the poor Arsenal district that reduced the cost of development. Begun in 1876, the project was accompanied in the same year by a much more prestigious and expensive scheme, the construction of the Avenue de l'Opéra. Looking onto the Opéra Garnier at its northern end, the avenue linked the thriving commercial activity of the Rue de Rivoli with that of the Boulevard Capucines and Boulevard de Madeleine. The Avenue de l'Opéra alone was funded by a massive loan that would not only compensate existing owners for their loss of property – a sum amounting to an average 225,000 francs per owner (a sum at least twice that on the Boulevard Henry IV), but also cover the cost of making the Avenue perfectly level. In total, the Avenue de l'Opéra cost the city the enormous sum of 45 million francs. However, the cost of constructing new buildings was borne largely by private builders who purchased lots from the city and were obliged to conform with Haussmann's building regulations. Overall, the avenue became an immediate commercial

132 *Avenue de l'Opéra, 1864-79*

success, as did its neighbouring streets that were funded in broadly the same way.

Paris enjoyed a long period of reconstruction and new development – not entirely continuously – over a period of forty years or more. Initially a new and radical city council re-built most of the key public buildings severely damaged by Prussian bombardment and by the conflict between the Commune and the Republican army, most notably the Hôtel de Ville that was completed in 1882. But the principal damaged legacy of the imperial years, the Tuileries remained in ruin before being demolished in 1883, though the Marsan and Flore pavilions of the edifice were restored.

THE NEW POLITICAL CONTEXT

As the monarchist threat subsided, Republicans were divided between pragmatic 'opportunists' on the one hand, and radicals on the other – the former supporting Grévy (1879-87) and the latter George Clemenceau, then the Mayor of Belleville but later prime minister (in 1906-09 and 1917-20). Further to the left, the socialists were also divided between moderates and supporters of the political system designed by Karl Marx[8] while on the right, royalists were split between authoritarian and antiparliamentarian forms of nationalism. In 1887 the 'Opportunist' administration was rocked by a scandal in the Grévy family when the president's son-in-law became involved in illegal wheeler-dealing, leaving the president himself to resign. Replaced as head of state by Marie-François Sadi-Carnot (1887-94), the 'Opportunist' party was involved in yet another scandal: this time concerning the Panama Canal Company where members of parliament (including Clemenceau) were bribed to overlook irregularities in the company's finances. Following this scandal, but not necessarily because of it, anarchists began attacking public figures throughout France, and as part of their anti-establishment campaign, Sadi-Carnot was assassinated in Lyon in 1894.[9]

It was foreign rather than domestic policy that became the focus of government activity from the latter years of the nineteenth century to the outbreak of the First World War in June 1914. It was recognised that new markets were now required for French trade and ports for the French navy, and as advocated by Jules Ferry (Minister of Public Instruction in the Grévy government) Tunisia was turned into a French protectorate in 1881, soon to be followed by colonies in West Africa (Senegal, Mauretania, Mali, Ivory Coast, Chad and Gabon), in the Indian Ocean (Madagascar and Réunion) and four protectorates in Indo-China: Annam, Tonkin, Cambodia and Laos. France had built up an enormous empire, second only to that of the United Kingdom, but it was in East Africa that French colonial ambitions were thwarted. In 1898, a small French expeditionary force was garrisoned in Foshoda in the Nile Valley, but its activities were halted by the arrival of the British Army that demanded that the French evacuate the area since it was occupied by British settlers. It was only after negotiations had taken place in Paris and London that war was averted, with the French humiliatingly having to withdraw.

Whilst taking place in Paris, the so-called 'Dreyfus Affair' was a reflection of foreign rather than domestic policy. Because many French politicians and much of the nation's army were obsessed with the perceived need to defend their country against future German aggression, they were particularly alarmed when they understood that one of their staff officers was supplying secret information to their former enemy. Suspicion fell on Captain Alfred Dreyfus who was court marshalled, found guilty and deported for life in December 1894 to Devil's Island in French Guinea. After a trial in Rennes in 1899, Dreyfus was eventually pardoned by President Emile Loubet in 1899, but was not reinstated until 1906.

In the early years of the twentieth century, there was a short respite in the political agenda being dominated by foreign policy. During this time the Radicals and Radical Socialists founded new parties and, supported by the lower middle classes, dominated French politics until 1940.[10] Even in the 12 years between 1902 and 1914, there were as many as seven Republican Socialist prime ministers and five Republican Democratic premiers. Their political agendas favoured moderate social reform rather than upheaval and revolution. Around the same time there was the growth of Socialism brought on by the development of Trade Unions which were instrumental in setting up the left wing SFIO (*Section Française de l'Internationale ouvriere*) whose leader was assassinated in July 1914 probably because of his opposition to Clemenceau, colonialism and war.[10]

But the defence of France remained an important political objective. Although war between France and the UK seemed remote, it was necessary to ensure that the two countries didn't drift accidentally into conflict. Therefore, Lord Lansdown, the UK's Foreign Secretary and Paul Cambon, the French ambassador to the UK, signed the Entente Cordiale in 1904. Possibly fearing French intensions in the wake of the Franco-Prussian war of 1871, a Triple Alliance had been formed between Germany, Austria and Italy in 1882, but it was not until 1914 that France, Russia and the UK sought to defend themselves by collectively establishing the Triple Entente (an amalgam of the earlier Entente Cordiale and a Franco-Russian agreement of 1893-4). On 1 August 1914, Germany declared war on Russia, and on France on the 3rd of the month, with the UK entering the conflict on 4 August.

THE RENEWED DEVELOPMENT OF THE PARISIAN BUILT ENVIRONMENT

Following the resignation of the first president of the Third Republic, Adolphe Thiers, in May 1873, the depression years of 1873-79, and the formulation of a new French constitution in 1875, Paris enjoyed a long period of reconstruction and development – not entirely continuously – over a period of forty years or more.

During this time new development was taking place on a much larger scale than the reconstruction of damaged buildings. Under the Presidency of Patrice MacMahon (1873-79), the National Assembly – still located in Versailles – funded the creation of a major landmark on the skyline of Paris, the Basilica of the Sacré Coeur. Situated on the peak of Montmartre, the Romano-Byzantine structure was not completed until 1923 and has for generations been unloved by the political Left since – in its view – it commemorates the demise of the Commune. As a moderate Monarchist, MacMahon also ordered the re-erection of the column in the Place de Vendome as a symbol of Imperial power but was unable to continue immediately with the Haussmannisation of Paris because of the shortage of funds, Paris being 2,500 million francs in debt in 1871. At first there was no immediate solution to this developmental constraint. Though many Parisians wished to preserve, at minimal expense, the heritage of their city as far as possible, others including architects, engineers, bureaucrats and above all Haussmann officials were in favour of modernising the capital's infrastructure and increasing its stock of buildings. The outcome of this dichotomy was that reconstruction and new development would be funded by private investors while construction would be managed by former Haussmann officials, many of whom were soon to be employed in a new radical council that inherited Haussmann's plan in 1874.

THE 1878 INTERNATIONAL EXPOSITION AND ITS AFTERMATH

During the final years of the MacMahon presidency, and substantially subsidised by both the National Assembly and City Council, the International Exposition of 1878 was designed to demonstrate to the world the extent to which France, and particularly Paris, had recovered from the ravages of the 'Terrible Year' at the beginning of the decade and to mark the hundred year anniversary of the outbreak of the French Revolution. The Exposition was located on both sides of the Seine – in temporary buildings on the Right Bank and in the Champs de Mar on the Left Bank, and in a more permanent building, the Palais de Trocadéro on the Right Bank. Designed by G.J.A. Davioud, and attracting thousands of visitors including Prince Edward, Queen Victoria's eldest son, the Trocadéro was both Moorish and Baroque in appearance and sported a huge rotunda topped by twin minarets, 9.5 metres high and flanked with twin semi-circular galleries. Of the temporary buildings, the most famous was the enormous iron and glass Galerie des Machines (demolished in 1910).

Because Paris had at last thrown off its politically precarious image, the Chamber of Deputies (formerly the National Assembly) moved from Versailles to the capital where it once again housed itself in its traditional venue, the Palais Bourbon in 1879, though as early as 1873 the President moved into the Palais d'Elysée, and in 1876 the Council of the Republic (later the *Senat*) occupied the Palais du Luxembourg – all three institutions continuing to occupy these buildings to the present day.

133   *Eiffel Tower, 1887-89*

By the early 1880s, and under a new president, Jules Grévy of the left-of-centre Opportunist Republican party, a new and radical city council had selectively rebuilt most of the key public buildings severely damaged by Prussian bombardment and by the conflict between the Commune and the Republic. Other notable public sector building projects of the 1880s included the construction of the Rue de Rivoli wing of the Louvre and the reduction in the size of the Palace Royale by stripping it of its monarchical functions to facilitate accommodating the Conseil d'État, Ministries de la Culture and the Conseil Constitutionnel, while the Halle aux Blés became the Bourse de Commerce in 1886.

THE 1889 WORLD EXPOSITION

In 1887 Grévy resigned as president in the light of his refusal to deny his innocence in the alleged corruption of his son-in-law in a matter of state procedure. Under the presidency of Grévy's successor, Marie François Sadi-Carnot (1887-94), the National Assembly and the Paris city council completed the subsidisation of a major international exhibition set in train by Grévy in a further attempt to glorify France, and to raise the profile of the capital, held as before on both the Champs de Mars and the Right Bank. In 1889 it was even more spectacular than its predecessor. Apart from a host of very diverse national pavilions, the most outstanding building was the Eiffel Tower. Designed by the civil engineer and architect Gustav Eiffel and built on the northern edge of the Champs de Mars overlooking the Seine, the extant 300m tower was assembled from prefabricated steel, is slightly concave and has three intermediate floors. However, the Gallery of Machines – a substantial iron and glass structure originally assembled for the 1878 exposition, the domed Palace of Fine Arts and Liberal Arts, and the widespread deployment of electric lighting (similarly used in 1878) were wonders of the world and highlighted Paris as the 'City of Light.'[11] Although the total cost of the exposition amounted to 41.5 million francs, its income from visitors was 49.5 million francs, the last Paris exhibition of its sort to make a profit. The exposition also brought forth some long-term enterprises away from its main site, for example 1889 saw the opening of the Moulin Rouge cabaret located on the southern edge of Montmartre and home of the can-can, while the Folies Bergère in the Rue Richer was at the height of its fame in the 1890s.

THE 1900 INTERNATIONAL EXPOSITION

During the presidencies of J.P.P. Casimir-Périer (1894-95) and Félix Faure (1895-99), the Opportunist-Republican government and the City of Paris, heavily subsidised the construction of the 1900 exposition, grandiloquently named 'Paris, Capital of the Civilised World.' Not only was Paris "the putative birthplace of democracy [it was also] the leading edge of modern civilisation," and put "its spectacular self on show in this two-edged period of *fin de siècle* and *belle epoque.*"[12] Whereas the Eiffel Tower epitomises the 1878 exposition, the Pont Alexander

III – Grand Palais – Petit Palace complex exemplifies the grandeur of its 1900 counterpart. Unlike the 1889 exposition, moreover, the 1900 exposition in its totality left a legacy of extant iconic buildings in central Paris, still in use to this day.

Connecting the Avenue Nicholas II (now the Avenue Winston Churchill) on the Right Bank of the Seine to the Quai d'Orsay on the Left, the Pont Alexander III (1896-1900) was designed in the neo-Baroque style by the architects Joseph Cassien Bernard and Gaston Cousin, and constructed by the engineers Jean Résel, Amédée Alby. With the ground broken by Czar Nicholas II to commemorate the signing of the Franco-Russian Alliance in 1892, the road and pedestrian bridge – "the most glorious and exuberant of all Parisian bridges",[13] – is a single-span cast iron arch (109 metres long and 40 metres wide) supported by two corner pylons at either end of the structure and illuminated at night by decorative gas lights.

Adorning the western edge of the Avenue Nicholas II, the Grand Palais (1896-1900) was designed by Charles Girault, Henry Deglane, Albert Thomas and Albert Louvet and is one of the finest examples of architecture in the Bell Epoque. Neo-Baroque in design, it was built for

134   *Pont Alexander III, 1896-1900*

135   *Grand Palais, 1896-1900*

the 1900 International Exposition as an events hall and has a huge stone façade displaying Corinthian columns and a decorative frieze. The interior consists of a large galleried hall of glass and iron, some 192 x 22 metres in dimension, and surmounted by the largest glass dome in Europe.

Built at the same time as the Grand Palace, the Petit Palace (1896-1900), also in the 8th *arrondissement* is situated immediately opposite its larger counterpart and is essentially an art gallery. Built in the eighteenth-century style, though with a hidden iron frame and an abundance of glass and iron, its façade features Ionic colonnades and corner pavilions, and the centre of the building is capped by a substantial dome. It is also marked by a large arched portal, and internally galleries surround a central garden.

The 1900 Exposition was an expensive exercise and unlike its 1888 counterpart exceedingly costly. Whereas 147 million francs was spent on its construction and management, its income from visitors was only 126 million francs, producing a loss of 21 million francs. But across central Paris, more viably constructed and less iconic buildings were being built during the last three decades of the nineteenth century and into the

136   *Petit Palais, 1896-1900*

twentieth. This was over a period when there were both Opportunist Republican and Democratic Republic Alliance presidencies, and largely after the depression of the 1870s had given way to a sustained growth associated with the latter years of the French industrial revolution.

Apart from the Théâtre de l'Opéra-Comique (1893-98), with its solid neo-Baroque structure and located in the 2nd *arrondissement*, most development focused on the construction of a wide range of buildings designed in the 'iron and glass' style of French architecture as displayed at the Expositions of 1878, 89 and 1900. Examples include: the department store, Au Bon Marché (opened in 1876) in the 7th *arrondissement*, the Muséum National d'Histoire Naturelle (1877-89, 1894-95) in the 5th *arrondissement*, the department store Au Printemps (1881-89) in the 9th arrondissement, the churches of Notre Dame-du-Travail (1897-1902) in the 14th *arrondissement* and St-Jean Evangeliste (1894-1904) in the 18th *arrondissement*, the Gare d'Orsay (1897-1900) in the 7th arrondissement and offices at 124 Rue Réaumur in the 2nd and 3rd *arrondissements*.

But, however innovative these buildings were in terms of design, their construction could not match the volume of building work involved in the completion of Haussmann's scheme for slum clearance, improved sanitation and access between 1885 and 1914, even though Haussmann himself had been relieved of his role as city planner in 1870. Within these three decades at the turn of the century, the Rue de

137   *Théatre de l'Opéra-Comique 1893-98*

138   *Au Printemps department store, 1881-89
(reconstructed 1907-11)*

Franche-Comté was connected to Boulevard du Temple, while the Rue des Filles-Dieu, Rue de Louvre, the Rue Jean-Jacque Rousseau and the Rue de Réaumur were – among others – widened and often increased in height by two further storeys and embellished with bay windows and balconies, taking advantage of the more relaxed building controls at the end of the century.

However, even before the turn of the century, the Haussmannisation of Paris proved a mixed blessing. Although his boulevards eradicated much of the city's squalor, they failed to connect rail termini; they didn't link central Paris to the *banlieue*, and massive traffic jams occurred at major crossroads. Congested boulevards could not have been foreseen since although there were only 45,000 vehicles on the streets of Paris in 1891, there were as many as 430,000 by 1910, with the principal means of transport across Paris evolving in turn from horse-drawn carriages to horse omnibuses, horse trams to electric trams and eventually to petrol-driven buses by the beginning of the twentieth century.[14]

In an attempt to ease congestion through the centre of Paris, *bateaux mooches* were deployed to carry commuters along the Seine to-and-from work and on shopping journeys, but the number of passengers using the *bateaux* was comparatively small compared to volume of passengers carried by the new Metropolitan system of largely underground railways. Opened in time for the 1900 exposition, after many years of opposition by central government, the city council and a variety of private interests, the first 'Metro' line cut "the journey from Maillot to Vincennes from ninety minutes to twenty-five."[15] By the 1930s, as many as 16 separate lines were running connecting a total of 302 stations, of which 245 were in the city. A feature common to most lines was that the sheltered passenger entrances (mostly painted green) were designed in the Art Nouveau style by Hector Guimard, and utilising iron and frosted glass, displayed a variety of floral forms with their lights resembling long-stemmed flowers.[16]

But for three decades before the introduction of the Metro, suburban Paris had been industrialising, partly because of skyrocketing rents, inadequate space and bankruptcies in the inner *arrondissements* of Paris subject to Haussmannian improvements. The production of carriages, bicycles, household goods and eventually motor vehicles was moving out to factories in, for example, Sant-Denis, Ivry-sur-Seine and

Alfortville but because of alleged exploitation, workers embarked on a long period of "industrial action and the formation of trade union organisations, such as the Confédération Générale du Travail (CGT),"[17] a union linked to the socialist Section Française de l'Internationale Ouvrière (SFIO), a nationwide organisation centred in Paris. Violent industrial action in both Alfortville and Saint-Denis in the 1880s was, to an extent, replaced in later years by organised strikes, for example in 1905 when "tens of thousands of construction, jewellery, cabinet and other workers joined car workers striking for the eight-hour day."[18]

Though Paris as a market location benefitted from the further development of nationwide railway routes and the reconstruction of some of the capital's major stations such as the Gare de l'Est in 1885 and 1900 and the Gare de Lyon also in 1900, the momentum of industrialisation in Paris was stimulated by the introduction of the Metro which helped to continue a major migration of blue-collared workers to the suburbs of Paris. At first, many industrial workers began to commute from their homes in inner Paris to the outer reaches of the city to obtain appropriate employment, but often found it impossible to obtain housing to suit their needs. Locating in the *banlieue*, and especially in the north and east of the city, industrial labour found the supply of adequate housing almost non-existent. It was ironic that at the same time as much of central Paris was being beautified by the 1900 Exposition, a belt of slums was emerging across many of its suburbs that over the years have shamed what many regard as the world's most beautiful city.

It was in Paris beyond the Thiers wall that the condition of housing was at its worst, for example in 1900 58 percent of households in Saint-Denis lived in insanitary dwellings, with 62 percent in Saint Ouen and 65 percent in Aubervillieres. *Banlieue* housing was also deficient in other amenities, for example as much as a fifth to a third of all dwellings lacked piped water in contrast to only 10 percent of homes in central Paris, while 50 percent of *banlieue* dwellings were without a private WC compared to around 20 percent in central Paris.[19] Conversely, there was a tendency for white-collar workers employed at the turn of the century in easily accessible commercial and service industries to remain within the inner *arrondissements*, most notably in their well-equipped boulevard apartments.

139   *Art Nouveau Metro station entrance 1900*

The spatial polarisation of the population of Paris had clearly arrived by 1900 if not before, a dichotomy that augured badly in the years to come. It is interesting to note that whereas the middle classes in the UK and USA, "relocated their residences away from city centres, [in] France, in contrast, Haussmann had cleaned up much of the centre of Paris in ways that made the middle classes remain there",[20] with the inner *arrondissements* "primed to become a showcase for consumption."[21] Designed in the Modernist style, a plethora of new or expanded commercial buildings were thus constructed in the central *arrondissements* of the capital, most notably: the department stores of Au Printemps (1907-11) and the Samaritaine (1904-19) which are both in the 1ˢᵗ *arrondissement* while the offices of the Société Générale (1906-12) and the Galeries Lafayette department store (1906-08, 1910-12) are in the 9ᵗʰ *arrondissement*. The Modernist style of architecture superseded the 'iron and glass' phase in the development of the Parisian cityscape during the first decade of the twentieth century. Among a number of early examples, the most notable is the Théâtre des Champs-Élysées (1906-13) in the 8ᵗʰ *arrondissement*, one of the first buildings of this

140   *Samaritaine department store, 1904-19 (reconstructed 1928-30)*

141   *Galeries Lafayette department store, 1906-08, 1910-12*

style that was to remain in vogue until at least the 1970s, while in 1913 Paris boasted thirty-seven cinemas, one of them, the Pathé, near the Invalides not only had an orchestra of sixty but claimed to have the world's largest screen.[22]

But war-clouds were rising. Though a major conflict between France and the UK seemed unlikely, it deemed prudent to ensure that the two countries didn't drift accidentally into conflict and therefore the UK's Foreign Secretary, Lord Lansdown and Paul Cambon, the French ambassador to the UK signed the Entente Cordiale in 1904. Possibly fearing French intensions in the wake of the Franco-Prussian war of 1871 particularly its lingering aim to regain Alsace-Lorraine, a Triple Alliance had been formed between Germany, Austria, Hungary and Italy in 1882, but it was not until 1914 that France, Russia and the UK sought to defend themselves by collectively establishing the Triple Entente (an amalgam of the earlier Entente Cordiale and a Franco-Russian agreement of 1893-94). On 1 August 1914, Germany declared war on Russia, and on France on 3 August, with the UK entering the conflict on 4 August. For over four years World War I raged, and after

142 *Théâtre des Champs-Élysées*

the armistice in November 1918, France, like all the other belligerent nations, entered a new age of hope and dissolution, of economic growth and depression, of laisser-faire and public control, but also of largely uncontrolled urban environments and decaying buildings and infrastructure.

REFERENCES

1. R. Cole, *Paris* (London: Phoenix, 1994), p.123
2. C. Jones, *Paris. Biography of a City*, (London: Penguin Books, 2006), p.376
3. C. Jones, opt. cit., p.376
4. Ibid
5. Ibid
6. Ibid
7. J.P. Gisserot, *The History of France,* (Paris: Editions Jean-Paul Gisserot, 2001), p.98
8. J.P. Gisserot, opt. cit., p.99
9. J.P. Gisserot, opt. cit., p.100
10. J.P. Gisserot, opt. cit., p.102
11. Ibid
12. C. Jones, opt. cit., p.396
13. C. Jones, opt. cit., p.408
14. C. Jones, opt. cit., p.420-21
15. A. Horne, *Seven Ages of Paris*, (London: Macmillan, 2002), p.335
16. H. Wischermann, *Paris. An Architecture Guide*, (Venice: arsenale editrice, 2005), p.115
17. R. Cole, opt. cit., p.194
18. Ibid
19. C. Jones, opt. cit., pp.419-20
20. C. Jones, opt. cit., pp.11-12
21. Horne, opt. cit., p.341
22. C. Jones, opt. cit., p. 461

CHRONOLOGY

1870-71	Paris Commune uprising. Paris besieged by Prussian forces, followed by the city being taken by French government forces **Destruction of many prominent buildings**
1871-73	Adolphe Thiers, President of France
1872	**Building of Sacré-Coeur-de-Montmartre, consecrated in 1919**
1873-79	Marshal MacMahon, President of France
1873-82	**Hôtel de Ville rebuilt after being burnt down during the Commune uprising**
1875	**Palais Garnier (Paris Opera) completed**
1876	**Au Bon Marché, first department store opens**
1878	**Paris International Exposition**
1879-87	Jules Grévy, President of France
1887-94	J.P.P. Casimir-Carnot, President of France
1889	**Eiffel Tower completed** **Paris International Exposition**
1893-98	**Théâtre de l'Opéra-Comique built**
1895-1900	**Metro stations built**
1895-99	Félix Faure, President of France
1896-1900	**Pont Alexander III constructed**
1897-1900	**Grand Palais and Petit Palais constructed**
1898	**Paris Metro opens**
1898-1900	**Gare d'Orsay built**
1899-1906	Emile Loubet, President of France
1900	**Paris International Exposition** Paris population passes 2 million
1906-08 and 1910-12	**Galeries Layfayette department store built**
1906-13	Armand Fallières. President of France
1911-13	**Théâtre de Champs Élysées constructed**
1913-20	Raymond Poincaré, President of France

13

RECOVERY AND DEPRESSION: 1918-39

INTRODUCTION

Fighting in World War I ceased on 11 November 1918 but it was not until 28 June 1919 that peace was secured by the Treaty of Versailles whose signatories were George Clemenceau (France), President Woodrow Wilson (USA), David Lloyd George (UK) and Vittorio Emanuele Orlando (Italy), together with the two dejected German delegates: Hermann Müller and Johannes Bell. While the political Left in France – the Communists, Internationalists and extreme Socialists – welcomed the treaty as they mistakenly saw it as a prelude to revolution, a large proportion of the French population were also dissatisfied with Versailles since they did not believe that, under the system of liberal democracy operating in the Third Republic, it would deter a further war with Germany in the not too distant future.

Although Paris suffered little material damage in World War I, one in ten of the city's conscripts never returned from the fighting,[1] and at the war's end, Paris "was shabby and run down and barely recognisable as the gleaming model city of the *belle époque*".[2] Nationally, the economy was in a bad way, France having spent a quarter of her gross domestic product on the war. But by the early 1920s there were clear signs of recovery both in the industrial and agricultural sectors. However, much of the vast supply of money issued to pay for the war remained in circulation and stoked up the fire of inflation.[3] Encouraged by the revolutionary Left, French workers militantly demanded higher wages and better working conditions,[4] but because the labour movement was seriously divided "union membership collapsed from around two million in 1919 to 600,000 in 1921."[5] The Communists succeeded in establishing a well-organised movement with its bastions in the grim industrial suburbs of Paris."[6] But whereas the Minister of Finance in Prime Minister Clemenceau's government, Louis-Lucien Klotz, had anticipated in 1919 that France's post-war budgetary deficits could be redeemed by German reparations, in 1923 Germany defaulted in her payments prompting Raymond Poincaré – then French Minister of Foreign Affairs – to send French forces to occupy the Ruhr and secure payment. When they soon withdrew because of international pressure, France was left with the task of 'tightening her belt' to balance her budget and ensure a degree of economic stability.

THE ECONOMIC DEPRESSION AND ITS AFTERMATH

But, beginning in the United States in 1929 with a New York stock market crash, the economic depression soon spread to Europe causing unemployment and hardship, particularly in Germany and the United Kingdom. France was at first unscathed since its economy was less developed than that of the United States, Germany and the UK, but when the depression arrived in 1931, France was hit even harder and took longer to recover,[7] lasting until 1938. Her industrial production fell by 17 percent between 1929 and 1934, her average incomes plummeted by 30 percent, and by the end of 1935, more than 800,000 were unemployed.[8] The depression gave "encouragement to those wanting a Communist revolution, and to others leaning towards a Fascist revolution, George Valois claimed that France, not Italy, was the birthplace of Fascism which he described as a fusion of socialism and nationalism."[9]

In the 1930s Paris's political unrest was an inevitable consequence of low wages and high unemployment particularly in its northern industrial suburbs. It was in such 'red suburbs' of Saint Denis and Belleville that Communists gained control of the municipal government in 1924,[10] and together had a succession of Communist mayors until 1932. There was a similar scenario in Ivry-sur-Seine where all mayors from 1925 to 2015 were members of the French Communist Party (the PCF), except during the war years, 1939-45. Some workers also turned towards the Right where there were many small disparate groups including Action Français, Jeunesses Patriotes and Croix de Feu, though Le Parti Social Français had 100,000 members by 1937. "On it went. Extremes of Left and Right spread across the country, but the proclivity for violence tended to be let out in Paris, the centre of government."[11]

In 1933 it came to light that a local financier, Serge Stavisky of central or east European origin, was alleged to have had "close links with many prominent figures in the worlds of property, politics and the law, [so much so] that . . . he came under police investigation for alleged corruption."[12] In response, violent agitation was initiated by right-wing factions since they believed that Stavisky was protected by a police cover-up.[13] A right-wing rally assembled on the Pont de la Concorde and aggressively targeted the National Assembly leaving sixteen dead and countless others wounded. This show of force encouraged the Left to be politically vigilant. The Communists signed an agreement with the French Section of the Workers International (SFIO) and the Radical Socialists on 14 July 1935, and on the same day staged a massive street procession through Paris. This grouping of parties secured victory at the election in May 1936, and governed as the Popular Front under the premiership of the Socialist Prime Minister Léon Blum. Immediately the front was faced with a "nationwide wave of strikes and spontaneous factory occupations by workers determined to see their electoral victory turn immediately into social gain."[14] In Paris alone 150,000 workers were on strike by mid-summer. With considerable help from the Communist leader, Maurice Thorez, negotiated agreements were made with employers across the economy but these triggered off an inflationary spiral as wage and salary increases were not reflected in increased production. Interest rates were therefore forced up, the balance of trade went into deficit, and real wages remained constant. A further round of strikes in the Paris car industry in 1938 led to a crisis in government in which the Blum government fell. After growing slightly from the end of the First World War to 1924, the French gross national product in real terms in 1939 was back to its 1913 level.[15]

REGIONAL PLANNING

Notwithstanding the political and economic upheavals of the 1920s and 30s, the population and the built economy of the Paris region as a whole grew substantially, but while there was an insufficient supply of housing and employment for those wishing to live and work in central Paris, there was a substantial development of unplanned and dispersed low-income *banlieue* (low-income housing estates) in the suburbs. With the absence of both central and local government control, urban sprawl soon spread over much of the region beyond the suburbs to envelop the neighbouring departments of Seine-et-Marne and Seine-et-Oise.[16] One solution to the problem of sprawl was well known, viz the development of garden cities. With the development of Welwyn Garden city and Letchworth on the outer fringe of London, Britain had pioneered the development of garden cities before the First World War, but this approach was largely disregarded in France. Instead the "extension of Paris . . . took place in a whirlwind of wide, unregulated initiatives. The most common form these took was a large estate – or *lottissement* – given over to one or two storey dwellings"[17] and driven by private property developers. But central government was not unaware of the advantages of urban and regional planning. National legislation in 1919 required all French cities to produce a development plan, but it took until 1934 before planning proposals for Greater Paris were published and until 1939 when they became law. But because of the hostility of many municipalities in the Île de France and a level of deadlock in Paris, very little was achieved[18], and in September 1939 the plan was derailed by the outbreak of World War II.

THE DEVELOPMENT OF THE BUILT ENVIRONMENT OF PARIS IN THE INTER-WAR YEARS

Political rivalry and the failure to achieve economic growth throughout much of the inter-war period did little to constrain the development of housing in Paris, but while the population of its twenty arrondissement in 1921 had only increased to 2.9 million, only slightly more than in 1900, the population of the Paris *banlieue* soared from 1.5 million inhabitants in the early 1920s to over two million by the late 1930s. Paris was clearly "on the point of being overtaken if not dwarfed by its suburbs."[19] To an extent this was recognised by presidents Raymond Poincaré (1913-20) and Paul Deschanel (1920), both of the centrist Democratic Republic Alliance party; Alexander Millerand (1920-24), an Independent; Gaston Doumergue (1924-31), a Radical Socialist; and Paul Doumer (1931-32), another Independent. However, because of the enormity of population pressure, an inadequate system of public finance and a less than efficient system of local planning, the shortage of low-cost housing of adequate standard remained largely unsolved through the 1920s-30s.

To help ease matters, the 34 kilometre-long and kilometre-wide fortifications of Adolphe Thiers that were built to encircle Paris in the 1840s were demolished in 1919-32, leaving an abundance of sites for the construction of housing. However, although a large proportion of the 40,000 new dwellings that were built around Paris by the end of the 1930s were situated along the route of the former wall, their provision did little to minimise city/*banlieue* antipathies. Although many had been built as desirable bourgeoise dwellings in such western suburbs as Auteuil and Clichy, most new housing took the form of Habitations à bon marché (HBMs). "The characteristic, seven-storey sets of buildings, solid rather than spectacular in appearance, were often designed around narrow alleys and courtyards,"[20] and were intended largely for relatively low-income tenants. Since their construction they have formed a 'red-brick belt' just beyond the circular *boulevards des maréchaux* (completed in 1939) and the circular *boulevard périphérique* (finished in the 1960s).[21] Such a co-location of low-income housing and urban motorways was barely conducive to the elimination of city/*banlieue* antipathies.

It was hoped that property development by the 1930s would be brought under control, by the Sarraut Law of 1928, and within new schemes the provision of roads and pavements, water supply, drainage and gas and electricity would soon become mandatory. But in 1931 and in the years immediately after, the downturn in the economy reduced the impact of such changes. Notwithstanding the development of HBMs, the supply of housing in the Paris region, and in the capital's *banlieue* in particular, remained inadequate and in a poor condition producing a low quality of life and a radicalisation of voting patterns.

Parisian municipal authorities in their *banlieue* were faced with what seemed an intractable problem. If they demolished poor quality

143   *Habitations à bon marché (HBM), social housing, 1930s*

housing prior to rebuilding, a temporary or not so temporary reduction in dwellings would either create even worse conditions in the housing stock that remained, or homelessness. But if the authorities attempted to create a market solution to housing need, higher rents "would trigger mass evictions and aggravate the very housing crisis they were trying to solve.[22] Backed by central government, the municipalities attempted to impose a solution, namely a rent freeze, but this meant that either private developers had little incentive to invest in new housing, or that existing landlords would either be disinclined to keep their properties in good condition or withdraw their properties from the rental market altogether.[23] The housing crisis was so dire that a municipal survey showed that "one third of Parisian dwellings were overcrowded [and] that some 30,000 dwellings were unoccupied and not on the market."[24]

   The overwhelming reason why housing in Paris presented what seemed to be intractable problems was the shortage of supply. In the inner areas of the capital, housebuilding almost came to a halt in the early-1920s since, with an outbreak of bubonic plague, there were serious "public health issues implicit in a decaying cityscape", [while

144 *An example of Modernist housing, Robert Mallet Stevens, 1926-27*

over a longer period, 1914-1942] instead of new housebuilding taking place in Paris, as many as 92 percent of all houses built in the Paris region were located in the *banlieue*."[25]

Despite the very uneven distribution of new houses across the Paris region, and deficiencies particularly within the *arrondissements*, a small number of dwellings of an innovative style were being constructed mainly within the outer reaches of the city. Designed by Le Corbusier (alias Charles-Édouard Jeanneret-Gris) of Swiss descent, a number of buildings in the Modernist style were being built largely within the private sector, among which the Villas La Roche and Jeanneret-Raff in the 16th *arrondissement* (1923-25), the Villa Savoye in the western suburb of Poissey (1928-31) and an apartment block in the 16th *arrondissement* (1933) are the best examples. Fortunately for Paris, Corbusier's proposal to rebuild much of the Right Bank of Paris with a series of megalithic blocks in the Modernist style was rejected by the city council, although the mayors of suburbs such as Drancy in the north, Suresnes in the west and Villejuif in the south authorised the construction of high-rise buildings as attractive alternatives to the 'red-brick belt' of the HBMs.[26] Among the other adherents to the Modernist style was Robert Mallet-Stevens noted for his design of a cul-de-sac of half a dozen diverse

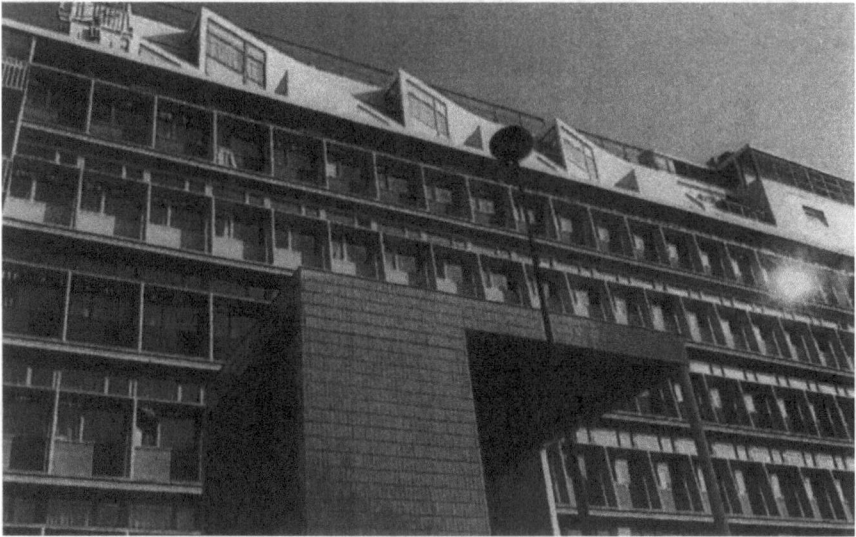

145   *The ten storey Salvation Army building, Corbusier, 1929-33*

apartments located in the 16th *arrondissement*. Constructed in 1926-27, each dwelling "is comprised of smooth white cubes with sharply cut window frames with hard projections and depressions."[27]

But Modernism was not confined to the residential sector. Auguste Perret – utilising reinforced concrete and an abundance of glass as building materials – designed the Église Notre Dame du Raincy (1922-23), and soon after Le Corbusier became the architect of the massive 10 storey Salvation Army building in the 13th *arrondissement* (1929-33), and the Fondation Suisse at the Cité Internationale Universitaire in the 14th *arrondissement* (1930-33). New factories and showrooms across Paris also began to be designed in the Modernist style, while a variant Art-Deco found expression in the design of the Grand Rex cinema in central Paris on the Boulevard Poissonière.

In the late 1930s the Art-Deco version of Modernist architecture was chosen for the development of two exhibition halls. In 1937 the Popular Front government promoted the Exposition des Arts et Techniques, an international exhibition on the Right Bank of the Seine immediately opposite the Eiffel Tower in the 16th *arrondissement*. With the nineteenth century Palais du Trocadéro demolished to provide a site, the exposition was housed in the newly constructed Palais de Chaillot. Designed by

146   *Fondation Suisse at the Cité Internationale Universitaire, Corbusier 1930- 33*

147   *Palais de Chaillot, 1937*

148   *Palais de Tokyo, 1937*

Jacques Carlu, Léon Azéma and Louis H. Boileau, the building currently houses the museums of the Marine and French Monuments as well as the Musée de l'Homme devoted to ethnography. The history of the palace is notorious. As if to compete ideologically with each other, two pavilions were built facing each other, one German (designed by Albert Speer, Hitler's architect) and the other Russian (by the state architect, Boris Iofan Vore Mukhini). On the German pavilion there stood a statue of an enormous Nazi eagle clutching a swastika, while on the Russian pavilion two Soviet workers, a man and a woman, yielding a hammer and sickle. All the 1937 exhibitions were dismantled within a year, and subsequently the palace reverted to its intended uses. Situated a short distance east of the Palais de Chaillot on the avenue du Président Wilson – and also looking onto the Seine – the Palais de Tokyo, designed by Jean-Claude Dondel, was also built for the 1937 exhibition. It contains both the national and city collections of modern art displayed in two separate single storey symmetrical wings separated by an open piazza. At the back of this space, it is connected by a *corps de logis* surrounded by columns. However, despite the continued existence of the Palais de Chaillot and Palais de Tokyo, the 1937 exposition "seemed to pale into comparison to earlier ones."[28]

REFERENCES

1. C. Jones, *Paris, Biography of a City* (London: Penguin Books, 2006), p.443
2. A. Hussey, *Paris, The Secret History* (London: Penguin Books, 2007), p.327
3. A. Horne, *Seven Ages of Paris* (London: Macmillan, 2002), p.373
4. A. Horne, opt. cit., pp.373-4
5. R. Price, *A Concise History of France*, (Cambridge: Cambridge University Press, 1992), p.127
6. Ibid
7. A. Horne, opt. cit., pp.373-374
8. Ibid
9. R. Cole, *Paris* (London: Phoenix, 2002), p.202
10. Ibid
11. R. Cole, opt. cit., p.203
12. A. Hussey, opt. cit., p.342
13. C. Jones, p.473
14. Ibid
15. C. Jones. opt. cit., p.475
16. C. Jones, opt. cit., p.467
17. C. Jones, opt. cit., p.470
18. C. Jones, opt. cit., p.489
19. C. Jones, opt. cit., p.453
20. C. Jones, opt. cit., p.455
21. Ibid
22. C. Jones, opt. cit., pp. 455-456
23. Ibid
24. C. Jones, opt. cit., p.456
25. C. Jones, opt. cit., pp.466-7
26. C. Jones, p.462
27. H. Wischermann, *Paris: An Architectural Guide*, (Venice: arsenale editrice, 2005)
28. Cole, opt. cit., p.207

CHRONOLOGY

1913-20	Raymond Poincaré, President of France
1914-18	First World War
1920	Paul Deschanel, President of France
1920-24	Alexander Millerand, President of France
1924-31	Gaston Doumergue, President of France
1926-27	**Rue Mallet-Stevens built**
1928-30	**'Samaritaine' department store updated**
1929-33	**Cité de Refuge de l'Armée constructed**
1930-33	**Fondation Suisse/Cité Internationale Universitaire built**
1931-32	Paul Doumer, President of France
1932-40	Albert Lebrun, President of France
1934-37	**Palais de Tokyo constructed**
1937	**Palais de Chaillot built**

14

MODERN PARIS

INTRODUCTION

In the wake of the German invasion of France in the early summer of 1940, Paris was declared an 'open city' on 11 June by the French Commander in Chief, General Maxime Weygand. The capital of France was thereby saved from being imminently destroyed by the advancing German armed forces and remained in occupation until 28 August 1944 when the city was liberated by Free French and US armies. Paris under its occupier's control retained most of the functions of a large peacetime city and became not only the centre of German administration in France and a leisure resort for German military personnel but also a centre for a compliant municipal government and police force. The city remained very much intact physically, though there was a major bombing raid by the RAF on the western suburb of Boulogne – Billancourt which caused considerable damage to the Renault vehicle plant on 3-4 March 1942, and by the USAAF on the marshalling yards at Porte de la Chapel on 21 April 1944. Later in the year in August 1944, just before the liberation, parts of the city were bombed by the Luftwaffe in an attempt to slow down the Allied advance. Subsequently, Paris was subjected to haphazard attacks by German V2 flying bombs, but in contrast to many other cities such as Warsaw, Rotterdam, London, Leningrad, Stalingrad and a host of German cities, total bomb damage to Paris throughout the war was negligible, although much of its built environment was in need of renewal. It was into this city that General Charles de Gaulle with representatives of the Free French army marched triumphantly down the Champs Élysées on 26 August 1944, a figurehead who was soon to become a dominant politician destined to play an important role in French politics on and off for 25 years.

THE IMMEDIATE POST-WAR YEARS

From September 1944 to late 1946 De Gaulle headed the Provisional Government of France but his party the 'Rassemblement du Peuple Français' (RPF) was rendered ineffective by unstable relations with the communists, socialists and radicals, leading – after only two years in office – to new elections and the creation of the Third Republic. But for the following eighteen years, political problems overseas overshadowed domestic policy, both environmental and economic.

From the outset, the French government was faced with demands for independence from within its overseas possession of Algeria and Vietnam. On 8 May (VE Day) Algerians rioted in Sétif in the Constantine area of their country resulting in one hundred Europeans being killed and many times that number of Moslems being slaughtered by the French army. Though an uneasy peace ensued, two new militant nationalist forces emerged in Algeria, the 'Parti du Peuple Algérian (PPA) and the much more militant 'Front de Libération Nationale' (FLN). Very soon, on 1 November 1945, the Algerian War broke out, with the FLN declaring that it was aiming at nothing short of restoring an Algerian State based on the principles of Islam that had been extinguished during and after the French conquest of Algeria in 1830-75. In Vietnam, a Communist regime under the leadership of Hô Chi Minh issued a proclamation of Independence from France in 1945. Being opposed by the colonial power, an eight-year guerrilla war began in 1946 with Viet-Minh guerrillas taking on French forces throughout the length and breadth of Vietnam, culminating in the defeat of French forces at the Battle of Dien Bién Phu in July 1954. Peace was brokered at a Geneva Peace Conference later in the year.

At home, and after four years of occupation, buildings, roads and bridges in Paris and throughout much of France needed substantial repair and maintenance. To make matters worse, France was incurring the cost of two further costly wars. Under the Blum-Byrnes agreement of 1946, therefore, public funds could to an extent be provided for a range of projects since the growth of the domestic economy was boosted by a loan of $650 million while the US government wrote off an existing debt of $2.8 billion dating back to the First World War.

The Fourth Republic

President Vincent Auriol – 1947-54 (French section of the Workers International)

After 1947 the French economy improved substantially. Under the government of President Vincent Auriol (1947-54), the Marshall Plan of 1947 injected a non-repayable $2.3 billion into the French economy, while during the premiership of Robert Schuman (1947-48) the Organisation of European Economic Cooperation was established putting the French economy within a west European context. More specifically, it was Jean Monnet's remarkable plan, based on Keynesian free trade ideas rather than state control, that put the French economy on a sound footing. At first, resources were to be focused on steel, energy, cement and transport equipment, but secondly priority would be given to urban development, housing construction, manufacturing and scientific research. Eventually in 1950, the French Foreign Minister, Robert Schuman, led the way amongst his counterparts in Western Germany, the Netherlands, Belgium, Luxembourg and Italy in setting up the European Coal and Steel Community (ECSC), strengthening the economies of its constituent members, not least France.

But within its capital, all was not well. At least 740,000 immigrants arrived from Algeria between 1947 and 1953. Many settled in the Place Maubert, rue des Anglais, Les Halles or the suburbs of Clichy and Gennevilliers where there were well established communities of Moroccans who had originally settled in these areas in the 1920s-30s.

Largely because of the high level of immigration, the Auriol government aimed to check the expansion of Paris since the capital with a population of around 2.8 million was thought to have grown to an excessive size. In attempting to put a cap on the further growth of the city, Auriol's Minister for Reconstruction, Eugene Claudius-Petit, "favoured the decentralisation of business and industry away from the capital into more distant *departements* and . . . also approved the idea of a 'green belt' on English lines: if there was to be further growth in the Île de France, it should be well away from Paris, and separated from the capital by definable green space."[1]

But decentralisation was a 'political pipe dream' with adverse effects on housing. Disastrously Claudius-Petit retained the current system of rent control, with dire effects on property investment in the capital and exacerbating the shortage of affordable dwellings. Recent immigrants not only sought accommodation in those areas of Paris where a generation of North Africans had settled in the 1920s and 1930 but were forced into assembling shanty towns (*bidonvilles*) made out of concrete and corrugated iron on any waste ground they could find behind the rail termini or on the fringes of the city at for example Noisy, Ivry, Villejuif and Nanterre.[2] At this time, and for good reason, the political Left was adamantly opposed to the redevelopment of the Parisian inner suburbs. It believed that new housing would be unaffordable to most low-income workers, forcing them into the *bidonvilles*.

After Claudius-Petit's resignation in 1953, housing policy in Paris became the responsibility of Yves Lancien as Deputy Councillor of Paris. He recognised that there had been no effective demand for major housing projects in Paris for decades and therefore introduced public subsidies for major housebuilding programmes that from very low beginnings in the early post-war years substantially increased the construction of HLMs (*habitations a loyer modere*) – the equivalent of UK council housing. Public housebuilding from the mid-1950s onward was helped greatly by the introduction of prefabricated parts and the development of *grands ensembles* – high rise apartment blocks surrounded by green space.

Because of the priority being given to housebuilding, there was comparatively little construction of non-residential buildings in Paris in the immediate post-war period. An exception was the Headquarters

149   *Radio-France, in middle distance, 1952-63*

of Radio-France, downstream on the Right Bank of the Seine built in 1952-63. With a reinforced concrete structure, the almost circular building comprises, like the rings of an onion: a 175 metre-wide outer ring 37 metres in height with a container wall of aluminium and glass; a middle ring 10.5 metres high accommodating the production departments, and an inner ring that houses transmission. At its core, the building is surmounted by a 70-metre tower for its archives.

President René Coty – 1954-59
(National Centre of Independents and Peasants)

Based on the general principles of the ECSC, the Treaty of Rome had established the European Economic Community (EEC)(the Common Market) in 1956 together with the European Atomic Energy Committee

150 *UNESCO's headquarters, 1955-58*

(EURATOM), and in 1959 De Gaulle was appointed Prime Minister by President Coty though it was only after he had been elected president in 1959 that he could effectively determine policy, regarding the role of France in an increasingly united Europe.

In Paris, the construction of the headquarters of the United Nations Education, Scientific and Cultural Organisation (UNESCO) in 1955-58 was arguably one of the most important projects undertaken in the city during René Coty's presidency. Designed by Marcel Breuer, Pier Luigi Nervi and Bernard Zehrfuss, the enormous complex is located in the Place de Fontenoy and is composed of three buildings. First, the Secretariat with seven screened floors on 72 V-shaped pilotis, a flat roof and over 800 rooms – all on a Y-shaped plot; second, a 70 metre span conference building with trapezoidal hall with fluted concrete walls, and third a cubic building accommodating the permanent delegations.

151   *CNIT exhibition hall, 1958*

Before the end of Coty's presidency, the shape of Paris was clearly beginning to change. Prime Minister Mendes-France's policy of controlling the growth of business premises in the French capital led to a ground-breaking expansion of commercial development on the western fringes of the city beyond its outer *arrondissements*. Though plans had been drawn up in 1950 to facilitate such development on a site referred to as La Défense (named after the eponymous bronze statue that commemorated the armed resistance of France against Prussian invasion in 1870), it was not until 1956 that construction began on the site. The first development of any note was the CNIT (Centre Nationale des Industries et Techniques) exhibition hall. Completed in 1958, the building "is a masterpiece of vaulting artistry on a triangular plot: three corner points – linked through steel cables spanning 220 metres – create the largest vaulting in the world."[3] Much more development on the site was to follow during De Gaulle's presidency and beyond.

The Fifth Republic

Charles De Gaulle, the *Union de* *Démocrates pour la République* (UDR)

De Gaulle and his party, the *Union de Démocrates pour la République* (UDR) won the November 1958 elections and duly formed a government in January 1959. Subsequently, as De Gaulle's prime minister from 1962 to 1968, Georges Pompidou – inspired by the post-war economic recovery of France (assisted greatly by the Marshall Plan) – introduced a meticulously planned programme of investment in energy, transport and heavy industry. In the context of a population boom unseen in France since the eighteenth century, the government intervened heavily in the economy using *dirigisme* – a unique combination of free-market and state-directed economy. This was followed by a rapid transformation and expansion of the French economy (e.g. by the extension of Marseille's harbour, the promotion of the Caravelle passenger jet airliner, the beginnings of the Franco-British Concorde airliner, the expansion of the French auto industry with the state-owned Renault at its centre, and the building of the first motorways between Paris and the provinces). Aided by these projects, the French economy recorded record growth rates unrivalled since the nineteenth century. In 1964, the French GDP overtook that of the UK. The period 1945-1974 has been referred to euphemistically as the "Thirty Glorious Years."

However, despite the growth of the French economy, "Paris was still a dirty and drab place in the early 1960s. This was partly due to the fact that since the end of the war, the authorities had been occupied with more pressing concerns than cleaning the city. The façades of most public buildings and even the grandest hotels were now black with soot."[4] There were two possible reasons for this: first, Parisians' love-affair with the car and the resulting traffic congestion and air pollution; and second, the boulevards of Haussmann still "left untouched a labyrinth of small streets, passages, dead ends and covered streets too narrow for traffic which rendered movement throughout the city painfully slow."[5]

In the late 1950s, the areas around Rue Lafayette and Gare Saint-Lazare were being cleaned up and modernised by public authorities.

Even if property owners resented paying additional tax for this purpose, the Parisian press were very much in favour and encouraged Pierre Sudreau, Minister of Construction, to extend it "to sand-blasting Notre Dame, the Louvre and Des Invalides, revealing complexities of colour in the stone which had not been seen for centuries".[6] Subsequently, De Gaulle's minister of culture, André Malraux, drew up a law in 1962 that identified areas in the central city of historic merit that would be preserved as *secteurs sauvegardés* (conservation sectors), for example the Marais and Les Halles.[7]

But, in the early 1960s, *grands ensemble* housing projects had penetrated into most of the twenty *arrondissements*,[8] but on the political Left there was still apprehension about the growth of Paris. It was thought that the development of employment opportunities in the central and inner-city *arrondissements* would render new housing

152 *Tour Noble (now the Tour Initiale) 1967*

in the *arrondissements* unaffordable because of increased land values "and lead to the relocation of Parisian workers in poor housing in the *banlieue*."[9]

In addition to a policy of decentralisation, it was decided to further develop La Défense as a site for new commercial and residential development on the western fringe of Paris. Following the completion of the CNIT exhibition hall in 1958, the first of several plans was approved in 1964. It "called for thirty towers, the highest to be just over 183 metres and the others 90 metres, with residential buildings limited to eight storeys."[10] Under a government agency, the Établissement Public pour l'Aménagement de la Défense (PAD), the buildings were intended to be built over a period of 30 years on nearly 1,000 hectares of land. By 1967 the first of the multi-storey tower blocks had been constructed: viz the Tour Noble (now the Tour Initiale) is 109 metres in height and accommodates 30 storeys, while in the same year, the Tour AIG was built, with a height of 99 metres and with 27 storeys. In 1969, the Tour Europe was completed with the same height as the Tour AIG but with 28 storeys.

DE GAULLE'S SECOND TERM, 1965-69

In December 1965, De Gaulle was returned as president ostensibly for a second seven-year term in which the French economy was booming largely as a result of an enormous increase in the export of manufactured goods and farm products to the other five members of the EEC, and the value of the franc remained remarkably strong for the first time in generations.

Otherwise, all was not well. The public were tired of his heavy-handed style. When a revolt against De Gaulle eventually occurred in March 1968, it was not modelled on the Revolution of 1789, or the insurrections of 1831 and 1848, or the Paris Commune of 1871. It was a "rebellion of middle-class students, the sons and daughters of those who had profited most from France's post-war recovery."[11] On the outskirts of Paris, some 12,000 students protested about overcrowded conditions and other deficiencies at the University of Nanterre on 22 March 1968, and on the 3 May Nanterre activists fought a violent street battle around noon against extreme right wing students at the Sorbonne. By the late afternoon the university was surrounded by the *Compagnies Républicaines de Sécurité* – well known for their brutal, strike-breaking methods. The fighting continued throughout the weekend of 4 and 5 May before the students dispersed.[12] Soon, on 14 May, there was an outbreak of strikes among workers demanding higher pay and improved working conditions. This was the moment the Gaullist politicians dreaded most. There was a strong possibility that an alliance of students and workers would bring the government down and lead to a period of anarchy and lawlessness not seen since 1870.[13] This nearly happened. On 24 May, some 30,000 demonstrators marched towards the Place de la Bastille, and after severe clashes with an overstretched police force at the Elysée Palace, Hôtel de Ville, and other main buildings of state, the demonstration subsided.

Hemmed in by events, De Gaulle spoke to the French nation on 30 May declaring that he would accept some of the reforms sought by the demonstrators, but instead of calling for a referendum to support his action, he was persuaded by Georges Pompidou (his Prime Minister) to dissolve parliament and hold new elections. There followed a

153   *Headquarters of the PCF (Communist Party of France), 1965-71*

triumphant parade of thousands up the Champs Élysées in support of De Gaulle. His party easily won the June 1968 election by 352 to 135 seats, the majority of the electorate, whatever their political predilection, fearing that the alternative would result in greater uncertainty or even revolution.

In contrast to later years, the PCF (the Communist Party of France) was quite a strong political force in the 1960s-70s, securing 20.8 percent of the votes in elections to the National Assembly in 1962 and 21.27 percent of the votes in the Presidential election of 1969. It is in this context that the PCF decided to build a new headquarters in expectation of expanding administrative functions in years to come. With plans produced by the Brazilian architect Oscar Niemeyer (with colleagues P. Chemetov, J. Deroche and J Prouvé), the building was constructed on a sloping site, with its main structure being a curved glass-clad structure, six storeys in height secured to five concrete supports. Extending beyond the front of this structure, a subterranean meeting hall is covered by a glass dome.

Attention was also paid to central Paris, particularly to the problem of easing traffic congestion. As a result of the initiative of Georges Pompidou, De Gaulle's prime minister, a dual carriageway was constructed in 1967 along the right bank of the Seine in an attempt to increase vehicular accessibility and enhance the commercial attributes of the capital.

No one really knows whether these developments were viewed favourably or unfavourably by the bulk of the Parisian electorate but, among French voters in general – where La Défense and other Parisian developments were not issues – De Gaulle received sufficient support to win the 1979 Presidential election. For a while, he clearly disregarded the belief among a proportion of the electorate that he was "too old, too self-centred, too authoritarian, too conservative and too anti-American"[13] to hold high office, but when his proposal to reform the Senate and local government was subsequently defeated in a nationwide referendum, he must have recognised that his popular appeal had at last evaporated and he duly resigned on 28April 1969. Two months later, Georges Pompidou was elected as his successor.

GEORGES POMPIDOU (1969-74) UNION OF DEMOCRATS FOR THE
REPUBLIC (*UNION DES DEMOCRATES POUR LA VE RÉ*) UDR

During Georges Pompidou's presidency, the French economy passed
through a period of recession in 1973-75 but this did not stop Pompidou
supporting the introduction of a number of iconic development
projects in the French capital, most notably the Parc-des-Princes
Stadium, Tour Montparnasse and Hôtel Méridien-Montparnasse; the
further development of La Défense; the Centre Beaubourg (known as
the Centre Pompidou after his death); the demolition of the open air
markets at Les Halles and its redevelopment as the Forum des Halles –
and constructing an expressway on the right bank of the Seine.

Built from 1967 to 1972, the Parc-des-Princes is an all-seater
football stadium, the home of the Paris Saint-Germain club since 1977,
and quite often the venue of French international football and rugby
matches. It can normally accommodate up to 47,929 spectators, but the
maximum number ever recorded was as many as 50,370. Owned by

154   *Tour Montparnasse, 1969-73*

Paris City Council, the stadium's architects were Roger Taillibert and Siavish Teimouri. The functionalist oval building that they designed was assembled from prefabricated concrete pieces of variable height which rest against 50 disc-shaped supports that also hold up the 48 metre-wide, overlapping roof.[14] Georges Pompidou duly inaugurated the new stadium in 1972.

Until 1969-73, when the Tour Montparnasse was built, no building in central Paris exceeded seven stories, the maximum height permitted by the city council. Although permission was granted in the late 1960s for its construction, it was feared that skyscrapers would become a common feature of Parisian skyline, but this was not to be. Instead, most future tall buildings in Paris would be confined to La Défense on the western fringe of the city proper or in the outer *banlieue*. Designed by Eugène Beaudouin, Urbain Cassan, Louis de Hoÿm de Marien and Jean Saubot, and located in the 15th *arrondissement* near the southern edge of the city, the tower was constructed on the northern side of the train station and is 210 metres in height and occupies a site surrounded by traffic, 62 metres x 39 metres in area. As an example of the International Style of architecture, its 58 storeys of mainly office accommodation are encased in a reinforced steel skeleton faced with brown glass curtain walls.

Constructed very close to the tower, but in the 14th *arrondissement*, the Hôtel Méridien-Montparnasse (built in 1971-74) is little over half the height of its tall neighbour rising to 116 metres and containing 31 floors. It has, however, a concrete skeleton and is faced with white-painted steel plates pierced by aluminium framed windows.

However, of all the new buildings constructed in Paris in the 1970s, perhaps the most famous is the Centre Pompidou (the Centre Nationale d'Art et de Culture). In principle, the president's decision in 1969 to proceed with this building was dependent upon an appropriate design being submitted by means of a design competition in 1971. Its winners were the architects Renzo Piano and Richard Rogers, and the engineer Ove Arup. Located in the Beaubourg in the rundown Marais district, and constructed from 1972-77, the six storey Centre Pompidou – 140 metres long and 50 metres wide – displays many of the hallmarks of Modernist architecture: open plan floors (of 7,500 square metres each), free façades, an open raised ground floor and a roof-top restaurant. In addition, its novel features include exterior escalators and plumbing

155   *Centre Pompidou (Central Nationale d'Art et de Culture), 1972-77*

(red for escalators, green for water, yellow for power, and blue for air) and it is these attributes that have given birth to the High Tech School of Architecture, though Renzo Piano denies the connection. However, in terms of town planning, the Centre Pompidou – with its extensive forecourt reminiscent of an Italian piazza – harps back to the Italian Renaissance or earlier, conceivably reflecting the Italian roots of the centre's architects.

The last of the major projects to be undertaken during the presidency of Georges Pompidou was the Forum des Halles. Designed by Claude Vasconi and George Pencreac'h the forum is located on the western edge of the Beaubourg on the site previously occupied by ten glass and iron market halls erected in the mid-eighteenth century. Constructed in 1973-79, the forum is both a major shopping centre and train station. Capped by a sprawling glass roof and spread over three levels, a major shopping centre accommodates a wide range of fashion shops together with a book shop, a swimming pool, a multi-screen cinema and a café. Below, at its lowest level, five Metro lines and three RER lines serve the forum rendering it a major commuter hub.

156   *Forum des Halles, 1973-79*

Though Georges Pompidou played a vital role in the development of major construction projects in Paris in the 1970s, and even had one named after him, he did not live to see the completion of most of them, dying in office on 2 April 1974. However, in the space of five years, he succeeded in changing the face of Paris more quickly and dramatically than any other public figure during the twentieth century, except perhaps President Mitterand towards the end of Millennium.

Valéry Giscard d'Estaing (1974-81) Republican Party 1974-78; Union for French Democracy 1978-81

From the outset of his presidency, Giscard d'Estaing made it clear that his main desire was to introduce various reforms to modernise the French economy. He instigated the development of nuclear power, promoted the development of the TGV high speed train and the Minitel (a precursor of the Internet), and in 1975 hosted a summit at Ramboullet whereby representatives of government of France, West Germany, the UK, Italy and Japan formed the Group of Six major economic powers (the G6) with the aim of discussing matters of mutual global concern (Canada joined in 1976 and Russia in 1994 to form G7 and G8). Overall, Giscard's economic policies were successful; personal incomes increased and the buying power of workers and pensioners rose substantially.

During Giscard's presidency a further ten high rise buildings were constructed at Le Défense, the three tallest buildings being the first to be completed in 1974; the Tour First rises to 231 metres and contains 52 storeys; the Tour Aveva is 184 metres in height and accommodates 44 storeys; and the CB 21 (formerly Tour Gan) is 179 metres high and has 42 storeys. Among the total buildings constructed, four are relatively low residential blocks. Most construction commenced before the full effects of the oil crisis of 1973 affected the national economy in general. It was doubly unfortunate for the president since he not only disliked much of the development of La Défense on aesthetic grounds, but his government had little control over the mounting cost of development, post 1973. Although Giscard showed some interest in other major projects such as the conversion of the Gare d'Orsay into an art gallery, economic conditions nationally were not conducive for major public sector initiatives.

Though a public building of a foreign country, Australia, its construction nevertheless helped to shape the French capital, some would say favourably. Built in 1975-77, the new embassy was located in a disused railway depot only 400 metres south-west from the Eiffel Tower and close to the Bir-Hakeim Bridge on the Seine. The 6,300 square metre site was purchased by the Australian government in 1972 whose commissioned architects Harry Seidler and Peter Hirst produced the designs for two edifices curved to form two quarter circles with both containing two 9-storey buildings – one being the Chancellery Building housing the ambassador and his country's mission to UNESCO and the Organisation of Economic Cooperation and Development (OECD), and the other accommodating 34 staff departments. Designed in the Modernist style, the embassy was built from pre-cast concrete modules with granite and quartz exteriors that provided the framework for an extensive provision of standard-size windows.

On a disused industrial site a short distance to the west of the embassy, a private developer in 1976-79 erected the Totem Tower, a high-rise block 98 metres in height and containing 207 luxury apartments. Designed by the architects Pierre Parat and Michel Andrault, the building is situated on a new 12-hectare strip of riverside land, the 'Font de Seine' – an

157   *Font de Seine housing and office development. 1970s-80s*

elevated esplanade containing 19 other towers of similar age. Brutalist in style, each column of the tower's concrete framework holds six 3-storey glass cubes accommodating a total of 207 apartments.[15] In 1978, political instability resulting from an inflationary overspend by the Giscard government brought about caution in the property market and a lull in new construction. But the economy didn't sink into recession since a right-wing coalition won the 1978 legislative election and prompted the president to increase his strength in the Elysée Palace by forming a central-right confederation, the Union of French Democracy (UDF). While this might have stabilised the economy, it was insufficient to prevent Giscard's defeat a few years later at the 1981 presidential election where he was defeated by the leader of the French Socialist Party, François Mitterrand, who went on to pursue a very pro-active approach to property development, particularly in the public sector.

FRANÇOIS MITTERRAND (1981-1988, 1988-1995) (*SOCIALIST PARTY*)

MITTERRAND'S FIRST TERM: 1981-1988

François Mitterrand was the first figure from the Left to be elected president under the Fifth Republic. He named Pierre Mauroy as PM (1981-84) and invited the Communist Party in his first government, but the CP was boxed in, and saw their support fall. However, because of the loss of parliamentary majorities, he was forced into 'cohabilitation governments' with conservative cabinets led by Jacques Chirac (1986-88) and Édouard Balladur (1993-95).

In his first term, he initially followed a radical programme, including the nationalisation of key firms, a 10% increase in the minimum wage (SMIC), a 39 hour working week, 5 weeks holiday a year, the creation of a solidarity tax on wealth, and increase in social benefits, and an extension of workers' rights to consultation and information about their employers (through the Auroux Act). Old age pensions were raised and health insurance benefits were made more widely available to unemployed persons and part-time employees. Major efforts were made to improve access to housing and healthcare, and the new technologies of Giscard d'Estaing were further promoted, e.g. the TGV and the Mintel, while government grants and loans for capital investment were significantly increased. His aim was to boost demand and economic activity by applying Keynesianism. But notwithstanding these initiatives Keynesianism was balanced to an extent by restraining monetary policy implemented by the Bank of France, unemployment continued to grow, and the franc was devalued three times.

After two years in office, Mitterrand made a substantial U-turn in economic policy. In March 1983 his government adopted the 'tournant de la rigueur' (austerity turn). Priority was given to the struggle against inflation in order to remain competitive in the European Monetary System. Although there were two periods of mild economic reflation (1984-86 and 1988-1990), fiscal and monetary restraint was the essential policy orientation of Mitterrand's presidency from 1983 onwards. But compared to the OECD average, fiscal policy in France remained relatively expansionary during the course of the two Mitterrand presidencies.

Almost regardless of the prevailing economic circumstances, Mitterrand was willing to see the further development of La Défense. Two further office blocks on the Défense site were thus constructed in 1983 and 1984, both of considerable height: the Tour Pascal which is 95 metres tall and accommodates 27 storeys, and the Tour Athena, 100 metres in height that contains 25 storeys. But one of Mitterrand's main legacies, if not his greatest, was his support (inspirational, financial and administrative) for a number of *Grands Projets*. Soon after taking office, he presided over the construction of the Institut du Monde Arabe

158 *Institut du Monde Arabe, 1982–87*

159 *Opéra de Bastille, 1982–89*

(1982-87), the Opéra de la Bastille (1982-89), the Parc de la Villette (1982-89), the Musée d'Orsay (1983-86) and the Louvre Pyramide (1984-93).

Funded by both the League of Arab States and the French government, the Institut du Monde Arabe was designed by Jean Nouvel, Henri Bernard, Pierre Soria and Gilbert Lézénès to become the cultural centre of the Arab world and to address some of the social tensions that exist between the Arab world and France. Located in the 5th *arrondissement* south-east of the Notre Dame and featuring a curved curtain façade of 25 metres in height with a shimmering skin of aluminium and glass, the building contains a museum, an auditorium, media centres, a screened library and a book tower.[16]

At around the same time as the Arab-French institute was being constructed, the Opéra de la Bastille was being built to the east in the 12th *arrondissement*. Situated on the old Bastille train station of 1859, the opera house was designed in Post-Modern style by the Uruguayan Carlos Ott, but with its rounded façade of glass, steel and stone, and columns reaching 50 metres, the axis of the building controversially pointed towards the Sacré Coeur to the north-west rather than to the middle of the Bastille plaza. Nevertheless, it can accommodate an audience over 2,700 in its auditorium and, being in the heart of a working-class area, to many it is a welcomed alternative to the Palais Garnier.[17]

Simultaneously, the imaginative Parc de Villette was being laid out in the 19th *arrondissement* on what was the site of a livestock market and slaughterhouse between 1867 and 1974. Acquired by the French government at no cost from the City of Paris, the 55-hectare site was comprehensively developed as a 'park for the future'. Designed overall by Bernard Tschumi, the park contains over sixty buildings and open spaces for a wide range of uses, most notably the Cité des Sciences et de l'Industrie, the largest science museum in Europe; La Géode, a Post-Modern 'omnimax' cinema housed in a 36 metre-wide sphere covered with 6,500 polished steel triangles, and 'Le Zenith', a concert hall of 75 by 75 metres for rock and other performances.

Although in principle favoured by President Valery Giscard d'Estaing, in the late 1970s it was the Mitterrand government that gave the 'green light' for the conversion of the Gare d'Orsay train station into a major gallery of international importance: the Musée d'Orsay.

160   *La Géode, Parc de Villette, 1985*

161   *Musée d'Orsay, 1983-86*

162   *Glass Pyramide at the Louvre. 1984-93*

Designed by Team ACT and the Milanese architect Gae Aulenti, the main hall of the building was converted into a gallery of 20,000 square metres dedicated to the display of nineteenth and early-twentieth century paintings and sculpture.

Perhaps the most iconic *grand projet* of the Mitterrand era is the glass Pyramide in the Louvre's Cour Napoleon. Commissioned by the president in 1984, the pyramid is based on the plans of the American-Chinese architect Ioeh Ming Pei (d. 1988). However, the detailed design of the outstanding glass structure was subsequently undertaken by G. Duval, M. Macary and Jean-Michel Wilmotte for the purpose of facilitating the expansion of exhibition space of the Louvre and its associated walkways and lighting effects. The Post-Modern edifice – surrounded by three much smaller pyramids – covers the new entrance hall on the lower floor of the complex and serves as the central point of entry into the Sully, Richelieu and Denon wings.

MITTERRAND'S SECOND TERM: 1988-95

In his second term, Mitterrand named Michel Rocard as Prime Minister (1988-91). Rocard led the moderate wing of the PS and was the most popular of the Socialist politicians. The government created the Insertion Minimum Revenue (RMI) which ensured a minimum level of income to those deprived of any other form of income; the restoring of the solidarity tax on wealth, (which had been abolished by Chirac's cabinet); the institution of the Generalized social tax; the extension of parental leave up to the child's third birthday; the reform of the Common Agricultural Policy; the 1990 Gayssot Act on hate speech and holocaust denial; the Mermaz Law of 1989; the Besson Law of 1990; the introduction of childcare allowances; the Urban Orientation Law of 1991; the Arpaillange Act on the financing of political parties; the reform of the Penal code; the Evin Act concerning smoking in public places; the extension of family allowances to 18 years in 1990; and the 1989 Education Act which, among other measures, obliged local authorities to educate all children with disabilities.

With regard to Paris, Mitterrand continued to preside over the continuing development of La Défense. From 1985 to 1990, a total of six tall office buildings were constructed most notably the Tour Alicante (Societé Général), 167 metres high and accommodating 37

163 *Grande Arche, La Défense, 1985-89*

storeys, and the Tour Chassagne (Societé Général) of the same height and number of storeys. It is, however, the Post-Modern Grande Arche that spectacularly completes the Louvre-Champs-Élysées-Défense axis. Completed in 1989, the edifice is an enormous open cube designed by the Danish architect Johann-Otto von Spreckelsen, and allegedly large enough to contain the whole of Notre Dame. Situated on the piazza below, it comprised two blocks of equal dimensions, both 110 metres in height and 30 storeys high, which together provide 80,000 square metres of office floor space. Capped by a roof terrace of one hectare, and with a podium of 15,000 square metres, the principal materials used in its construction were glass and Carrara marble. By the early 1990s, and covering 560 hectares, La Défense had become Europe's largest purpose-built business district.

In contrast to the development of La Défense to the west of central Paris, the construction of the Economic and Financial Ministry (1988-89) took place at Bercy upstream from the centre. Designed by Paul Chemetov and Borja Huidobro, the building replaces ministerial accommodation in the Richelieu wing of the Louvre. Since it occupies

164   *Economic and Financial Ministry, Bercy, 1988-89*

a narrow site on the Right Bank of the Seine, it projects outwards over the river to provide the office space required. Resembling a viaduct, it is only 21 metres wide but 360 metres long whilst the outer edge of the building is supported by a pair of pillars that stand in the water.

A further development to emanate from Mitterrand's second term in office was the Cinematheque Française. Located in the Rue de Bercy, designed by Frank Gehry and built in 1988-94, the cinema is attached to the former American Centre and from the outset it has been funded by the French government. Its entrance displays a freely arranged collection of shapes displaying the Deconstructiveness style of the architect.

Located in the Tobiac quarter of the Left Bank, the new Bibliothèque Nationale de France was built in 1991-95 and was intended to replace an earlier and over-stocked city-centre complex of Labrouste and Pascal in the Rue de Richelieu. Designed by Dominique Perrault, the new library comprises four 80 metre towers of steel and glass, each containing 25 storeys, with the plan of each tower being L-shaped and situated at each of the four corners of a sunken garden. The building, however, "proved one of the most controversial of the *grands projets* due to its cost and technical failings,"[18] most notably "the anticipated storage of the light- and temperature-

165   *Bibliottheque Nationale de France, 1991-95*

166   *Fondation Cartier exhibition and office centre, 1991-94*

sensitive books in the glass towers was [without remedial action] unworkable for reasons of preservation [while] darkness plagues the underground reading rooms which are supposed to accommodate 10,000 users per day."[19]

Mitterrand's support for *Grands Projets* was now over. For better or worse it had cost the French taxpayer a sum of €4.6 billion, and its effect on Paris will remain for generations to come.

One of the last major developments of the Mitterrand era was a privately funded project aimed at satisfying the exhibition and office needs of the Fondation Cartier. Located in the boulevard Raspail, designed by Jean Nouvel and Emmanuel Cattani and built in 1991-94, the front and back walls of the building are composed almost entirely of glass secured to steel frameworks.[20]

Jacques Chirac (1995-2002)
Rally for the Republic Party (RPR); (2002-2007)
Union for a Popular Movement (UMP)

After François Mitterrand's death in 1995, Jacques Chirac of the RPR won the Presidential election in May of that year promising to bring in tax cuts and introduce job programmes. But soon his neo-liberal economic austerity measures – including budgetary cutbacks – were highly unpopular. By the autumn, a number of major workers' strikes turned into a general strike in November-December 1995, reminiscent of events in 1968. But at the presidential election of April 2002, Chirac won a further term in office, partly because his opponent, the far-Right candidate Jean-Marie Le Pen, attracted very little support from the electorate that preferred – all things considered – to retain the status quo. Although Chirac triumphantly won 90 percent of the votes in Paris, it was not long before he too became unpopular, some might say he was the least popular occupant of the Elysée Palace since the Second World War. With his reformed and newly named Union for a Popular Movement (UMP), he antagonised public sector employees by reducing hiring and firing rights, scaling back pensions and unemployment benefits, and limiting the scope of the nation's health service. But by the beginning of 2007, Chirac's health deteriorated and he decided not to stand for a third term at the presidential elections in May of that year. Throughout his term as president, Chirac was generally reluctant to promote and fund the development of the built environment across Paris. Unless previously planned, there were to be no more *Grands Projets* at the public's expense.

He was, however, in favour of private sector initiatives across the capital, and during his second term in office presided over a start being made of a number of iconic buildings across Paris such as the sales headquarters of Citroën 42, the Galeo Bouygues, and the Fondation Louis Vuitton. Only with the Philharmonie de Paris was he willing to sponsor the development of a major public sector building.

The car manufacturer Citroën re-established its presence in the Champs Élysées among the designer fashion stores, restaurants and hotels by commissioning a new 'vertical' showroom in 2002. Inheriting

167   *Headquarters of Fondation Louis Vuitton, started 2006*

the glamour of motoring between the wars, when art deco architecture helped to sell a dream, the twenty-first century Modernist building employs "cutting edge architecture and presentation techniques to create what are in reality three-dimensional adverts for [the company's] brand."[21] Completed in 2007, a novel feature of the building is that the cars are displayed on "a stack of eight cantilevered rotating platforms, while the cascading glass façade billows out to cover [an] extended ground floor." From 2004 to 2010, the French construction and property giant Bouygues developed an office complex – the Galeo Bouygues Immobilier – in the boulevard Gallieni on the periphery of the Boulevard Periphérique. Consisting of a trio of buildings that accommodate the developer's office and other offices for rental, and shaped like a *galet* (a beach pebble), the "quiet design and the project's environmental credentials are typical of the current state of corporate workplace architecture",[22] for example the curved upper floors of the Galeo Bouygues are not only demonstrations of technical prowess, they are also a means of securing public acceptability.

However, two buildings by respectively Frank Gehry and Jean

168   *Philharmonie de Paris, begun 2006*

Nouvel are notably controversial. The first is the headquarters of the Fondation Louis Vuitton, located at the edge of the Bois de Boulogne and begun in 2006. It is a startling example of Deconstruction, with a structure comprising a framework of laminated timber beams bolted together by steel plates and covered by 3,500 laminated glass panels set within twelve glass sails that appear to collapse to the ground in no specific order. The second building was the Philharmonie de Paris. It too was begun in 2006, but unlike the Louis Vuitton, it was funded by the public sector: 45 percent by the French government, 45 percent by the City of Paris and 10 percent by the Region of Paris. It too is an example of Deconstruction, and, located in the Parc de la Villette, sits among an array of other public sector buildings, including its failed predecessor completed only a few years earlier. Its huge concrete shell contains the auditorium and insulates the interior of the building from the noise of the nearby Périphérique ring road, and the exterior of the building is clad in thousands of white, black and grey aluminium tiles, each shaped like a bird in flight which gives the illusion of movement. Both buildings were completed after the presidency of Jacques Chirac, the Louis Vuitton building in 2014 and the Philharmonie concert hall in 2015. It will probably be many years before most Parisians look with affection at these buildings.

NICHOLAS SARKOZY (2007-12) *(UMP)*

In 2011, four years into the presidency of Nicolas Sarkozy, the city council of Paris relaxed its strict planning controls and henceforth permitted buildings of up to 180 metres in height to be constructed. In principal the freeing of controls was in keeping with the president's initial attachment to neo-liberal policies, but when the global financial crisis occurred in 2008-09, Sarkozy was obliged to adopt an interventionalist approach to economic management though he ensured that the relaxed height controls of buildings were maintained. There followed a flux of high-rise developments in the outer fringe of the city, the most notable being: the Tour Triangle, a 42-storey tower at the Porte de Versailles in the 15th *arrondissement* and designed by the architectural agency Herzog and de Meuron to accommodate offices and street level shops; a 160 metre tower at the Porte de Clichy in the 17th *arrondissement*, consisting of steel and glass boxes designed by Renzo Piano to accommodate a new Palais de Justice; and located in the 13th *arrondissement* and designed by Jean Nouvel – the Tours Duo comprising edifices 180 metres and 125 metres in height, a development that

169   *Residential blocks in the 17th arrondissement, 2015*

only got off the ground in 2017 during the final year of the Socialist administration of **François Holland's (2012-17) presidency.** In the same *arrondissement*, two 50-metre tall residential blocks in the public sector had been constructed two years earlier to help satisfy the housing needs of the local population.

By the beginning of the twenty-first century, and for the first time, the city government of Paris put the improvement of the physical environment firmly on its agenda. Elected in 2001, Bertrand Delanoe, the first Socialist mayor since 1870, began a policy of reducing traffic congestion and creating cycle lanes, bus lanes and pedestrianised areas including a 2km stretch along the Seine. He also introduced free hop-on and hop-off community bicycles, electric rental cars, new tramway lines extending out to the suburbs, and long stretches of riverbank roads were converted into the Paris Plage (Paris Beach) each summer. By 2008 29 kilometres of specially marked bus lanes had been scheduled for completion by 2020, while under its next Socialist mayor, Anne Hidalgo, an upgraded environmental policy for the capital was introduced at the beginning of her first term in office in June 2014. Named '*Paris Respire*' (Paris Breathes), it focussed on improving the environment within the central areas of the capital (*arrondissements* 1-4), and had five specific aims: (1) It banned all cars from certain areas of Paris (including the Champs Élysées, roads along the River Seine, in the Marais, along the Canal St-Martin and in Montmartre) on the first Sunday of each month; (2) It introduced free public transport for that day; (3) It increased parking meter prices for the rest of the week; (4) It set out to convert certain sections of the highway along the Right Bank of the Seine with a riverside park; and (5) It proposed creating 1,400 km of cycle lanes by 2020. Partly because of the general popularity of these measure (that were largely implemented), Anne Hidalgo was swept back into power in the local elections of June 2020, in alliance with the Green Party. But her victory was also attributable to her proposed policy for her following six years in office, specifically her promise to continue to rid the capital of cars, greatly extend the provision of bike lanes, to designate new pedestrianised areas, to provide more parks and greenery, and increase the provision of new social housing. Public sector improvement in the shaping of Paris is clearly no longer concerned with the construction of major buildings or provision of new public open spaces, as had been the case for the best part of two millennium. It is now far more concerned with enhancing the use and enjoyment of the built environment that already exists, an approach that should immeasurably benefit Paris and ensure that it will continue to remain one of the world's greatest centres of economic development, and one of its most beautiful cities.

REFERENCES

1. C. Jones, *Paris. Biography of a City* (London: Penguin Books, 2006), p.504
2. H. Wischermann, *Paris. An Architectural Guide* (Verona: Arsenale Editrice, 2005), p.126
3. A. Hussey, *Paris. The Secret History* (London: Penguin Books, 2007), p.405.
4. Ibid
5. Ibid
6. C. Jones, opt. cit., p.506
7. C. Jones, opt. cit., p.505
8. R. Cole, *Paris* (London: Phoenix, 2005), p.279
9. C. Jones, opt. cit., p.505
10. A. Hussey, opt. cit., p.414
11. C. Rogers, *How to Read Paris* (Brighton: Ivy Press, 2016), pp.2160-17
    H. Wischermann, opt. cit., p.133
12. Ibid
13. C. Rogers, opt. cit., p.226
14. M. Padberg, *Paris* (Königswinter: Tandem Verlag GmbH, 2007), p.407
15. C. Rogers, opt. cit., p.232
16. C. Rogers, opt. cit., p.233
17. C. Rogers, opt. cit., p.234

CHRONOLOGY

1947-54	Vincent Auriol, President of France
1952-63	**Radio-France Headquarters constructed**
1954-59	René Coty, President of France
1955-58	**UNESCO headquarters built**
1956	**Development of La Défense begins with the construction of the CNIT exhibition hall**
1959-69	Charles de Gaulle, President of France
1965-71	**Headquarters of the French Communist Party built**
1967-70	**Maisons des Sciences de l'Homme built**
1969-74	Georges Pompidou, President of France
1969-72	**Parc des Prince Stadium constructed**
1969-73	**Montparnasse Tower built**
1971-72	**Hôtel Méridien-Montparnasse built**
1972-77	**Centre Nationale d'Art et de Culture constructed**
1973-79	**Forum des Halles developed**
1974-81	Valérie Giscard d'Estaing, President of France
1977	**Decision to convert the Gare d'Orsay to the Musée d'Orsay**
1978	**Australian Embassy built**
1981-95	François Mitterrand, President of France. Establishes a number of *Grands Projets*
1982-89	**Opéra de la Bastille built**
1982-87	**Institut du Monde Arabe constructed**
1982-89	**The Parc de la Vilette amusement park developed**
1983-85	**"La Geode" in the Parc de la Vilette built**
1983-86	**Musée d'Orsay established**
1984-85	**Renovation of the Louvre and construction of its glass pyramid**
1988-89	**Economic and Financial Ministry constructed**
1988-94	**American Centre built (later to become**

	the Cinémathèque Français)
1989	**Grande Arche de la Défense built**
1991-95	**Bilbiothèque de France constructed**
1994-95	**Cartier House built**
1995-2004	Jacques Chirac, President of France
2002-07	**Citroën 42 constructed**
2004-10	**Galeo Bouygues Immobilier built**
2006-14	**Fondation Louis Vuitton built**
2006-15	**Philharmonie de Paris constructed**
2007-2012	Nicholas Sarkozy, President of France
2012-2017	François Holland, President of France
2014	Anne Hidalgo becomes Mayor
2017	Emmanuel Macron, President of France
2020	Anne Hidalgo begins her second term as Mayor

15

CONCLUSION

For a thousand or more years, the townscape of Paris has been substantially influenced by the development of grandiose buildings and public open spaces funded or promoted by French heads of state eager to consolidate or strengthen their political power, or by leading churchmen intent on enhancing their influence over their spiritual flocks. Examples of the former are very numerous and include among many others the Palais de la Cité (the Conciergerie) of Philippe IV, the Palais du Louvre of François I, the Place des Vosges of Henri IV, the Place Vendôme of Louis XIV, the Place de Concorde of Louis XV, the Arc de Triomphe of Napoleon I, the boulevards and Palais Garnier of Napoleon III and the Grande Arche de la Défense of President Mitterrand. Among the many churches built by their incumbents and other patrons, Abbot Suger's Abbey of St-Denis and Bishop de Sully's Cathedral of Notre Dame de Paris have few rivals. It must be recognised, however, that a number of churches were also funded by heads of state, possibly – for political reasons – to empathise with the faithful, the Pantheon, for example, was built by Louis XV in honour of Paris's patron saint, St-Geneviève.

It might have been expected that during the First Republic (1792-99), and in the years of the Second and Third Republics (respectively 1848-53 and 1871-1940), the political leadership of France would have discontinued the age-old practice of using architecture and urban planning as a means of psychologically strengthening its political hold on the capital's population. It might have been thought that Republican governments instead would have focussed on urban development that democratically reflected the interests of newly enfranchised electorates. But this was not necessarily the case. Elected for the first time in 1848, the French president as head of state had supreme executive authority and significant policy-making power not very different from that of an absolute monarch of the *ancien régime* though, since 2000, intervals between presidential elections have been reduced from seven years to five slightly reducing the presidential hold on policy. Nonetheless, even under the Fifth Republic there remains in many quarters a strong attachment to some of the vestiges of monarchical rule. Founded in 1958, the Assemblée Nationale – the country's lower house of parliament – is based in the Palais Bourbon, formerly the home of Louis XIV's daughter, the Princess Louise-Françoise de Bourbon, while the French President's sumptuous residence – the Elysée Palace – was once home to the mistress of Louis XV and later the residence of Emperor Napoleon III. Some presidents, moreover, deliberately or by nature, have adopted a regal manner, for example François Mitterrand who was satirically dubbed 'the last king of France'. It remains to be seen whether the planning powers of the mayor of Paris produce a built environment more in keeping with the interests of the majority of the capital's population than that achieved by monarchs and presidents past. Judging from mayoral policy in recent years, one can only be optimistic.

However, on the night of 15-16 April 2019, an event occurred that altered the whole relationship between public and private sector funding of major development or redevelopment schemes in the French capital, Notre Dame Cathedral was seriously devastated by fire. Its roof and spire were completely destroyed and the rest of the iconic building was only saved by the efficiency and bravery of 500 members of the Paris fire brigade. But although French secular laws had transferred the ownership of the cathedral from the Catholic church to the state as long ago as 1911, the French Ministry of Culture made only a paltry 2 million euros available for the cathedral's restoration while the Île de France region contributed a meagre 10 million euros and the City of Paris some 50 million, very small sums since it was estimated that the total cost of restoration would amount to at least one billion euros. Following President Macron's promise on the night of the fire that restoration work be completed by 2024, in time for the Paris Summer Olympics, a Bill was passed in July 2019 aimed at dispensing 850 million euros in private donations. By October 350,000 donations had been received of which Bernard Arnault (Chairman of the company that owns Luis Vuiton, Marc Jacobs and Möet) contributed 200 euros, the Bettancourt family (who own L'Oréal cosmetics) also promised 200 euros, and François-Henri Pinault (Chairman of Kering, the owners of Yves Saint Laurent, Gucci and Alexander Mc Queen) donated 100 million euros. In addition the oil giant Total pledged around 100 million euros, and other large sums were pledged for example by Apple and Disney. If this rescue scheme is successful, it seems very probable that the private sector will assume a much greater rôle than in the past in the development of major development or restoration schemes in Paris, a rôle that historically was very largely the monopoly of the French monarchy or republic, or more recently the office of the Mayor.

But in the short to medium term future, the public sector is likely to take the lead in redeveloping the urban environment.

In January 2021, the mayor of Paris, Anne Hildalgo, approved plans that had been made by the Parisian architects PCA-Stream - working in liaison with the city's Champs-Élysées Committee - to redevelop the 1.9km long Champs-Élysées at a total (public and private) cost of 250 million euros. Aware that the environment of the boulevard had seriously deteriorated over the three decades 1990-2020 as a result of heavy traffic and that pavements heaving with large crowds of tourists, PCA-Stream proclaimed that the boulevard would be converted into an enormous park stretching from the Place de la Concorde to the Arc de Triomphe. This would facilitate the provision of ample green spaces, play areas, museums and cafes spilling out on to the pavements, as well as accommodating the redevelopment of existing buildings where necessary. Traffic would be halved by narrowing road space, and more cycle routes and pedestrianized areas would be provided. At the western end of the boulevard. the Étoile (the site of the Arc de Triomphe) would be transformed into public piazza with a considerable reduction in the volume of circulating traffic. Although the plan is intended to be implemented after the 2024 Paris Olympics, prior to this, the Place de la Concorde at the eastern end of the Champs Élysées will become a largely traffic-free area adorned with ample green spaces extending seemlessly from the Jardin des Tuilleries. By contrast the public sector is also getting involved in promoting small scale development projects of cultural importance. At the beginning of 2022, a new city-sponsored gallery for the exhibition of contemporary art was opened in the former Bourse de Commerce, close to Les Halles. Previously in 2016, Anne Hildalgo had granted a 50 year lease to businessman Francois Pinault for 15 million euros, and in return he transformed the building with its nineteenth century glass dome into a gallery spanning more than 10,500 square metres with an exhibition space of more than 3000 square metres, much of which being dedicated to the display of Pinault's private collection. Thus in both large and smaller projects, the City of Paris is gearing itself up to perform an important enabling role in determining the capital's future built environment.

APPENDIX 1

PRINCIPAL NEW AND IMPROVED CARRIAGEWAYS AND BRIDGES, 1852-60

	Year when building started	Arrondissement (post 1860 numeration)
Boulevards		
Right Bank:		
Strasbourg	1852	10
Diderot	1853	12
Pereire	1853	17
Sébastopol	1854	2 & 3
Magenta	1855	10
Haussmann	1857	8 & 9
Prince Eugène (Voltaire after 1870)	1859	11
Île de la Cité:		
Palais	1858	1 & 4

Left Bank:

Du Montparnasse	1767	6, 12 & 15
St-Germain	1852	7
St-Michel	1855	6
Arago	1857	14
St-Marcel	1860	5 & 13

Improvement of Grands Boulevards
Right Bank:

Temple	1656-1705★	3 & 4
Beaumarchais	1670★	3, 6 & 9
Filles-du-Calvaire	1670★	3
St-Martin	1685★	3 & 10
Bonne Nouvelle	1685★	10
Montmartre	1676★	2 & 9
Des Italiens	1676 & 1704★	2 & 9
Madeleine	1676★	1 & 9
Poisonnieres	1685★	2
Capucines	1685★	2 & 9

Avenues
Right Bank:

Carnot	1854	17
L'Impératrice (now Foch)	1854	16
Essling (now MacMahon)	1854	17
Boulevard l'Étoile (now Avenue Wagram)	1854	8 & 17
Malakoff	1854	16
Republique	1857	11
D'Iena	1858	8
Victoria	1858	4
Daumesnil	1859	12

Left Bank:

Gobelins	1850	5 & 15

Streets

Right Bank:

Rue de LaFayette	1823 (improved in 1850s)	8 & 9
Rue de Rivoli	(extended 1852-59)	1
Rue St-Antoine	(extended 1852-59)	4
Rue Reaumur	1854	2 & 3
Rue Turbigo	1854	1, 2 & 3
Rue Étienne Marcel	1858	1 & 2

Left Bank:

Rue de Rennes	1853	6
Rue des Ecoles	1852 & 1855	5
Rue Monge	1859	5

Bridges

Pont Napoleon III (now Nationale)	1853	Links 12 & 13
Pont Notre Dame	1853	4
Pont d'Austerlitz	1854	Links 13
Pont d'Alma	1856	Links 7 & 8
Pont d'Arcole	1856	4
Pont au Change	1858	1
Pont St-Michel	1857	1, 4 & 5
Pont des Invalides	1859	Links 7 & 8

*The redevelopment of the Grands Boulevards of the seventeenth century was begun by Haussmann in the 1850s-60s.

APPENDIX 2

PRINCIPAL NEW AND IMPROVED BOULEVARDS, AVENUES AND STREETS, 1861-70

	Year when building started	Arrondissement
Boulevards		
Right Bank:		
Malesherbes	1863	8 & 17
Clichy	1864	9 & 18
Rochechouart	1864	9
de la Chapelle	1860s	10 & 18
de Belleville	1864	19 & 20
Haussmann	1864	9 & 10
de la Villette	1864	10 & 19
Henri IV	1866	4
Barbes	1867	18
Ornano	1867	18

Left Bank:

St-Jacques	1860s redeveloped	5
Raspail	1869	6 & 14
de Grenelle	1864	15
Massena	1861	13
Kellerman	1864	13
Jourdan	1868	14

Avenues

Right Bank:

Beaujon (now Avenue Friedland)	1863	8
Kleber	1863	16

South Bank:

Orléans (now General Leclerc)	(redeveloped 1860s)	14
Montsouris (now Reny Coty)	1865	14
Denfert-Rochereau	1866	14
Observatoire	(extended 1866)	5, 6 & 14

Streets

Right Bank:

Rue Faubourg-St-Antoine	1865	12

Left Bank:

Rue Gay-Lussac	1864	5

Bridges

Pont Louis Philippe	1862 (rebuilt)	4 & 5
Pont St-Louis	1862	4
Pont Bercy	1864	12 & 13

Appendix 3

PRINCIPAL ROND-POINTS IN PARIS, 1777-1860S

Rond-points	Arrondissement	Initially laid out	Later radiating thoroughfares
Place de l'Étoile	8e, 7e	1777	Avenue d'Essling
			Avenue MacMahon
(now Place de Charles de Gaulle)			Boulevard Étoile
			Avenue Wagram
			Avenue Reine-Hortense★
			Avenue Hoche
			Boulevard Beaujon★
			Avenue de Friedland
			Avenue de Champs Élysées★
			Avenue Joséphine
			Avenue Marceau

Avenue d'Iena

Avenue Roi de Rome
Avenue Kleber

Avenue d'Eylau★
Avenue Victor Hugo

Avenue l'Impératrice
Avenue Foch

Avenue de Neuilly★
Avenue la Grande Armée

Avenue Carnot

Place de la Bastille   43, 113, 12e   1792   Boulevard Beaumarchais

Boulevard Richard Lenoir

Rue de Roquette

Rue de Faubourg St-Antoine

Rue de Lyon and Avenue Daumesnil

Boulevard de la Bastille

Boulevard Bourbon

Boulevard Henry IV

Rue St-Antoine

Place de la Trône-Renvensé (Place de la Nation)	113, 12e	1792	Avenue Philippe Auguste (now Avenue Trône)
			Avenue du Belle Air
			Boulevard Diderot
			Faubourg St-Antoine
			Boulevard Prince Eugene Boulevard Voltaire
Place du Châtelet	1e, 4e	1802-10	Boulevard de Sébastopol
			Avenue Victoria
			Rue de Rivoli
Place d'Italie	13e	1850s	Boulevard August Blanqui
			Boulevard de la Gare Boulevard Vincent Autiol
			Boulevard d l'Hôpital
			Avenue de Choisy
			Avenue des Gobelins
			Avenue d'Italie

Place du Châteaux-d'Eau 3e, 10e, 11e **(now Place de la République)**		1850s	Boulevard de Magenta
			Boulevard Prince Eugene Boulevard Voltaire
			Boulevard St-Martin
			Boulevard de Temple
			Avenue de la Republique
			Rue de Faubourg de Temple
			Rue de Temple
Place de l'Opera	9e	1860s	Rue Aubert
			Rue Halevy
			Boulevard des Capucines
			Rue du Quatre Septembre
			Rue de l'Opera
			Rue de la Paix

Place d'Enfer   14e   1863   Boulevard Raspail
(now Place Denfert-Rochereau)

Avenue Denfert-Rochereau

Boulevard Arago

Boulevard St-Jacques

Avenue Montsouris (Avenue René Coty)

Avenue d'Orléans (now Avenue du General Leclerc)

Rue Protovaux

[NOTE: *Original numeration]

BIBLIOGRAPHY

Ayers, A, *The Architecture of Paris*, (Fellbach, Stuttgart, 2003)

Baldwin, J.W., *The Government of Philip Augustus*, (Berkeley, CA, 1986)

Ballon, H., *The Paris of Henri IV. Architecture and Urbanism,* (Cambridge, 1991)

Bazin, G., *Baroque and Rococco*, (London, 1964)

Bergdoll, B., *European Architecture 1750-1890*, (Oxford, 2000)

Bernard, L., *The Emerging City. Paris in the Age of Louis XIV*, (Durham, NC, 1970)

Blunt, A., (revised by Beresford, B.), *Art and Architecture in France 1500-1700*, (Newhaven CT and London, 1999)

Bony, J., *The French Gothic Architecture of the 12th and 13th centuries*, (Oakland, CA, 1983)

Borrus, K., *Five Hundred Buildings of Paris*, (New York, 2003)

Braham, A., *The Architecture of the French Enlightenment*, (Berkeley, CA, 1992)

Burton, R., *Blood in the City. Violence and Revolutions in Paris. 1789-1945*, (Ithaca, NY, 2001)

Chemetov, P., and Marley, B., *Architectures: Paris 1848-1914*, (Paris, 1983)

Chevalier, L., *The Assassination of Paris,* (Chicago, 1994)

Cole, R., *A Traveller's History of Paris*, (reprint edition, Moreton in the Marsh, 2005)

Cronan, V., *Paris on the Eve, 1900-1914*, (London, 1989)

Paris, City of Light (1919-39), (London, 1994)

Edwards, S., *The Paris Commune, 1871*, (Chicago, 1971)

The Communards of Paris, (Ithaca, NY, 1973)

Eriksen, S., *Early Neo-Classicism in France*, (London, 1974)

Evenson, N., *Paris. A Century of Change, 1878-1978*, (Newhaven CT and London, 1979)

Fierro, A., *The Glass State, The Technology of the Spectacle, 1981-98*, (Cambridge, MA, 1983)

Furneaux, Jordan, R., *A Concise History of Western Architecture*, (London, 1969)

Higonnet, P., *Paris. Capital of the World*, (Cambridge, MA, 2000)

Horne, A., *The Fall of Paris: The Siege and the Commune, 1870-1871*, (New York, 1965)

Seven Ages of Paris, (London, 2002)

Friend or Foe. An Anglo-Saxon History of France, (London, 2004)

Hussey, A., *Paris, The Secret History*, (London, 2007)

Jones, C., *Paris, Biography of a City*, (London, 2006)

Jordan, D. P., *Transforming Paris: Life and Labours of Baron Haussmann*, (New York, 1994)

Kirkland, S., *Paris Reborn: Napoleon III, Baron Haussmann*, (New York, 2014)

Lavedan, P., *French Architecture*, (London, 1956)

Loyer, F., *Paris. Nineteenth Century: Architecture and Urbanism*, (New York, 1988)

McAuliffe, M., *Paris. City of Dreams, Napoleon III, Baron Haussmann and the creation of Paris*, (Lanham, MD, 2020)

Mansel, P., *Partis between Empires, 1814-52*, (London, 2000)

Murray, P., *Renaissance Architecture*, (New York, 1977)

Pinkney, D.H., *Napoleon III and the Rebuilding of Paris*, (Princeton, NJ, 1958)

Price, R., *A Concise History of France*, (Cambridge, 1993)

Ranum, O., *Paris in the Age of Absolutism*, (new edition, Philadelphia, 2002)

Rapport, M., *Rebel Cities. Paris, London and New York in the Age of Revolution*, (London, 2017)

Roche, D., *France in the Enlightenment*, (Cambridge, MA, 1998)

Rogers, C., *How to Read Paris,* (Brighton, 2016)

Russell, J., *Paris,* (New York, 1960)

Salvadori, R., *Architects Guide to Paris,* (London, 1990)

Schama, S., *Citizens. A Chronicle of the French Revolution,* (London, 1989)

Strayer, J.R., *The Reign of Philippe the Fair,* (Princeton, NJ, 1980)

Summerson, J., *The Classical Language of Architecture,* (London, 1980)

The Architecture of the Eighteenth Century, (London, 1986)

Sutcliffe, A., *The Autumn of Central Paris. The Defeat of Town Planning, 1850-1970,* (1970)

Paris: An Architectural History, (Newhaven and London, 1996)

Sutton, I., *Western Architecture,* (London, 1999)

Thomson, D., *Renaissance Paris: Architecture and Growth 1475-1600,* (London, 1984)

Trout, A., *City on the Seine: Paris in the time of Richelieu and Louis IV,* (new edition, London, 1996)

Van Uffolen, C., & Golser, M., *Paris – The Architectural Guide,* (Salenstein, 2009)

Van Zanten, D., *Building Paris, Architectural Institutions and the Transformation of the French Capital,* (Cambridge, 1994)

Velay, P., *From Lutetia to Paris. The Island and the Two Banks,* (Paris, 1992)

Watkin, D., *A History of Western Architecture,* (5th Edition, London, 2011)

Wischermann, H., *Paris. An Architectural Guide,* (Venice, 1997)

INDEX OF PLACES

Page numbers in *italics* refer to figures or maps; pages with a suffix *t* indicate a table. Pages with a suffix *a* refer to pages in the appendices (though individual roads and bridges in the appendices are not indexed). Roman numerals refer to pages at the front of the book. The index does not cover the chronologies at the end of each chapter.

INDEX OF PEOPLE

Page numbers in *italics* refer to figures or maps; pages with a suffix *t* indicate a table. Roman numerals refer to pages at the front of the book. The index does not cover the chronologies at the end of each chapter.